BEYOND MARX AND TITO

THEORY AND PRACTICE IN YUGOSLAV SOCIALISM

BEYOND MARX AND TITO

THEORY AND PRACTICE IN YUGOSLAV SOCIALISM

SHARON ZUKIN

Assistant Professor, Departments of Sociology and Political Science
Brooklyn College, City University of New York

CAMBRIDGE UNIVERSITY PRESS

Published by the Syndics of the Cambridge University Press
Bentley House, 200 Euston Road, London NW1 2DB
American Branch: 32 East 57th Street, New York, N.Y. 10022

© Cambridge University Press 1975

Library of Congress Catalogue Card Number: 74–12978

ISBN: 0 521 20630 8

First published 1975

Printed in the United States of America
by The Colonial Press Inc., Clinton, Mass.

CONTENTS

Contents

FOR MY GRANDPARENTS

PREFACE

This work offers neither a chronological narrative of recent Yugoslav history nor a diagrammatic analysis of Yugoslav political institutions. Rather, it is an exercise in interpretation, in which I have tried to cross the distance between theory and practice in Yugoslav socialism and to speculate on alternative resolutions to the problems involved. Because much of my research was based on interviews and conversations with, as well as observations of, ordinary Yugoslavs, I wish to acknowledge my debt to the ten Belgrade families and to the many other Yugoslav friends and colleagues who helped me during my year in Yugoslavia by opening up themselves and their society to me. Even though my conclusions may differ from many of theirs, I hope that I have presented their views fairly.

Two of my former professors at Columbia University have helped me greatly with their friendship, their advice, and their encouragement: Dankwart A. Rustow, now at The City University of New York, whose own work acts as a model of breadth of knowledge and clarity of style, and Donald J. Puchala, who exemplifies the ideal of a good teacher. I wish to thank another of my former professors, Zbigniew Brzezinski, director of the Research Institute on Communist Affairs at Columbia University, for his continued support and encouragement, and to acknowledge guidance from two Yugoslav mentors, Professor Najdan Pašić of Belgrade University and Professor Josip Županov of Zagreb University. John C. Leggett of Rutgers University carefully read the manuscript and offered helpful suggestions. The book is better for their help, but they should not be blamed for its shortcomings.

During the past few years, I have talked over many of the points in this book with Richard Rosen. I am glad to be able

ix

Preface

to count on both his continual challenges and his continued help.

Finally, I am grateful to the Foreign Area Fellowship Program and the International Research and Exchanges Board for supporting my field work in Yugoslavia and to the Research Institute on Communist Affairs for financial support while I was writing this book.

S. Z.

1
YUGOSLAV SOCIALISM:
A CRITICAL INTRODUCTION

The most important thing . . . that we can know about a
man is what he takes for granted, and the most elemental and
important facts about a society are those that are seldom
debated and generally regarded as settled.

Louis Wirth

From the beginning, the purpose of this study has been to find
out and to demonstrate rather than to prove. Often in reading
about socialism and revolution, I had come upon references to
'the Yugoslav way' and the political institutions — workers'
councils and communes — associated with it. Theoretically, the
institutions of what the Yugoslavs called 'self-management' were
based on the concept of participatory democracy; in practice,
Yugoslavs and foreigners agreed that they worked. Some foreign
observers went so far as to advocate the spread of the Yugoslav
system to their own countries, indicating that only this kind of
participation could eradicate the alienation and loss of social
purpose that have afflicted the highly industrialized societies.[1]

Saturated but not satisfied with these general statements, I
started to question what 'self-management' really meant to people's lives. Perhaps I was reacting with the American distrust of
(another country's) political slogans, or with my generation's
disillusionment with established priorities, but I wondered how
far institutionalized self-management had reached into the lives
of ordinary citizens. If the concept is to be applied to very different societies, then we should know whether citizens living
under the Yugoslav system come to feel that they are indeed
managing their 'selves' and their problems. In short, when a
journalist says that 'workers' councils in Yugoslavia seem to be

---

1 See Roger Garaudy, *The Crisis in Communism: The Turning-Point of
Socialism*, trans. Peter and Betty Ross (New York: Grove Press, 1970),
ch. 4 and Robert A. Dahl, *After the Revolution?* (New Haven: Yale
University Press, 1970), ch. 3.

successful',[2] we have to know *how* successful and *at what*. Until now, these have been open questions.

These questions coincided with an interest in studying alternative forms of socialism. A possible approach, indicated by the methodology of Alfred Schutz and the empirical work of Oscar Lewis and Robert Lane, involved trying to define the meaning of a socialist society in terms of its subjects' lives and perceptions.[3] Basically, this sort of study would present an idea of how the whole social system works in a socialist country, as well as how ordinary persons perceive it, relate to it, and evaluate its working. In this way the student of a socialist society would be able to come to grips with the dichotomy between theory and practice on many levels, as well as to assess the relative impact of cultural and ideological norms on social change. The work of Schutz, Lewis, and Lane also suggests that a good medium for this sort of research is that of intensive conversation and participant-observation, working with a small number of people chosen to represent various parts of the social structure. Examining the everyday life and the life-experiences of these representative individuals — as well as public statements by political leaders, public opinion surveys, economic data, and studies of specific locales — should enable the social scientist to make a concrete, critical analysis of particular forms of socialism and the conditions surrounding their implementation. In contrast to studies of elites, processes, and institutions, a firm grounding in the real 'mass base' of politics would shed light on conflicts and contradictions in both theory and practice. Through collecting and reproducing the citizens' social reality, students of socialist societies could offer a clearer idea of the dynamic which lies behind often confusing accounts, say, of the ' "enemies" [who] constitute

2 Jack Newfield, 'A Populist Manifesto: The Making of a New Majority', *New York*, 19 July 1971, p. 43. Cf. the argument by a British student of participatory democracy that Yugoslav workers' councils have been functional to the country's economic growth. Carole Pateman, *Participation and Democratic Theory* (Cambridge University Press, 1970).

3 Alfred Schutz, *Collected Papers*, 2 vols. (The Hague: Martinus Nijhoff, 1964–7); Oscar Lewis, *La Vida* (New York: Random House, 1966); Robert E. Lane, *Political Ideology* (New York: Free Press, 1962). For methodology, see appendix. 'Meaning' here denotes the interpretation that specified subjects develop to explain the way their social institutions work, the way their society hangs together, and the social purpose that they find in their own lives.

a seemingly incompatible horde, described [by the Yugoslav leadership] as anarcho-liberals, pseudo-liberals, technocratic managers, Stalinists, petit bourgeois democrats, bureaucratic centralists, Cominformists, ethnic chauvinists in the various republics and emigré intriguers abroad'.[4]

This sort of direct documentation of life under socialism had not yet been attempted, but Yugoslavia seemed a likely place to try it. First, the concept of self-management as their ideological linchpin makes Yugoslavs particularly conscious of and willing to talk about their political needs and activities. Because they are proud of self-management and its potential, through workers' councils and decentralized local government, for the realization of Marx's ideals, they are amenable to explaining their society and their beliefs to outsiders. Second, the degree of political freedom is relatively high, and the distrust of foreigners relatively low, for a socialist country. So I had some confidence that Yugoslavs would talk to me about politics.

My plan was to live in Yugoslavia for a year (1970–1): participating as much as possible in daily life, observing the kinds of public and political interaction which characterize the society, and reading about everything else I did not see directly. Following Schutz, Lewis, and Lane, I tried not to start out with preconceived analytic categories. Instead, I tried to open myself to Yugoslav ways of thinking. Although the problems and vocabulary of social science eventually shaped my writing, my concerns for the most part coincided with questions that Yugoslavs — citizens and leaders alike — are asking themselves.

A significant part of their self-examination concerns the relationship between Marxist theory and Yugoslav practice. Despite domestic critiques of 'the Yugoslav way', foreign observers have been either unable or unwilling to confront this question. Perhaps those Western writers who, as I do, favor the idea of socialist self-management fear that criticism in this area would either cast doubt on the general principle of self-management or cause the Yugoslav government to react defensively. Moreover, as foreigners, they may recognize that Yugoslavs perceive such remarks as gratuitous, if not also harmful. Nevertheless, it is crucial that students of socialist societies join Yugoslav thinkers in examining

4 Raymond H. Anderson, 'A New Political Orthodoxy is Asserting Itself in Liberal Yugoslavia', *New York Times*, 2 January 1973.

how everyday practice diverges not only from Marxist theory, but also from official Yugoslav ideology.

Surely the discrepancy between theory and practice is common to all political systems. It would be foolish to lash at the Yugoslavs — no matter how grand the claims of their official ideology — on this score. So instead of asking *why* the Yugoslavs have experienced a gap between theory and practice, we should consider *how* they have arrived at their particular form of this relationship. Indeed, this is the critical purpose behind the present work.

We might find it helpful to think of the relationship between theory and practice as a particular interplay between leaders and masses in which both sides act on the basis of expectations and calculations. Within this relationship, motivations of self-interest mix with definitions of collective goals and visions of future society. Neither pure altruism nor pure egotism causes the divergence between stated theory and experienced practice: this is a fact of social life for both capitalists and socialists, although capitalists prefer to work from implicit, rather than explicit, theory. However, in all societies we can separate empirically a 'founding' ideology or myth, current official ideology, formal or legal norms of institutions, actual institutional norms, perceptions of both formal and actual norms, and behavior of individuals within institutions. Although the leadership group usually determines the official ideology and establishes the institutions, the masses respond to their efforts with degrees of belief or disbelief, participation or withdrawal. This combination of the leadership's efforts and the masses' response makes for the changing relationship between theory and practice. So we may regard socialist self-management in Yugoslavia less as a full-blown ideological or institutional system than as an ever-emerging chain of choice and response under certain conditions.

In their choices within and responses to recent historical situations, both Yugoslav leaders and masses have shown a great deal of independence and initiative. On the one hand, the nation has been noted for its self-liberation from Hitler's army in a guerrilla war; on the other hand, the leadership has been cited for its defiance of Stalin, its defense of democratization and self-management, its renunciation of Communist Party dictatorship in 1958, and its denunciation of bureaucracy and other entrenched interests. But if we look at the goals and policies as-

4

sociated with Yugoslav socialism over the past twenty-five years, then we find that the choice has remained overwhelmingly the leaders' and the response the masses'.

Indeed, most analyses of the evolution of Yugoslav socialism — even those offered by Yugoslavs — are based on interpretation and evaluation of key choices that the leaders have made. To pursue the relationship between theory and practice in Yugoslavia, it will be helpful to review three of these analyses and to suggest a fourth. The three Yugoslav analyses are those of the dissenting former leader Milovan Djilas; the philosopher whom the leadership now accuses of harmful dissent, Svetozar Stojanović; and several political scientists and economists (notably Najdan Pašić, editor of *Socijalizam*) who represent the current official line.

The new class

Milovan Djilas is the former Yugoslav communist leader who, during the postwar period of consolidating power, began to question publicly the ethics of his associates. This sort of criticism resulted, over the next ten years, in his expulsion from the Yugoslav Communist Party and two imprisonments. Eventually Djilas renounced communism for a type of socialist democracy. Although he was removed from both leadership and Party for a series of critical articles that he published in Yugoslavia in 1954, significant parts of his critique have apparently been accepted by makers of official ideology. Aside from the Bolshevik leader Bukharin, whose observations were appreciated by a more limited public, Djilas was the first writer to alert widespread critical attention to the effects of leadership behavior on the communist social system. As Djilas did in his early writings, so subsequent Yugoslavs have also defined the stages of the communist revolution in terms of the leadership's choices in — or responses to — successive historical situations. Later writers have also shared Djilas' concern with the connection between state ownership and bureaucracy. The point on which these Yugoslavs diverge from Djilas is his condemnation of communist leaders as a distinct personality type (hungry for power, dependent on authority structures) with a preference for certain forms of or-

5

ganization (cliques within the leadership, oppressive apparatuses toward the rest of society). Once in power, according to Djilas, communist leaders constitute the modern form of despotism. This is obviously a view that the makers of official ideology cannot accept.

Djilas depicts the leaders of a ruling Communist Party as 'the new class' — the group which directs the society through its exclusive and total control of power, ownership, and ideology.[5] The key term here is ownership, which encompasses and symbolizes the extent to which 'the new class', in Djilas' view, has betrayed its revolutionary ideals. Once in power, Djilas states, the new class's sole motivation lies in 'strengthening its property holdings and its political positions'. But the 'strengthening' for which they aim is unquestioned and absolute control. Whether all property is under 'state ownership', as in the Soviet Union, or 'social ownership' as in Yugoslavia, the new class makes a mockery of socialist revolution. Thus the first premise of the official ideology of the new socialist state — 'socialization' of the means of production — does not mean what it implies, that is, the extension of all ownership functions to the collective citizenry. Nor do the stated corollaries of 'socialization', such as decentralization, liberalization, and self-management, really apply. As Djilas warns, 'Decentralization in the economy does not mean a change in ownership, but only gives greater rights to the lower strata of the bureaucracy or of the new class.' For Djilas, real decentralization or liberalization — in the economy as in the polity — would extend to free discussion of the leadership and open consideration of alternative systems. As he puts it, in the communist state 'liberalization and decentralization are in force only for Communists'. Similarly, Djilas goes on, the Yugoslav communist leadership has used workers' self-management as an ideological smokescreen. The leaders' original intention, in the 1950 adoption of self-management, was to make 'a concession to the masses' during the stressful period after Yugoslavia's break with Stalin. When Djilas wrote four years later, the measure had not been put into practice. From its inception, he states, self-management was 'increasingly relegated to one of the areas of party work'. Thus, self-management, like decentralization, be-

5 The exposition here follows Milovan Djilas, *The New Class* (New York: Praeger, 1957). For the convenience of the reader, all citations are from section 7 of the essay 'The New Class'.

comes another property of the new class, to be managed, dispensed with, and distorted in its own interest. 'Without universal freedom', Djilas says, 'not even workers' management can become free.'

Djilas' general statements about the intention behind the leadership's adoption of various policies, such as decentralization and self-management, may well be accurate. He may also be right about the leaders' subsequent unwillingness to implement these decisions. After all, Djilas remained a member of the communist leadership from the prerevolutionary (prewar) period of clandestine organization and student agitation until 1955. However, several of his specific criticisms about the lack of policy implementation may have been rendered obsolete by the leadership's responses to new situations. Indeed, Djilas' subsequent writings have often modified his original critique. The indictment that he brings against the early non-implementation of workers' self-management is of particular interest for an examination of 'the Yugoslav way'. Djilas states that workers' self-management has not resulted in a real sharing of profits on any level, that the bureaucracy has levied taxes which leave nothing to the workers but 'crumbs . . . and illusions'. This point has been refuted not only by the official Yugoslav ideology, but also by numerous studies of domestic and foreign observers.[6] Still, two of Djilas' questions about self-management remain unanswered: What is the influence of the Communist Party leadership on self-management? Can self-management be realized without total freedom in society?

Although twenty years have passed since Djilas first expressed his theory of the new class, his statement continues to exert an influence on attempts to analyze socialist societies in general, and 'the Yugoslav way' in particular. In terms of our immediate concerns, it is significant that Djilas' theory documents a distance not only between Marxist theory and Yugoslav practice, but also between (stated) official ideology and (observed) Yugoslav practice. According to Djilas, this gap is created and perpetuated by the communist leadership.

6 See, for example, Josip Županov, 'Samoupravljanje i društvena moć' [Self-management and social power], in *Samoupravljanje i društvena moć* (Zagreb: Naše teme, 1969). Cf. F. Singleton and A. Topham, *Workers' Control in Yugoslavia*, Fabian Research Series, no. 223 (London: Fabian Society, 1963), p. 23, cited in Pateman, *Participation and Democratic Theory*, p. 97.

Yugoslav socialism: a critical introduction

Ideals and reality

Svetozar Stojanović, a philosophy professor at Belgrade University, shares Djilas' concern about the distance between Marxist theory and Yugoslav practice. This concern is revealed not only in his writing, but also in the title of a collection of his essays which was published in 1969: *Between Ideals and Reality*.[7] Like Djilas, Stojanović traces a departure from prerevolutionary theory to postrevolutionary realities. Stojanović also sees continuity broken and congruence shattered by the revolutionary leadership's assumption of power and the perquisites of power. This results in a double standard, sanctioned by the leadership, of impoverishing the masses and enriching the political elite in the name of socialism. But Stojanović differs from Djilas on two major points which deepen and broaden the common concern of their analyses. First, Stojanović does not condemn the communist leadership for a lack of morality. Rather, he blames the postrevolutionary leadership for perpetuating and enforcing a revolutionary ethic which is no longer relevant to social conditions. Thus, according to Stojanović, the communist leadership must respond to a changed historical situation by revising its theoretical assumptions. In Stojanović's terms, the leadership must make the transition from a theory of 'underdeveloped' to a theory of 'developed' communism.

According to Stojanović, the prerevolutionary and revolutionary situations — particularly the struggle for power — spawn an ethic of deprivation which becomes the norm for all relationships between the individual and society. Because it applies to all spheres of social action and belief, including individual motivation, economic relationships, and political institutions, its influence may be compared to that of the Protestant Ethic. In tone also, though not in content, the two ideologies show similarities, for the revolutionary ethic consists of 'solidarity, cooperation, general interests, discipline, moral stimulation, renunciation, equality in distribution'. In short, the revolutionary ethic replaces the ascetic individualism of the Protestant ethic with

7 Svetozar Stojanović, *Izmedju ideala i stvarnosti* [Between ideals and reality] (Belgrade: Prosveta, 1969). Except as noted, citations in this section are from the essay 'Ka razvijenom komunizmu' [Toward a developed communism]. As cited here, Stojanović seems to appreciate and to justify the direction that the official ideology took after 1965; as events have proved, however, the leadership rejected Stojanović's analysis and its implications. See below, chapter 8.

'collectivist and ascetic egalitarianism'. It directs individuals to work for the success of the new social order; it justifies economic relationships based on mass needs and equal distribution; but it accepts the domination of political institutions by a monolithic state and its oligarchic elite. Essentially, Stojanović's Revolutionary Ethic accounts for the combination of moral fervor, collectivism and egalitarianism, and subjection to political controls which characterizes the 'Stalinist' period of Yugoslav socialism (1945–50).

Unfortunately, Stojanović says, during the early postrevolutionary period the leadership of the new communist state acts to negate its own ideals. In the material sense, the leaders siphon off the country's meager resources; morally, they contradict the egalitarianism of socialism; politically, they emasculate all institutions save those which transmit their will down to the masses. These institutions trace their roots to the prerevolutionary period, when the clandestine revolutionary movement needs a 'centralized, hierarchical, and, in many ways, undemocratic organization' — in short, when the movement sets up a Leninist-type party. Once power has been attained, Stojanović says, these organizational forms have outlived their usefulness. But in the meantime the leadership has become wedded to its organization, and it is reluctant to give up these forms. What a paradox this is, says Stojanović, for the communist leadership to rely on an undemocratic organization not only before and during, but even after the struggle for power.

> The revolutionaries got together of their own free will to fight for de-alienation, but the revolutionary organization has alienated itself from them and become the center of new forms of alienation in the whole society . . . Even more grotesque, such a party often carries out 'reorganizations', which turn in a circle, for they change the organizational chart but don't challenge the principles of organization and action.[8]

If this situation is allowed to continue, Stojanović warns, the society will degenerate. As the Russian, Chinese, Yugoslav, and probably the Cuban, experiences show, 'the positive revolutionary tradition can be safeguarded only if it is accommodated to

---

8 Stojanović, 'Revolucionarna teleologija i etika' [Revolutionary teleology and ethics], in *Izmedju ideala i stvarnosti*, pp. 193–4.

9

changed conditions; otherwise, it is transformed into a conservative force'.

Stojanović asserts that the Yugoslav leadership has indeed responded to new conditions. Thus he identifies the stage of 'primitive' communism with Stalinism (even after Stalin's death) in the Soviet Union and with the 'Stalinist' postrevolutionary period (1945–50) in Yugoslavia. For Stojanović, the Yugoslav leadership's subsequent choice of decentralization and liberalizaion indicates that it has made the transition to 'developed' communism. In contrast to the collectivist and ascetic Revolutionary Ethic, the principles of 'developed' communism consist of 'Marxist personalism, humanistic hedonism, and stimulating material reward according to work'. Such norms are irrelevant to the first phase of revolution in underdeveloped countries. But once the country has crossed a threshold of survival — both economic and political — conditions have changed and the revolution must change its approach. To save the revolution, Stojanović argues, the leadership must reinterpret its ideology and organization so that they adapt to the new social conditions. Politically, this means moving from 'primitive politocratic etatism' to 'modern technocratic etatism', loosening up controls and sharing the direction of society with all those who are equipped for making decisions. Economically, this change implies granting material incentives and rewards, raising the standard of living, and accepting increased social differentiation not between the leaders and the masses but among the people themselves. Such changes imply a redirection of emphasis from collectivism to self-interest. The general interest of the society as a whole can be protected by nonpolitical coordination, especially by the self-management system and by a market mechanism. In this phase of socialism, the market will insure that reward is really commensurate with the quantity and quality of work performed. But Stojanović also points out the danger that the market mechanism could assume predominance over deliberate planning and conscious controlling of social development. Because a socialist society must provide for the welfare of its citizens without regard to their individual earning power, limitations must be set on the market's sphere of influence.

By and large, Stojanović's analysis of the transition from 'primitive' to 'developed' communism seems to describe the Yugoslav leadership's pattern of choice and response from 1950 through

Interpretations: the leaders

1970. However, as the Party's attacks on his reputation and attempts to have him dismissed from his teaching position (from 1972 through 1974) indicate, the leaders unalterably reject a depiction of their earlier model as Stalinist. As a socialist humanist and philosopher of ethics, Stojanović obviously prefers 'developed' communism's relatively congenial atmosphere. His argument suggests a socialist society in which theory would approach practice: there would be equality on basics, differentiation on luxuries, under a democratic leadership.

The long transition

In contrast to Djilas and Stojanović, writers and professors who occupy positions in which they edit theoretical journals sponsored by the mass political organizations, or write for such journals, or sit on state planning committees, may be viewed as spokesmen for the official ideology. Although they are not so gustily critical as writers who are not associated with the leadership, they too are concerned with the distance between Marxist theory and socialist practice. On several points, their analyses bear some similarity to their critics'. First, exponents of the official ideology also divide the progress of the socialist revolution into phases which are inaugurated by changes in the leadership's responses to social conditions. The second point of similarity is that writers, planners, and economists associated with the official ideology also judge as progressive the shift from collectivist to individual social action — bearing in mind, of course, that this individualism is expressed in 'socialist' forms. Third, both official ideologists and dissenters are searching for the best means of regulating the new social order. Having rejected the bureaucratic state apparatus, they seem to have adopted the market mechanism in place of the Plan. The status of the League of Communists (the Party) in the area of social control is not well defined.

Najdan Pašić, a professor who has written extensively on Yugoslav socialist theory, is the author of a textbook which sets forth the 'Elements of a Marxist political science'.[9] In this work, he comes to grips with the same leadership phenomenon that concerns Djilas and Stojanović: that the communist leadership,

9 Najdan Pašić, *Klase i politika: Elementi marksističke političke nauke* [Classes and politics: Elements of a Marxist political science] (Belgrade: Rad, 1968). This section is drawn from pp. 109–10, 360–5, 370–1, 381–7.

11

which purports to rule in the interests of the working class, may act 'so as to change the objective laws of social life by the subjective will of the leading stratum'. Pašić calls this phenomenon 'bureaucratic subjectivism' and identifies it with the first phase of the socialist state, i.e. with the 1945–50 period in Yugoslavia. If the leadership continues to act in this way, Pašić says, then the society will tend toward inertia. Working people, bereft of influence on the social conditions of life and work, lose interest in contributing to the economy and the polity, so that these two systems stagnate. In other words, the leadership's monopoly over social power leads to widespread apathy — apathy toward work, apathy toward politics — which in turn causes economic and political stagnation. It is interesting, in comparison with Djilas and Stojanović, that Pašić criticizes the leadership as representative not of the Communist Party, but of the state bureaucracy. He impugns neither their morality nor their Ethic — but their politics.

According to Pašić, the turning-point comes when the leadership realizes it must make a choice between two kinds of response to the new situation: the leadership must either rely even more on the bureaucratic controls of 'etatism' or turn toward self-management. For him, of course, the latter represents the only possible decision. Thus the second, or self-management, phase of socialist development begins with the leadership's conscious decision to treat political power as a means rather than an end. This means that the leaders loosen up the state's controls over economic and political life, which should encourage the workers to transform their apathy into activism. By the same token, the leaders reorganize the Communist Party on a more democratic basis, which should lead to renewed activism among ordinary members. Self-management spreads from enterprises to communes to the Party, from the economic to the political sphere, and soon dominates all social action.

> Instead of direct state management of the basic social processes in the name of the working class, [Pašić says,] the apparatus of state power increasingly limits itself to assuring the general conditions for the freer and more autonomous development of self-managing relations and for the freer, real activism of working people on the basis of their direct management of the social means of production.

The 'administrative' manner of making decisions and resolving conflicts becomes 'a process of free expression and direct-democratic confrontation and reconciliation of various social interests and needs'. Within this system of expression, confrontation, and reconciliation, the Communist Party performs a necessary function, that of ideologically and politically guiding the society toward its ultimate goal, communism. Admittedly, the present transitional phase will last a long time — until conditions are ripe for the 'new historical form of nonparty democracy' at which Pašić hints.[10]

In the meantime, decisions must be made and conflicts resolved. Pašić explicitly warns against the assumption that, even under self-management, such action occurs spontaneously or automatically. Apparently there remains the need for what non-Marxist sociologists call an integrating and coordinating mechanism. In part, the Communist Party fulfills this need — but indirectly, in the sense of socializing people to make the proper decisions and resolutions. A more direct role is played by planning. This is not the rigid planning procedure of the 'administrative' period, but, according to Pašić, it is 'self-managing planning'. Such a process cannot completely eliminate hierarchical or bureaucratic decision making. However, if each community, each economic enterprise, and each political organ can determine the conditions under which it operates, then there is no need for an overbearing state planning organization. For Pašić, this represents a concrete example of how the state can wither away under self-management. But while the state plan is disappearing and the 'self-management' plan is gaining, there is still need for a decisive and authoritative means of making allocations between self-managing units, resolving conflicts of interest and defining the general interest, and enforcing such decisions. The Yugoslavs have determined that, in this transitional period, the only possible institution which could perform these functions is a market mechanism.

Yugoslav economists view the market as a rational, relatively nonpolitical, i.e. nonadministrative and nonbureaucratic, means of regulating economic processes such as commodity production, distribution, work, and development in a transitional phase of socialism. As such, the market represents 'the only alternative'

10 For a fuller exposition of the official ideology of self-management, based on Pašić and others, see chapter 2.

to 'the rigid etatist-bureaucratic system' symbolized by the Five-Year Plan.[11] Moreover, these economists argue, the dominant norm of a market system — modernize or die from the competition — forces the elimination of certain habits and customs which hinder overall economic development. Thus the market should prove instrumental in the 'huge effort to push aside and change the numerous relations still in existence of primary communities, primitive accumulation, and political voluntarism (which have lingered too long and actually flourished under social ownership)'.[12] Furthermore, those Yugoslav economists who defend the use of the market mechanism, at least in a relatively underdeveloped country such as theirs, feel that it does not necessarily threaten the Marxist goal of 'socializing' all aspects of life. As a Yugoslav economist says, 'If socialism is conceived of as the complex socialization of living conditions, and not as some *a priori*, moralistic fiction, then a high degree of socialization of all living conditions can be attained within the conditions of a goods-money [i.e. a market] economy.' [13]

Reactions to market socialism usually fail to make a distinction between its theory and its practice on two levels: that of economics and that of ideology. The question of the market's efficacy should be kept separate from the question of its compatibility with the goal of building a socialist society. Analytically as well as empirically, however, many Yugoslavs identify the theory of the market with current economic practices and find that neither theory nor practice conforms to visions of socialism. This kind of thinking has prompted Yugoslav sociologist Josip Županov to remind his colleagues that to speak of a 'market economy' in Yugoslavia is to speak more 'of ideology than [of] an economic reality'.[14] In other words, Županov is saying, Yugoslavia has not yet been able to implement anything approaching either a pure or a real market economy, so much of the criticism of Yugoslav market socialism is fallacious. But even economists who are involved in policy-making find themselves caught by the double-barreled question, on the one hand, of whether

11 Sime Djodan, 'Socijalizam i robno-novčani odnosi' [Socialism and goods-money relations], *Praxis* 5: 161.
12 Rudolf Bićanić, 'Proces podruštvljenja i socijalizam' [The socialization process and socialism], *Praxis* 5: 181.
13 Djodan, 'Socijalism', p. 161.
14 Josip Županov, 'Neke dileme u vezi s robno-novčanim odosima' [Some dilemmas in connection with goods-money relations], *Praxis* 5: 165.

the Yugoslav market system is working, and, on the other, of whether the Yugoslav market, such as it is, is compatible with socialism. The only point of agreement seems to be that the current situation will last a long time. In this light it is instructive to follow a 1970 discussion on market socialism between several prominent Yugoslavs who participate in economic decision-making, including Vojislav Rakić, then president of the Federal Economic Council; Dr Živojin Rakočević, Belgrade University political science professor; Roman Albreht, president of the Parliamentary Commission on the Revision and Codification of Laws in the Field of Social Labor; and Dr Miladin Korać, Belgrade University economics professor.[15]

> Mr Rakić: I'm thinking . . . about the dilemmas about
> what 'goods production' means . . . For us here, at least,
> it is indisputable that in our form of a market economy,
> of goods production, we have socialist relations, as well
> as social ownership and workers' self-management . . .

> Dr Rakočević: But only by tendencies.

> Mr Rakić: No, not only by tendencies . . . Today, in our
> forms that we call market forms, we nonetheless have
> socialist relations. And today, we have accepted market
> relations in practice, rightfully, I think — and this is
> neither practice nor theory — as the only possible alterna-
> tive to etatist socialism. We took that merely as a form,
> as the basis for the affirmation of self-management . . .
> And today it's obvious that the whole thing wouldn't
> work without [the market mechanism] . . .

> But . . . I would say that . . . the concrete form in
> which we can have socialist relations today is limited by
> historical conditions, and that socialism cannot be only
> that which we have today. I don't know how far history
> will bear me out . . . but I'm sure that a developed
> communist society will not know [the market]. But it will
> have social ownership and self-management and so on . . .

> Mr Albreht: . . . It's a different thing to criticize a model
> that hasn't been applied. We're talking as if we had a
> self-managing goods economy, but the state still has the

15 From 'Razgovor u studiju: "Koncepcije robne privrede u socijalizmu"'
[Conversation in the studio: 'Some conceptions of a goods economy in
socialism'], *Treći program* 2, no. 3: 198–202.

disposal of 70 percent of profits. The indirect role of the state, in my opinion, is larger than in a capitalist state, and many autonomous structures are functioning . . .

Dr Korać: While we're speaking about [Yugoslav] goods production, I don't agree with what Comrade Albreht said a little while ago: we have not yet developed to the nth degree . . . the model of a self-managing goods economy that we have chosen.

Mr Rakić: That's just what I wanted to say . . . In my opinion, the mere fact of goods production, its existence, shows that production is not directly or completely socialized, in the sense of being the negation of the capitalist system that Marx intended for future communist society.

Dr Korać: In other words, you mean that we don't have communism. Well, that's for sure . . . But we have a socialist production [system].

Mr Rakić: That might be debatable inasmuch as we're talking about socialism as both a constructed system of relations and . . . a system which indicates the full negation of capitalism. Be careful, we're still — at least in my opinion — we're still in the period of transition from capitalism to communism . . .

Dr Korać: . . . Here's where we can agree: even though socialist goods production is still underdeveloped in Yugoslavia, we nevertheless have its basic, elementary forms.

Mr Rakić: Not only socialist goods production, but, above all, socialism is underdeveloped. And it'll remain underdeveloped as long as we have the forms of the market.

Dr Korać: No, we differ there. In your opinion, does socialist goods production offer any possibilities for developed socialism?

Mr Rakić: First of all, what does 'developed socialism' mean? If 'developed socialism' is communism, then it doesn't.

Dr Korać: Of course it doesn't. Only you're talking about communism, and I'm talking about socialism. And, like you, I believe that communism may mean the negation of goods production. But by some accounts, according to

16

present trends, we're going to need something like 250 years for the profit motive to go down to zero. That means that the type of socialist goods production that we're developing now will be around for at least some time. Do we then have the right to consider this goods production as something really new which exists between capitalism and communism?

Mr Rakić: Of course.

So, within the common desire for socialism and the agreement that full socialization takes a long time, there is much room for uncertainty and controversy. Examination of the views of Yugoslav political theorists, political scientists, and economists yields at least three conclusions. First, in the Yugoslavs' attempts to create what they consider to be a new system, they show a tendency to confuse ideology and economics, on the one hand, and theory and practice, on the other. While theory varies to justify practice and practice labors to emulate theory, the public discussion veers between ideological and economic arguments. The Yugoslavs seem not to have decided whether to use economic or ideological criteria for evaluating current practice. If they want to combine the two types of analysis in some way, they must answer definitively the difficult questions of exactly what kind of practice they are creating and whether it is economically efficacious or ideologically legitimate.

The second conclusion is that Yugoslavs are very much aware of the significance of political decision-making. Although decision-making supposedly rests on the Marxist axiom that material conditions determine social action, the Yugoslavs implicitly recognize that their leaders' responses to given situations have played the largest role in creating their social system. To this point we have noted how Djilas, Stojanović, and Pašić all build their analyses around key leadership decisions or attributes.

The third conclusion is that the Yugoslavs show much uncertainty about where to go from here in both practical and theoretical terms. Should they strengthen or de-emphasize the market mechanism? What would be the practical consequences of either action? Behind all this questioning lies a realistic concern about the nature of stimulation and response: in this case, whether it is possible to build 'socialist' responses in human beings despite long-term exposure to market stimulation.

Yugoslav socialism: a critical introduction

Choice and response

Every analysis of Yugoslav socialism underlines the significance of the leadership's response to the challenges of the late 1940s–early 1950s period.[16] Without doubt, this was a time of domestic and international conflict in which the Communist Party leaders had to justify their ideas, their right to rule, and their existence as part of an independent state. Although Yugoslavs point, quite rightfully, with pride to the announcement of independence from Stalinist domination and the concept of self-management, it is in this period that they took the first step away from the founding myth of Marxism. Since that time, they have moved steadily toward a formulation of official ideology based on the Western model of development, including acceptance of the unanticipated consequences of that model, and efforts to accommodate the resulting model with the founding myth. In contrast to their contemporaries the Chinese, the Yugoslavs have developed a theory *a posteriori*, which has led to both confusion and contradiction. Yugoslavs now wonder how their society could have become more 'developed' but less 'socialist'. Moreover, the theory that Yugoslavs have created to 'cover' existing practice shows inconsistencies from the attempt to join Marxist axioms with the Western developmental model and its economic and social consequences.[17]

Certainly, the Yugoslavs have tried to create an internally consistent official ideology, mainly under the 'umbrella' concept of self-management. In this attempt, they have borrowed certain ideas from Marxist theory, ideas such as socialist humanism, reward according to work performed, and direct democracy. Unfortunately, these concepts are subject to so many different interpretations, and their application to the Yugoslav situation is so problematic, that their adoption has had several deleterious effects. Their incorporation into the official ideology has resulted in an inflation of ideological argument and a divisiveness among the political and intellectual leadership. Together with other, often contradictory policies, they have also prevented the leader-

16 See the discussion on the formulation of the concept of self-management in chapter 2.
17 Lasswell and Kaplan briefly discuss the problem of developing a consistent ideology and relate 'uniformity of ideology' to both 'other [ideological] perspectives and . . . nonsymbolic "material" uniformities'. Harold D. Lasswell and Abraham Kaplan, *Power and Society* (New Haven: Yale University Press, 1950), p. 124.

18

ship from setting standards of overall social development within the framework of the drive toward communism. Without such overall criteria, the Yugoslav leaders find it difficult to determine, except perhaps by instinct, which elements of their ideology are responsible for which undesirable practices. So the leaders' disapproval of such 'unsocialist' behavior as amassing a commercial fortune or expressing political dissent causes them to retreat from the most recently and most tentatively adopted, least well-defined concepts, e.g. socialist humanism, and to reiterate those concepts, e.g. self-management, which have long been unquestioningly accepted as part of 'the Yugoslav way'.

Over the past twenty years, four concepts and the policies that they represent have shaped Yugoslav theory and practice. These concepts are industrialization, self-management, market socialism, and social differentiation. Behind each of these concepts lies a series of assumptions, beliefs, and consequences linking economic policy, political order, and social structure. Sometimes the political or economic assumptions behind one of the four concepts are contradicted by its social consequences, as with policies of rapid industrialization. Occasionally, social assumptions or beliefs are belied by political and economic consequences, as in Yugoslavia's persistent national–ethnic–republican problems. Frequently, the contradictory consequences of policy in one area are reinforced by the contradictory consequences of policy in another area, as, for example, gaps between richer and poorer individuals, regions, and republics may be created by industrialization policy, reinforced by self-management, intensified by market socialism, and justified by social differentiation. The consequences — both planned and unplanned — of these four concepts have often formed a bone of contention in struggles within the Yugoslav leadership and between social groups.

Industrialization, chronologically the first concept to influence Yugoslav ideology and behavior, impressed the leadership as being necessary to the creation of the new social order that they envisioned. They felt, first of all, that Yugoslavia had to develop itself economically, i.e. industrially, to maintain its autonomy from the Soviet Union. They also believed that industrial wealth and industrial work represented the only way of eradicating the habits and the mentality of a long-oppressed peasantry. Finally, following Marx's writings, industrialization seemed to provide the requisite basis for a socialist transformation. In the early postwar period, industrialism probably appeared to most Yugoslavs, masses as well as leaders, as a tremendous boon. Establishing control over their own resources raised expectations on all levels. Except for those Yugoslavs who had collaborated with the Germans, most social groups — the small, educated bourgeoisie; the somewhat larger working class; and the peasant masses — looked forward to a place in an industrializing society with an expanding economy. This appetite for change coincided with a lingering spirit of victory from the end of the Partisan War. Together, they enabled the Yugoslav leaders to encourage mobilization based on enthusiasm rather than coercion. In this new situation, the ex-Partisan masses seemingly stood in a direct relationship with their leaders, which affected expectations and calculations on both sides. Previously, the masses had expected nothing from the state; now they expected all. This is part of what Djilas describes as the symbiotic relationship between the masses and the new class.[18]

Although industrialization undoubtedly has improved opportunities for all Yugoslavs, it seems to have benefited social groups differentially.[19] First of all, the necessity of overseeing plans, allocations, and construction contributed to the predominance of state organs and government personnel. Furthermore, the political criteria which influenced decisions associated with industrial policy — demonstrated by the 'political factories' which were located and built for other than economic reasons — assured the rise of ex-Partisans and Communist Party cadres. Moreover, the economic needs of industrialization encouraged the division of the work force into three social strata: highly-valued workers with prewar white-collar or blue-collar training and skills; verbally lauded but less concretely valued unskilled workers; and undervalued peasants. In retrospect, it appears that the leadership's initial choice of rapid industrialization without coercion made possible emphasizing the social contribution, and enhancing the relative position, of the middle strata. These

18 'Most important of all, the new class cannot achieve industrialization and consolidate its power without the help of the working class. On the other hand, the working class sees in expanded industry the salvation from its poverty and despair.' Djilas, 'The New Class', section 2, in *The New Class*.

19 For a model of the differential benefits of social mobility in conditions of economic development, see Eugene A. Hammel, *The Pink Yo-Yo*, Institute of International Studies (Berkeley), Research Series, no. 13 (1969).

in turn had consequences for both the social structure and the official ideology.

Around 1950, the idea of workers' self-management emerged as the leadership's response to the masses' flagging activism and lagging belief.[20] It developed into such a potent idea, domestically as well as internationally, that it soon became a canon of the official ideology. But at the beginning, self-management indicated its value chiefly as a new form of noncoercive mobilization. It also represented a means of imposing unity on a growing diversity among the masses. Over time, the institutions of workers' self-management acquired legitimacy and authority. They became instrumental not only in rallying the population, but also in rationalizing industrial management. To do this, the ideology as well as the norms of all social institutions de-emphasized politics and stressed economics. Thus, beginning in the economic sector, criteria for making specific decisions became less 'political', that is, less influenced by prior decisions taken in branches of the Communist Party, especially within the small leadership cliques or *aktivs* within these branches. While decision-making criteria were becoming less dependent on the Party, in general, and its leadership cliques, in particular, they were supposedly becoming more 'rational'.

This change also affected personnel policy, permitting an upsurge of managerial over Party cadres. Within ten years of the adoption of workers' self-management, many former Partisans were shunted out of their executive positions and replaced by directors with some administrative or economic training. These new directors relied upon professional and expert advice and tried to assure their advisers predominance within the enterprises. To this end the official ideology aided them, for around this time the political leadership began to define self-management in terms of enterprise and community autonomy. Autonomy in this case meant self-sufficiency, 'making a go' of the company or the commune without further straining the state's resources. Survival would no longer be hinged on the stability to make 'connections', but the ability to make a profit. For this reason, persons in managerial and staff positions developed social value and social power. In an arrangement of mutual convenience, the managers and their advisers developed means of informally controlling the self-management organs, while those institutions nominally con-

20 On the waning of revolutionary enthusiasm, see chapter 4.

trolled the enterprise as a whole.[21] Although workers' self-management achieved its legitimacy in terms of representing the
masses of workers, it attained its authority by stressing administrative and technological expertise.

By 1965, the concept of self-managing autonomy had developed logically, though not without a great deal of debate
within the leadership, into market socialism. As we have seen,
the Yugoslavs hoped that the market would act as a less 'political', more 'rational' sort of coordinating mechanism than the
state plan or Party directives. Under Yugoslav conditions, the
'laws of the market place' operated so as to maintain and
strengthen certain social tendencies that industrialization and
self-management had created. First, market socialism increased
the dependence upon highly-skilled, technical, and professional
workers. As the need for such work increased, so the reward also
rose. Materially and financially, the middle strata of the population prospered; at the same time, the official ideology accorded
them a higher status. Also related to the market was a new
juxtaposition of social consciousness, individual initiative, and
the profit motive. Enterprises geared to market success emerged,
through their workers' councils, as collective entrepreneurs. In
this environment, a desire for individual or group advancement
superseded a willingness to sacrifice for the common good. Of
course, not every individual or every workers' council began to
act as 'economic man'. Some resisted socialization by market
norms for ethical or political reasons. But because the laws of
the market place became the more or less accepted paradigm for
economic development, most residential and work communities
tended to tie the allocation of societal resources to competition
rather than cooperation.

The Yugoslav leadership did not intend to relinquish social
responsibility to the vagaries of the market place. Their society
still guaranteed the satisfaction of basic needs, such as food,
housing, health care, and schooling. Nevertheless, competitive
market norms may have had the unanticipated consequence of
restricting the availability of certain goods and services to those
parts of the public which were able to pay for them. Such a
consequence has little direct relationship with the major intended effects of market socialism, i.e., the elimination of un-
profitable enterprises and activities (such as the remaining 'po-

21 See chapter 5.

22

litical factories') which continued to block economic development and the improvement of existing, or surviving, products offered for mass consumption. But because funds for their development were supposed to come from the profits of enterprises, communes, and even republics, the people behind these organizations connected their long-term survival with winning a large share of the public's purse. Furthermore, they understood this connection to imply that, the more profit-oriented an organization, the more successful it would be at operating 'in the black'; therefore, the more it would have funds to plow back into both capital investment and research and development. So, for example, many Yugoslav doctors supported the private practice of medicine, which became legally permitted in the late 1960s in two of the western republics and caused much discussion in the other four republics. Some physicians believed that, if they could sell their services on the open market, then they could make a higher profit which they would use, not necessarily for personal enrichment, but to buy equipment that the social medicine system could not afford. But — to take an extreme case — if all health services were sold on an open market, then many Yugoslavs would not be able to procure the care they needed while some Yugoslavs would be able to buy the finest care.

The Yugoslav experience with market socialism suggests some caveats. In conditions of general economic underdevelopment and possible psychological unreadiness for market norms, the combination of anticipated and unanticipated consequences of market socialism may create an unintended, problematic situation which demands further resolution by the leadership. The intended effects of market socialism, at least in Yugoslavia, concerned (1) the availability of goods and services of high quality at low prices, (2) support for the innovation and the expansion of successful producers, which in turn are expected to aid economic development, and (3) reward for individual initiative and skill. Because of the socialist premises of Yugoslav society, each of these goals had to be modified. Otherwise, a free or an open market would have resulted in (1) the sale of basic goods and services to those who could pay most, (2) expansion in the form of monopolies, corporations, and trusts, and (3) personal enrichment. Indeed, a review of the Yugoslav press indicates that, by the early 1970s, all three types of phenomena were in practice. This situation required the political leadership to modify the market mechanism by imposing various limitations: on prices; on individual accumulation of consumer goods; on regional, local, and enterprise forms of self-expansion.

Until the early 1970s, the leadership tolerated such forms of self-interest and self-expansion as they deemed necessary for economic development. The official ideology justified this line by publicizing the norm, 'Reward according to the results of work'. On the one hand, the norm represented an attempt to associate the evolving practice of Yugoslav market socialism with the older body of Marxist theory, particularly with the envisioned transition toward the distributive norm, 'From each according to his ability, to each according to his need'. On the other hand, the norm promised a more immediate reward to those individuals and enterprises who worked harder, better, and more profitably. The leadership intended this norm to structure the society into occupational and income strata which would not, however, bear the stigmata of classes. They considered social differentiation of this sort a necessary and even a desirable concomitant of economic development. Egalitarianism, particularly as it appeared to have been enforced in such countries as China and Bulgaria, connoted equality in conditions of poverty or misery or both. From this viewpoint, most Yugoslavs began to regard egalitarianism as dysfunctional to development.

In the short run, the market face of the Janus-like concept of market socialism seemed to triumph. Yugoslavs grew increasingly conscious of the need — not particularly to work harder and better, but — to work more profitably. Many came to view life as a commercial treadmill, a *trka za dinarom,* a 'struggle to make a buck'. While some merely survived the struggle, others succeeded markedly. Inevitably, the survivors were many but the successes were few. Social differentials, most visibly in the form of consumer goods, had been translated into exclusions and restrictions: friendship and business cliques, special vacations, opportunities for children. Given the relative openness of their society, many Yugoslavs considered it obvious to wonder, in one form or another, whether the different lifestyles of social strata would become permanent and transmittable perquisites. In short, many ordinary people asked whether Yugoslavia would take on some of the attributes of a class society. Although all Yugoslavs recognized that the exclusive and restricted forms of social differentiation were not 'right', some defended them as 'natural' in

24

terms of human nature, the level of Yugoslav economic development, the laws of the market place.

The persistence of such forms of behavior poses both practical and theoretical problems. Yugoslavs argue that these forms are related to norms of selfishness and greed, which are in turn related to the objective conditions of economic underdevelopment and peasant society. According to this line of thought, rich countries like America or France would not experience the same difficulties in striving for socialism. But non-Yugoslavs may question this argument. If the profit motive, even under conditions of self-management, can exert great influence on Yugoslav attitudes and behavior in only twenty years, then how can we eradicate the effects of 400 years of capitalism? The Yugoslav experience indicates that, over and above the benefits of a welfare state, material incentives and social differentials play a powerful role in shaping people's motivations, social norms, and the structure of the society as a whole. It may be true, as the Yugoslavs say, that such norms and forms represent only a stage in the historical unfolding of socialism, particularly in underdeveloped countries. But it is also possible that the social inequalities which exist today, reinforced by societal priorities, will endure. Moreover, the Yugoslav experience suggests that the unanticipated consequences of a sequence of pragmatically dictated policies may undermine the intended effects of the leadership's actions. Ironically, for example, the inclusive norms and groupings — the solidarity — of an earlier period, with a lower level of economic development, have evolved through policies of industrialization, self-management, market socialism and social differentiation into exclusive forms of social behavior. We must hope that this is not an inevitable part of the process of modernization. But posing the problem in these terms indicates that we should rethink the implications not only of specific policies, but of general orientations such as liberalization and control.

The answers to questions about the future of Yugoslav socialism must rely on interpretation of today's social practice: ideology, norms, perceptions, and action. So far this discussion has focused on the leadership's role in defining the norms of social practice. But this represents only half the reality. To understand the way practice develops, we must also examine the masses' responses to the leadership's choices.

INTERPRETATIONS: THE MASSES

Although we may take for granted that, in any society, something is lost in the translation from official ideology to everyday reality, it is not readily apparent *what* is lost and *how*. Does the problem turn, as Djilas suggested, on the malevolence of a leadership which never intends to implement its slogans? Or should we blame norms which arise as 'aberrations' but, reinforced by acceptance, eventually shape the social reality in which most people live? To resolve these questions, it is crucial to determine what this social reality is and how people relate themselves to it. We might begin as skeptics, by asking what part of the official ideology trickles down to the level of individual belief. Do institutions really operate the way they claim to work? In a society such as Yugoslavia, where the ideology and the institutions of self-management claim to have eliminated the problem of an alienated citizenry, these questions assume great significance.

Yugoslavia's form of socialism prompts three general questions about the relationship between the masses and the organization of society. First, how has social change, especially revolution, affected individual lives? Second, how are individual citizens and workers integrated into the political system? Third, how do individuals internalize the norms of socialist society, in general, and of self-management, in particular?

Postrevolutionary change

Even casual visitors to Yugoslavia have noted the absence of signs of full political mobilization which are typical of other communist party states. Externally, no banners and slogans are displayed except on national holidays; as evidence of internal concerns, conversations and art forms are apolitical. Obviously, Yugoslavs have made a transition from the full mobilization of revolution to selective mobilization, perhaps even immobilization. Although this shift to a lower gear of revolutionary activism does not necessarily imply a lack of support for the social order, the change in behavior must be related to a change in attitude. Surely both of these reflect the perception, on the part of masses of people, that society itself has changed. Just as the social system has undergone revision, so individuals have reordered their priorities.

Because more than twenty-five years have passed since the creation of a socialist Yugoslavia, this change in priorities may correspond to a change in generations. So it is reasonable to expect differences between the Partisan generation, now in their forties, and their children, many of whom are passing from adolescence to young adulthood. Like many middle-aged generations, the Partisan parents have struggled to give their children a better world. The two great efforts of their lives have taken — and continue to take — the forms of a struggle for socialism (*borba za socijalizam*) and the struggle to make a buck (*trka za dinarom*). Along with improvements in the standard of living, their children have inherited both struggles. But, as Karl Mannheim has said about all generations, children cannot fight the same battles their parents fought when they were young adults.[22] If children grow up in relative comfort and security, then they do not perceive the salience of self-sacrifice. For them, 'struggle' connotes a parental memory, a sermonized value, a virtue or a necessity practiced in a place or at a time distant from their own. From this viewpoint, the children of Yugoslav Partisans may regard the struggle to make a dinar as more salient than the struggle for socialism.

The implied differences between these two forms of collective social action suggest that the Partisan generation and their children have been socialized by different sets of norms in different social environments. Perhaps the children of former revolutionaries like the Partisans lack the key experiences which welded their parents' individual wills into a collective revolutionary vision. According to Mannheim, conditions of relative social destabilization produce generations with distinctive modes of thinking and acting. The generation is formed among individuals of the same age group, on the threshold of young adulthood, who apprehend reality from similar 'social locations', such as class or geographical position. To the extent that these individuals share the experience of confronting the same social conditions and enunciating the same response, they become a generation — or more properly, in Mannheim's terms, a generational unit. Age-cohorts who face conditions of the time from different social locations tend to work up the material of their common percep-

22 References to Mannheim on generations from Karl Mannheim, 'The Problem of Generations', in *Essays on the Sociology of Knowledge*, ed. Paul Kecskemeti (New York: Oxford University Press, 1952), pp. 276–322. On political generations, see Maurice Zeitlin, *Revolutionary Politics and the Cuban Working Class* (Princeton University Press, 1967), ch. 9.

tions in different ways, and so to form different generational units. Following this line of thought, we can speak of those Yugoslavs who fought in the Partisan War (World War II) as a unified generation. But as for their children, it is less clear what forms of collective response to social conditions are most common to young adults in Yugoslavia. The ideology and institutions of self-management are intended to offer both a generational ethos to succeeding postrevolutionary generations and a source of continuity between them, for they are supposed to make appropriate for 'normal' times the shared experience and the collective action of revolution which made the Partisans a generation. If self-management does not work in this way, then the Partisan generation has failed in bequeathing to its successors a basis for social solidarity.

Not only have the Partisans' children been born and socialized into a different social order, but the parents themselves have been affected by the new reality. After all, they have adopted the lifestyle into which their children are born, and they have worked out the norms and roles into which their children are socialized. Although they might cling to the memories of the Partisan past, they have adapted their attitudes and behavior, over the years, to conditions quite different from those of their youth. So the Partisan generation has been socialized partly by Partisan norms and partly by the new norms that they have created. We might ask whether this combination of influences and environments has enabled the Partisan generation to retain its sense of social solidarity. On the one hand, the former Partisans have had to respond to a changing social environment and to the demands and expectations voiced by the children whom they brought into that environment. On the other hand, the former Partisans have had to adapt to the process of growing old. Could aging have made them adopt different orientations toward society, or would growing old have confirmed and hardened their earlier beliefs? It may be true, as Mannheim says, that the earliest or 'primary stratum of experiences' becomes the most significant part of the individual's mental framework for organizing reality, for 'early impressions tend to coalesce into a *natural view* of the world' against which the individual tests all his later experiences. Yet people continue to grow, to learn, even to reinterpret their opinions as they get older. We cannot automatically say that aging brings more conservative orientations for, as both Mannheim and Zeitlin have shown, an older generation may be more progressive than their successors. Nor can we say that changes are merely measurable results of the burden of years, so that 'aging may simply mean the cumulative influence of *more* exposure to the *same* kind of environment',[23] for the world around us, and around the Partisans, is constantly changing.

A major form of postrevolutionary change to which the ex-Partisans have had to adjust has been the increasing differentiation of social groups. The classes or strata, ethnic groups, and activist and apathetic individuals which had formerly been united by revolutionary purpose have been broken apart. Their social differentiation has resulted not only in a political expression of their separate needs and wants, but also in a tension between their competing, even conflicting, views of social reality. Thus the brief unanimity of publicly-expressed opinion in the revolutionary and postrevolutionary periods has yielded to different political orientations, both within an aging Partisan generation and between their generation and their children's.

The older Yugoslavs have also had to reconcile the social change of the past twenty-five years with the revolutionary ideology of their youth. They have done this in two ways. On the one hand, as some members of the Partisan generation have aged, they have tried to protect themselves against the barrage of social change by developing defenses such as psychic fatigue, physical withdrawal, and insistence upon the values of their youth, which they may also tend to perceive in an increasingly idealized way. On the other hand, some older Yugoslavs have accepted the new, postrevolutionary values and attributes, which they view as consistent with the ideology of their youth.

Thinking about life processes in general and about the lives of former revolutionaries in particular indicates that, to consider the effect of social change on people's lives, attitudes, and behavior, we must come to terms with several processes: the differentiation of social groups, especially generations; the transmission of perceptions, rules, and norms from a generation to its successors; the determination, by each generation, of the salience of social learn-

23 Herbert Hyman, *Political Socialization* (New York: Free Press, 1959), pp. 102–3, 119, at 103. Hyman points out that no one has demonstrated what general effects aging, or growing old, has on attitudes and behavior. Emphasis in original.

ing that it receives in this way; and the reconciliation, by an aging generation, of past experiences with new social values.

Writers who want to study these processes in their own society have an advantage over foreign observers, for they have lived the social reality and experienced the generational change: theirs is a job of interpretation. Those who have not lived the reality that they want to analyze must first document it, preferably by 'going to the people', whose everyday lives and life stories represent the best source of data on social change. The lives of ordinary people are repositories of social changes. Indeed, the stories of ordinary lives have always provided a mechanism for the transmission of learning about culture and society — from oral tradition to oral history, from grandmothers' tales to documentary photography. Similarly, a study of change in any society must begin by documenting the social reality reflected in the lives of its ordinary citizens. Documenting social change within the framework of life stories and other oral 'ramblings' permits us, the observers — as it has countless generations of children — to leap from the present to a past we can never share. This method of listening enables us to compare in a moment the pleasures of then and now, and to understand a little better how people have responded to social conditions that we have only read about.

Just as the life stories of ordinary Yugoslavs reflect revolutionary and postrevolutionary times, so talking with them today brings up current social problems. Reflections as well as reminiscences indicate how people 'make sense' of their society. Thus a good method of getting to the way people think about society is simply to draw them out in conversation about their lives and the world in which they live. As they talk about their problems and preoccupations, they do naturally what the observer is trying to do analytically: they reproduce the meaning that political acts and social institutions have for them. Their on-going explanation and rationalization — for the benefit of the outsider — reveal how they have 'made' and continue to 'make sense' of their society.[24]

24 This is how Lewis and Lane have successfully conveyed the social reality of specific strata of societies in Latin America and the United States, respectively. Many other social researchers are following this path, e.g. Danilo Dolci, *Report from Palermo*, trans. P. D. Cummins (New York: Viking Press, 1970 [1959]); Studs Terkel, *Division Street: America* (New York: Pantheon Books, 1967); Todd Gitlin and Nanci Hollander, *Uptown: Poor Whites In Chicago* (New York: Harper and Row, 1970); Tony Parker, *The Frying-Pan: A Prison and Its Prisoners* (New York: Basic Books, 1970).

Interpretations: the masses

Integration

Along with social change, the integration of citizens into political society represents a problem which can be approached within the context of ordinary lives. The concept of political integration, especially according to the Yugoslav model of de-alienation through self-management, implies that the individual citizen identifies his social self with the workings of political institutions and the outcomes of specifically political processes. Ideally, this self-identification should take both active and reflective forms: with the citizen participating in political activities and thinking about political issues. In short, integration guarantees that 'politics' as a form of social action is and will remain salient to the citizen's life.

For this to be so, without a great deal of either mystification or self-delusion, requires individuals to believe that political institutions work for them. The belief, like the institutions, must operate on many levels, but it must rely on two major points: That individuals have, or consider that they have, access *to* the political system; and that individuals enjoy, or consider that they enjoy, access to the benefits available *through* the political system. Political structures as diverse as 'the Machine', the 'lobby', and the *soviet* work according to these principles. Such institutions appear — at least, in many people's eyes — to balance the self-interest of individual citizens or social groups with the general interest of the whole society. Moreover, although people realize that these institutions must make their accommodations with other organizations, whose goals possibly contradict their own, most people tend to believe in the integrity of political institutions. Thus, integrated citizens view political institutions as pursuing their stated or accepted goals without unnecessary coercion, chicanery, or subterfuge. In the citizens' eyes, whatever corruption exists serves to lubricate the wheels, rather than to bog down the works, of the political machinery. If the citizens see that the situation is otherwise, then their attitudes and behavior will reflect cynicism, apathy, and alienation. In short, this indicates a failure of the political institutions to communicate and to integrate.

For some years, social scientists have tried to find indicators for, and to measure, the dimensions of alienation, but their research has concentrated on its reflective, rather than its active, elements. Thus, many of them have focused too much attention on isolating stated opinions instead of looking for a site in which citizens dynamically work out their perceptions and 'make sense' of political

31

phenomena. Too often, for sociologists and political scientists, asking people what they think and what they do takes the place of observing people as they engage in social action, drawing out their arguments and reasons, and reconstructing the political system as it appears to them.

This argument suggests that talking to people should be combined with a methodology which would construe 'politics' as a relatively structured field of observable social action. A good site for the sort of research that this implies would appear to be those low-level situations, such as meetings, which are structured by political institutions.[25] At meetings, for example, people gather and interact in an established way, i.e. through discussion, usually on a predetermined agenda. Within this format, leaders and citizens at meetings should indicate how open political institutions are to individuals and social groups. So interaction at the meeting should reflect the nature of control in the political society. Because participants in the meetings voice to some degree an evaluation of their fellow political actors, comparing their respective stakes in and benefits from 'politics', the observer should find in political meetings a useful starting-point for a critical analysis of the political system. In the Yugoslav case, meetings offer a chance to observe how various institutions and ideological norms work in practice: the 'leading role' of the Communist Party, the 'initiatives from below', the balance between authority and community. Moreover, since a Yugoslav legal authority has called meetings 'the basic form of self-managing decision-making',[26] any judgment about the self-management system must take them into account.

In Yugoslavia, one of these 'basic forms' of self-management is the voters' meeting (*zbor birača*). It is part of the communal system of self-government rather than the better-known system of workers' self-management. Held every other month in the local residential community (the *mesna zajednica*), which is a division

25 Erving Goffman's work, such as *Behavior in Public Places* (New York: Free Press, 1963) would be suggestive here, but it has to be made explicitly political. Sheldon Wolin refers to political institutions and the situations that they set up, such as a courtroom, a legislature, an administrative hearing, in *Politics and Vision* (Boston: Little, Brown, 1960), p. 7. It must be borne in mind, through the following discussion, that some distinctions obtain between higher and lower political meetings, i.e. between forums of elite and mass behavior.
26 Dragoljub Kavran, *Sastanci i odlučivanje* [Meetings and decision-making] (Belgrade: Radnička štampa, 1968), p. 3.

of the Yugoslav commune rather like an American ward or election district, the voters' meeting provides all citizens over the age of eighteen with a chance to participate in politics. At the voters' meeting they are expected to discuss and resolve problems which in America comprise the stuff of local politics, e.g. schools, taxes, transportation, and sanitation. According to a Yugoslav political scientist, 'The *mesna zajednica* is the first level of territorial community in whose framework citizens can directly decide or primarily influence decisions which regulate communal questions.' [27] At these meetings the citizens also hear proposals from higher organs, such as the Commune Assembly (to which the *mesna zajednica* sends two representatives) and the Municipal Assembly (one representative); they discuss these proposals and offer their own suggestions. Because the meetings offer a site for citizens to learn how to 'self-manage' their communal affairs, they potentially have great salience to people's lives.[28] So the discussion and the physical behavior — in short, the action and interaction — at voters' meetings should suggest how political integration through self-management works on a very basic level. Whether we can extrapolate significant political norms, especially those concerning control, authority, and community, from meetings such as these depends on indications from other sources, including sociological and political studies and public statements. But if the practice of self-management is half as potent as the theory, then ordinary political meetings should indicate relationships which are quite different from those of local politics as we know them.

Internalization of new norms

The long-ranging significance of revolutions lies in the changes they effect in private values and public lives. In this sense of revolutionary change, it would be worthwhile to ask how a formerly peasant society like Yugoslavia has adapted to the new social norms implied by the official ideology and institutions, particularly those of socialist self-management. Given the historical experiences of 500 years of Ottoman and Austro-Hungarian colonialism, the bureaucracy of these and Stalin's empires, and the *Gemeinschaft* of a traditional peasant economy, we would expect

27 Radivoje Marinković, *Ko odlučuje u komuni* [Who decides in the commune] (Belgrade: Institut društvenih nauka, 1971), pp. 220–1.
28 Cf. the suggestion that people might be more interested in self-management on lower levels with more immediate salience to their everyday activities. Pateman, *Participation and Democratic Theory*, p. 100.

that twenty-five years of socialism and self-management — despite
the explicit ideology-making and propagandizing that they entail
— have not been long enough to build a new consciousness.

The transformation of consciousness from peasant individualism to self-managing collectivism requires deliberate, delicate, and
continual balancing of stability and change, habit and improvement, security and risk. The political leadership which must attempt this feat is, itself, subject to the strains of conflicting norms
and values. Leaders as well as masses must suspend their belief in
the demonstrated certainty of traditional culture for the theoretical certainty of official ideology. In the transitional period, the
predominance of one or the other way of thinking depends on its
acceptance in and relevance to ordinary, everyday acts. So interaction between people, between people and institutions, between
officials and citizens or executives and workers, should show in
various milieux how Yugoslavs are working out the relevance and
the acceptance of new social norms. If strangers bound by neither
tradition nor kinship react to each other with mutual respect and
trust, if institutions as well as individuals carry out their functions with a sense of social obligation and objectivity, then we
can say that people are living up to the formal norms of socialist
self-management. However, if venality and *veze* ('connections')
predominate in public life, then we must conclude that self-management has not yet supplanted traditional behavior patterns.

The consciousness of social responsibility implied by socialist
self-management suggests a conception of self which is quite different from that of Yugoslav peasant society. In that world, the
self is defined by local traditions and face-to-face relations. For
each self, the relevant public is comprised of, first, the family,
then, the other villagers, and, ultimately, the far-flung fellow
members of the ethnic group. But it is the first of these, the
family, which constitutes the major relevant or 'critical other' for
each self. It is within the family that individuals must moderate
their behavior so as not to threaten the needs of other people,
including the ethical or psychological need for respect of self. In
contrast to the narrow social milieu in which the peasant feels
constrained by relevant others, Western urban society sets standards, at least ideally, for interaction in large social groups. These
standards or norms require the creation of a public self which acts
to minimize the personalism of interaction. Generally, becoming
a member of large, modern, social groups, such as highly urban-

ized cities and wealthy industrialized societies, has meant that
people assume in public a depersonalized, hence more 'objective'
and less 'offensive', self and revert in private, among close relatives
and peers, to a self which is permitted greater sloppiness of form.
Thus in peasant society the individual feels more constrained to
offer a polite or unobjectionable self in a narrow, rather private,
social milieu: his critical others are his family, his fellow villagers,
and his ethnic brothers. Conversely, in Western urban society the
individual tends to constrain his self-expression in a wider milieu:
his critical others are the strangers with whom he temporarily
shares a public place.[29]

Certainly, the official norms of socialist self-management seem
to encourage the construction of a public self familiar to urban-
ized, industrialized, Western societies. Relations among self-managers are supposedly based on the individual's independence from
traditional and personal, familial, or other narrowly-defined ties
which would prevent innovation and open-mindedness. Self-
management also demands cooperative or comradely relationships
based on lack of prejudice or favoritism, incorruptibility, and
mutual respect. The self-manager's public self denotes responsibility to other persons, *all* of whom are regarded as relevant
others, and to the society as a whole.

These norms, especially the transformation of parochial loyalties based on primary groups into social responsibility based on
national and working-class solidarity, apply not only to the ideology of self-management but also to the practical tasks of political integration and political development in relatively new states
such as Yugoslavia. The significance of these tasks is not lost on
the Yugoslav leadership, who have often made an issue of the
problem of responsibility. The mass media show increasing concern with 'irresponsible' behavior on many levels, and a well-
known professor, Jovan Djordjević of the Political Science Faculty
in Belgrade, has published a book entitled *Self-management and
a responsible society*. The publicity and the public opinion
aroused in connection with the topic of responsibility — and no
society, even one associated with a 'rule of law', appears to be
immune from the irresponsible excesses which arouse both publicity and public opinion — suggest that accepted norms and ma-

29 Cf. Erving Goffman, *The Presentation of Self in Everyday Life* (New
York: Doubleday, Anchor Books, 1959) and Edward T. Hall, *The Hidden Dimension* (Garden City, New York: Anchor Books, 1969).

terial rewards are not sufficient to insure responsible social behavior.

The simplest question we could ask about whether Yugoslavs have internalized the norms of socialist self-management has been put, in a different context, by a social psychologist from Slovenia: he asks, 'How do self-managers act when they are self-managing?' [30] To answer the question requires observation of Yugoslavs behaving 'naturally' in various social situations, interacting with other persons, especially in public places. Political meetings, as discussed in the previous section, offer a specialized type of milieu for this sort of observation. Other, nonpolitical public places for observation are wherever Yugoslavs gather: in *kafanas* (cafes), in work groups, on buses. In all these places a mode of interacting is worked out, through negotiation between the self and the relevant others, and a form of social order is established. By the same token, interaction between corporate social actors, such as the state and its institutions, economic associations like enterprises, and leadership groups, also creates a certain social order through accommodation to or adjustment of the official norms. Public life between corporate actors exerts a powerful influence on individuals, who perceive that this order indeed represents 'the way things are'. Whether this form of social order has anything to do with socialist self-management is a serious question for the future of 'the Yugoslav way'.

As the previous discussion shows, three general questions seem to pinpoint major problems in both the theory and the practice of Yugoslav socialism: How has social change, especially the revolution, affected individual lives? How are individual citizens and workers integrated into the political system? How do individuals internalize the norms of socialist society, in general, and of self-management, in particular? For the answers to these questions, we must deal with the social reality of the masses, on their own grounds.

SUBJECTS

Following this approach, we return to the purpose of the study: the direct documentation of life under socialism in the words

30 Vladimir Arzenšek, 'Samoupravljanje kao motiv i socijalna vrednost' [Self-management as a motivation and a social value], *Moderna organizacija* 2, no. 1 (1969): 32.

of people who live that way. So it is appropriate to end an introduction to the subject by introducing the subjects on whom much of this study is based. These are members of ten families whose life-stories and opinions appear at length in the text. All the families belong to the same ethnic group (Serb) and all reside in Belgrade. Aside from these similarities, they represent various income levels, occupations, educational achievements, and experience in an urban milieu. In terms of political activity, they are, on the average, rather more inclined to Communist Party membership than the population as a whole, but most of them are not active. A couple of them have been communists since before the war while others were attracted by the fact and then the successes of the socialist regime; still others do not even think about themselves in these terms. The middle-aged adults among them have lived through the Partisan War (World War II), and their children have grown to young adulthood in the era of socialism and workers' self-management.

The first five families, whose fictitious names in this study start with letters A through F, represent the Belgrade middle class — neither so rich as directors, administrators, and political leaders, nor so poor as workers and pensioners. The main wage earner in each of these five families earns over 2,000 dinars ($133) a month, which alone puts him in the top five to ten percent of Yugoslav wage earners. The last five families, whose names here start with letters P through Z, represent the working class. Their highest monthly salary is drawn by a highly-skilled machinist (1,800 dinars or $120), and the lowest is the unemployment compensation of an elderly semiskilled worker (800 dinars or $53). This range of salary puts these families within that half of the labor force which lives just above and below the poverty line, estimated at 1,000 dinars ($60) a month.[31]

31 In contrast to the middle class represented in this sample, a Yugoslav upper class consists of political officials and enterprise directors who earn monthly salaries greater than 4,000 dinars. According to published figures on base salaries, Belgrade political officials (in city government, the Party organization, and the unions) earn between 4,000 and 7,000 dinars a month, federal political officials (in the executive, legislative, and judicial branches of the government) from 5,000 to 8,000, and Belgrade directors between 6,000 and 9,000, with the salaries of some Serbian directors rising as high as 17,000 dinars a month. Thus a successful director of a profitable enterprise may earn twenty times as much as an unskilled worker. We can only imagine the salaries of the highest Party leaders and the directors of resort complexes on the coast. See Radivoj Cvetičanin, 'Društvo: Koliko zaradjuju rukovodioci'

Yugoslav socialism: a critical introduction

Aside from income, other factors of their lifestyle indicate differences — as well as similarities — between the middle-class and the working-class families. The location of their residence, for example, is beginning to take on more social significance. Although the destruction of German bombing and postwar reconstruction eliminated most of the old character and social homogeneity of neighborhoods, some areas are still known or are becoming known by the social status of their inhabitants. Thus some Belgrade neighborhoods are populated primarily by top-ranking political leaders; businessmen; successful artists and actors; up-and-coming administrators, technical cadres, and scientists; or workers and pensioners. Furthermore, in the semisuburban areas which have opened up for development since the war, the price of land and building costs have restricted home-ownership to the middle class. Workers have to wait for apartments to become available in socially- or enterprise-owned housing. Thus semisuburban areas become known by either their middle-class houses or their workers' housing projects. Several areas on the outskirts of the city have developed into 'wild settlements', where people, usually workers who have migrated to Belgrade, buy land from peasants and throw up a one-story house without getting the necessary building permit from municipal authorities. In contrast, suburban middle-class houses have two stories, perhaps a garage, and, certainly indoor conveniences for bathing and cooking.

Danilo Arandjelović, the head of the first family, moved to Belgrade from his village in western Serbia in 1945 for medical treatment of a war-related injury. (These and the following data on the sample are summarized in table 1.) He now earns 4,500 dinars a month as a journalist. His wife, a teacher, probably earns about 1,500 dinars a month. They have two young children. Recently they built a home in a semisuburban area known as an upper middle-class neighborhood. They own no other real property, but they drive a large Peugeot. Their home is equipped

[Society: How much do leaders earn] *NIN*, 16 April 1972, pp. 18–19 and Vuk Drašković, 'Društvo: Vrh platna nije na vrhu' [Society: The highest salaries aren't at the top], *NIN*, 23 April 1972, pp. 18–19. Also, Toma Džadžić, 'Ispod granice života' [Below the threshold of living], *NIN*, 6 June 1971, pp. 16–18, and Nenad Zirojević, 'U trci za dinarom: Šta je to zarada' [In the race for a dinar: What is a salary], *Politika*, 18 October 1970, p. 9. At the current exchange rate, one dollar is equal to fifteen dinars.

with many conveniences, including a telephone, television, record player, and tape recorder. Their furniture consists of the kind of set that Jugoexport makes in various period styles, e.g. Louis XV, 'Como', or 'Colonial', but they 'have not yet had time' to buy paintings and accessories to complement it.

Sretan and Beba Belić, a retired engineer and pharmacist respectively, moved to Belgrade in 1955 from a small town in Serbia. Originally, he comes from an old commercial port on the Dalmatian coast and she from a town in western Serbia. Both families belonged to the middle class, his containing admirals and churchmen and hers merchants. When Beba works, as she does occasionally, despite growing old, she earns 3,300 dinars a month. Their younger son Branislav, a lawyer, lived with them at the time of the interviews, but he has since married and moved away. He earns a salary of 1,500 dinars a month but supplements that with fees from his own clients, which often add 1,800 dinars a month. The Belić family owns three pieces of property. First, they own the land on which their Belgrade house is built and an adjoining fruit and vegetable garden. Located in a semisuburban area which retains its prewar character as a white-collar 'colony', the house has two stories and a garage. The Belićes share the house with another family which lives downstairs, and they also rent out a studio apartment on their floor. The second piece of real property that they own is a house on the Dalmatian coast, and they also have a plot of land near Belgrade where they are planning to built a week-end cottage. Their Belgrade house contains not only household conveniences (except a telephone), but also has walls of built-in storage space in dark wood panelling. There are always bowls of fresh flowers placed around the sets of furniture. Old silver and family crystal are displayed in a glass chest.

Miša Cvijić lives with his mother and younger sister in a spacious apartment across the street from the Serbian Orthodox cathedral. His father has retired to a village about a hundred kilometers from Belgrade, but because of his position in the state administration the Cvijićes had got a place in this building, which is restricted to government employees. Miša earns 2,700 dinars a month as service representative for a travel company. His mother probably earns about 2,000 dinars a month as a secondary-school teacher. Their apartment has many conveniences, including an extension telephone. During the course of inter-

Table 1 *Social attributes of sample families*

Attribute	Aranđelović	Belić	Cvijić	Đorđević	Filipović	Popović	Ristić	Stojanović	Vuković	Živković
Family										
National-ethnic identification	Serb	Serb	Serb	Yugoslav (Serb + Croat)	Serb	Serb	Serb	Serb	Serb (Montenegrin)	Serb
Year moved to city	1945	1955	Native	1961	1964	1950	Native	1964	1946	1966
Income from wages or pension (dinars/month)										
Father	4,500	3,300 *	*	2,500	2,240	1,400	945	800		1,200
Mother	*	3,000		1,200					1,000	
Child			2,700				2,700			
Home location										
Historic center	X									
Wider center			X	X	X				X	
Semisuburb		X				X	X	X		X
Middle-class										
Workers'										
Home-ownership										
Built and own home	X	X					X	X		X
Rent socially-owned apartment			X	X		X				
Rent privately-owned apartment									X	

40

Item								
Other real property								
Week-end and/or summer cottage	X	X				X		X
Rent out part of own living space					X (Illegal)		X	X
Rent out separate apartment(s)		X						
Field in country			X		X		X	
Car	Peugeot	Fiat		Fiat		Fiat	Fiat	
Household equipment								
Inside water and toilet	X	X	X	X	X	X	X	X
Stove-oven	X	X	X	X	X	X	X	X
Refrigerator	X	X	X	X	X	X	X	
Radio and television	X	X	X	X	X	X	X	X
Telephone		X		X	X		X	
Tape recorder	X	X		X				
Paintings, etc.	X	X	X					
Furniture set(s)	X	X	X	X	X	X		
Furniture fair								
Furniture makeshift		X				X	X	X

* Additional data unavailable.

41

viewing, they redecorated their living room, changing from one type of period furniture to another, more ornate style with more delicate chair legs. Their walls are hung with many fine paintings, and they have much crystal and silver. Miša's grandparents also lived and worked in Belgrade as part of the state bureaucracy, and in the Cvijić home I came to understand accessories like paintings and crystal as status symbols of the prewar bourgeoisie.

Josip and Milica Djordjević moved to Belgrade from Niš in 1961, when Josip retired from the army. Originally, he comes from a village on the Dalmatian coast; he is the only Croat in the sample. She comes from a village near Novi Sad, in the Vojvodina, north of Belgrade. While his family was poor, hers was a relatively prosperous peasant family. Her father was a respected man in the area, well read and involved in politics, and had even been elected to the legislature in the prewar Democratic Party. Josip's army pension is 2,500 dinars a month. Vesna, the elder daughter, earns 1,200 dinars a month as a clerk-typist, but she does not pay for room or board. The younger daughter is in a commercial high school. The Djordjevićes have a two-bedroom apartment in a fairly new building in New Belgrade which is restricted to army officers. Milica also owns a field in the country that she inherited from her father. They drive a *Crvena zastava* (a Yugoslav-made Fiat). They have many household conveniences, but their furniture is not the same quality as that of the first three families. The Djordjevićes' furniture is an assortment of serviceable pieces.

Moving to Belgrade from the Serbian town of Valjevo in 1964, Milutin and Zora Filipović soon bought a piece of land and erected a two-family house with another family in a semisuburban area. Milutin earns 2,240 dinars a month as an accountant, supplemented — so I heard from one of his co-workers — by rent from a field that he owns in the country and his wife's taking in sewing. However, Milutin says that they can not afford a car. The area in which they live seems to have a half middle-class, half working-class character. The Filipović household has all the necessities but no luxuries like a telephone or paintings. Their furniture is comfortable but varied in style.

It is a step down in social status from the Filipovićes to the Popović family. Rade Popović came to Belgrade from Niš in 1950, and a few years later he married Branka, whose father was

Subjects

a well-to-do peasant near Belgrade. They live with their two young children in an enterprise-owned apartment in a workers' settlement some distance from Belgrade. They also own a small plot in the 'wild settlement' where I first met Rade. The two-room, whitewashed cottage that he has built there is still unfurnished. Rade earns 1,400 dinars a month which was supplemented last year, a good year for his enterprise, by a bonus of 400 dinars a month. Rade rides a bicycle. But his apartment has many conveniences, though not a telephone, and the furniture is comfortable.

The Ristić family straddles the lower middle class and the professional middle class, although the elderly father's pension of 945 dinars a month would place him in the working class. Marko, the father and head of the household, was born in Belgrade over seventy years ago. His father was also a native of Belgrade, so his is an unusually urban family, at least on one side. Both he and his father were railroad clerks. The house that Marko built in the 1930s in a working-class neighborhood on the old outskirts of the city is large enough to accommodate, besides the parents, a divorced son and a married son and his family. Both sons contribute to household expenses. Steva, the divorced son, makes 2,700 dinars a month as an engineer. The other son owns a *Crvena zastava*. Their house has many conveniences, including two telephone lines, and the furniture is comfortable.

The Stojanović family moved to Belgrade from a farm in the Vojvodina in 1964. Originally, the parents are from southern Serbia. Miodrag, the father, is almost old enough to retire. Presently he is unemployed and, as a semiskilled worker, gets compensation of 800 dinars a month for himself and his wife. They own a plot of land on which they built a two-story, two-family house. They rent out an apartment and live in the remaining space with a married son and his wife and baby, two unmarried sons, and an unmarried daughter. Their house is adjacent to a fairly new workers' settlement. The Stojanović household has all the necessary equipment except a telephone. Their furniture, however, is old, in poor condition, and makeshift.

The Vuković household consists of the widow Dušica and her divorced brother Janko. Both Dušica and Janko are retired, she from a job ironing at the socially-owned dry-cleaning and laundering enterprise and he from an unspecified routine clerical job with the secret police. She lives on a combination of her own and her husband's pensions, which total about 1,000 dinars a month. At the time of the interviews, she leased her two-room house, on a working-class block near a big outdoor market, from a private landlord. For extra money, she rented out a bed in her brother's room to a young baker. Dušica and Janko had lived in the same neighborhood since moving to Belgrade from a Montenegrin town in 1946. Neither of them owned any property. Their house did not have an indoor water supply, but Dušica had a television and a radio, bought on credit and paid for when her husband died five years ago. Her furniture was makeshift and in poor condition. However, Dušica and Janko had the good luck to live in a house which was designated for demolition in 1971, probably so that a tall modern apartment house could be erected on the site. The city, which is obliged to compensate residents in this predicament, assigned them a new apartment in a middle-class, semisuburban neighborhood of brand-new apartment houses with all the conveniences. Many of our conversations concerned their enthusiastic preparations for moving to the new apartment. At last contact, Dušica and Janko had moved in and were quite content.

The last family is that of Jovan Živković, an invalid who lost a leg during the last days of the war. He and his wife, Slavka, both originally from southern Serbia, moved to Belgrade in 1966 from a village in the Vojvodina. After boarding with their three children for a year with a peasant family in a village just on the city's borders, they bought a plot of land and threw up a small house in the 'wild settlement' where Rade Popović built his cottage. They live on Jovan's pension of 1,200 dinars a month. Their house has few conveniences, lacking an indoor water supply and a toilet, but they do have electricity, a television, and a small record player. Their furniture is makeshift and old.

Not only in lifestyle, but also in political involvement, these ten families represent ordinary citizens. It is quite possible that the opinions and orientations that they express would appear differently in other milieux, specifically, if I had chosen a sample of government and Party leaders or successful enterprise directors. To repeat, however, this study is concerned with the lives of ordinary citizens. The sample's political activism — in terms of membership in political organizations and attendance at political meetings — is actually higher than the Yugoslav average

Subjects

Table 2 *Political activism of ten Belgrade families*

Family	Number of adults	League of Communists		Socialist Alliance		*Mesna zajednica*		Workers' self-management	
	Status:	Hd. Ldr.	Mem- ber	Hd. Ldr.	Mem- ber	Hd. Ldr.	At- tend	Hd. Ldr.	At- tend
Arandjelović	2	×	×			×		×	
Belić	3								
Cvijić	4	×	×						
Djordjević	3	×	×			×			
Filipović	2				×		×		
Popović	2		/						/
Ristić	3	×	/						
Stojanović	6								
Vuković	2	×							
Živković	2	×							

×   Presently or in past (indicates continuous involvement).
/   Broke off involvement.

(see table 2). While nine of the twenty-nine adults (31 percent) in the sample belong to the League of Communists, roughly one out of every eleven adults (about 10 percent) in the total Yugoslav population is a Party member, according to figures in the 1971 Statistical Yearbook. Moreover, one member of the sample (Danilo Arandjelović) has continuously been elected to office in his Party unit and his workers' self-management organization. Another respondent (Josip Djordjević) is a leader in his local community. Despite the small size of the sample, it is suggestive that these two most active respondents tend to reiterate the official ideology in their political attitudes.

The object of using this sample is to delve into social reality from Arandjelović to Živković, to discern what 'the Yugoslav way' means to people living and working with it. This chapter, which offered a 'critical introduction to Yugoslav socialism', presented several of the problems, and many of the questions, which may occur to outsiders seeking to understand the system. Just as the introduction began by reviewing the relationship between theory and practice in Yugoslav socialism from the standpoint of policy choices made by the leadership, so the rest of the study considers this relationship from the viewpoint of the subjects. Each question posed in the introduction describes an ever-widening circle in the pool of social reality, as we move from official ideology to life experiences, to perceptions of society, to generational changes, to political meetings, to public places, to cultural norms. This particular order takes us from a level of generality — that of official ideology — down to many kinds of specific data, from private lives and individual statements, then up again to the general level of cultural norms.

That part of the official ideology which is held to be not only unique but also most indicative of the sort of socialism that Yugoslavia represents is the concept of self-management. Accordingly, the next chapter examines the history of this idea and the institutions which it has inspired. This discussion should be especially useful to foreign students of self-management who are curious about the conditions under which the concept has been applied and extended.

From an explanation of official ideology, the study moves into an interpretation of how the revolution has affected people's lives. Thus, chapter 3 considers the perceptions of ordinary Yugoslavs and the social conditions which have influenced these perceptions. Here is where we enter into the life experiences of the Arandjelovićes, the Popovićes, the Živkovićes, and their peers. The comparison between Partisan parents and modern children, as well as between the Partisans in youth and in middle age, takes us into chapter 4. In that part of the study we consider changes in attitudes and behavior within a single generation and across generations. Through the statements of the Belgrade sample we attempt some generalizations about these kinds of changes in a postrevolutionary society. That chapter also offers a categorization of Yugoslav political attitudes which enables us to understand the divisions between 'official' and 'dissenting' opinions.

Chapter 5 turns from the Belgrade sample to political meetings in that city. Taking off from participant-observation, the chapter also uses Yugoslav studies of decision-making and political influence, surveys, and statements in the Yugoslav press to analyze the extent to which self-management has strengthened political integration. Chapter 6 uses participant-observation of a different type of social action, that of behavior in public places, to draw inferences about the internalization of the norms of socialist self-management in a Balkan peasant society. That discussion requires a general consideration of Balkan peasant culture, particularly the self-concepts and the norms engendered by the collective, historical experiences of colonialism, bureaucratism, and dependence on all levels of society. Thus chapter 7 indicates to what extent change has been possible within the parameters of cultural norms. Following the empirical body of the study, chapter 8 offers a consideration of the problems that Yugoslav socialism has had to face and a partial assessment of its successes and failures. The discussion returns, in many ways, to the problems and questions posed in the introduction. This return to the starting-point indicates the salience of these questions not only for Yugoslavs, but for all their contemporaries who are searching for an egalitarian but democratic 'way' of their own.

2

THE OFFICIAL IDEOLOGY
OF SELF-MANAGEMENT

Today we already know enough about etatism. Socialism, however, is only now seeking its substance.

Svetozar Stojanović,
Izmedju ideala i stvarnosti

For the past twenty years, Yugoslavs have proclaimed that *samoupravljanje* ('self-management' or 'self-government', pronounced säm″-ŏ-ōō′-präv-lyä-nye)[1] is their gift not only to world socialism but also to all countries of the world. Although *samoupravljanje* is the most popular word in their official vocabulary, Yugoslavs have never defined exactly what it means. It remains — like 'democracy' in Western societies — praised for excesses and damned for failures, assumed to be both institutionalized and immanent, protected by law yet vulnerable to enemies of the state. We in the West know about *samoupravljanje* in the form of workers' councils. Indeed, some foreigners have even advocated the adoption of workers' councils in their own countries to lessen the malaise of workers in industrial society.[2] But although we may have a glimmer of recognition to the term 'workers' self-management', we are lost when the Yugoslavs claim to have pioneered a true system of 'social self-government'. What is this system? How does it carry over from industry to society? Perhaps most important to Westerners, does it work?

1 I use the Serbo-Croatian term because it carries the double meaning of self-management and self-government, which I distinguish for the sake of conceptual clarity. In this chapter 'self-management' refers to the political system in work units like enterprises and self-government to residential units like communes and *mesna zajednicas* ('local communities'). In the following chapters I shall use 'self-management'.

2 Dahl, *After the Revolution?* ch. 3. See also Michel Crozier, *La société bloquée* (Paris: Editions du Seuil, 1970), ch. 4.

Introduction

In theory *samoupravljanje* is man's effort to control every aspect of his own life: to crawl out, historically speaking, from under the domination of tribal chiefs, feudal lords, infallible monarchs, fascist governments, various bosses, big businessmen, and, in Yugoslav experience, centralist bureaucratic states. Thus *samoupravljanje* stands for de-alienation, the liberation of work, and direct democracy. In essence, *samoupravljanje* means self-government or self-determination. Workers' self-management means the right of the workers (producers, experts, and administrators) in enterprises or firms to control the means and resources at their disposal without harassment from the state or from any other economic interest. Organized in an elected, representative council, the workers make their own economic plans, determine their own salaries (above a government-set minimum), distribute their own benefits like apartments and vacation plans, and nominate their own directors. In contrast to American propositions about workers' councils, workers' self-management presupposes a socialist property system, that is, a system in which the means of production, public transportation and communications, and most housing are owned — not privately, not even by the state, but — socially, by all the people in society.

Social self-government is a concept both more inclusive and more elusive. Just as workers' self-management applies to man's work problems, so social self-government applies to the multitude of intricate communications and relationships which surround man in contemporary society. In practice, though, workers' self-management applies to the work unit and social self-government to the residential community. What Yugoslavs mean by social self-government is what the workers' representatives in the Paris Commune of 1871 called political unity: 'The voluntary association of all local initiatives, the spontaneous and free swelling of all individual forces toward a mutual goal — the well-being, freedom and security of all'.[3] For social self-government, according to a recent, authoritative Yugoslav text,

3 From the Manifesto of the Federal Chamber of Workers' Societies (1871), reprinted in Radoš Smiljković and Milan Petrović, *Samoupravljanje i socijalizam: Čitanka samoupravljača* [Self-management and socialism: A self-managers' reader] (Sarajevo: Zavod za izdavanje udžbenika, 1970), p. 57.

it is indispensable that [man] is integrated in the self-governing [*samoupravni*] mechanism of the local community so that he may already exert — at that level, in those surroundings — his influence not only on the reproduction of his naked existence and the existence of his narrower work community, but also on the resolution of other social needs, social services, and all the other fields of social work . . .[4]

What this boils down to in practice is like local politics as we know it in America, with locally-elected and locally-responsible school and draft boards, a mayor, a town council. Yugoslavs, however, emphasize the independence of the local unit — the commune — and its theoretical self-sufficiency and autonomy. Like the enterprises governed by workers' self-management, communes are supposed to provide most of their own income (usually from taxes on firms and individual salaries and from additional taxes, called 'contributions' [*doprinosi*], on residents), to improve their own facilities and services, and to realize the wishes of the citizens living there.[5]

The official Yugoslav ideology of self-management consists of the oral and written statements of the political leadership and their advisers, as well as the laws that they have enacted under this rubric. They refer to the writings of utopians like More, Fourier, and Owen; early socialists like Baboeuf, Saint-Simon, and the Paris Communards; Marx and Engels; Lenin; and Rosa Luxemburg, Antonio Gramsci, and Bela Kun, the unsuccessful or briefly successful socialist revolutionaries. The official ideology also refers to the work of Svetozar Marković, a Serbian communist and a contemporary of Marx. Although some Yugoslavs, such as the trade unionist Dimitrije Tucović, were writing about socialism at the beginning of this century, their work has not been

4 Najdan Pašić, *Političko organizovanje samoupravnog društva* [Political organization of self-managing society] (Belgrade: Komunist, 1970), p. 67.
5 For an explanation of the organization of workers' self-management, see *Workers' Management in Yugoslavia: 1950–1970*, Stanko Grozdanić and Momčilo Radosavljević, eds., (Belgrade: Medjunarodna politika, 1970); Gerry Hunnius, 'Workers' Self-Management in Yugoslavia', in *Workers' Control: A Reader on Labor and Social Change*, Gerry Hunnius, G. David Garson and John Case, eds. (New York: Vintage Books, 1973), pp. 268–321; and Ichak Adizes, *Industrial Democracy: Yugoslav Style* (New York: Free Press, 1971). On social self-government, see Pašić, *Političko organizovanje*, pts. 1 and 3, and Dragoljub Milivojević, *The Yugoslav Commune* (Belgrade: Medjunarodna Politika, 1965).

published or publicized since around 1950. Finally, the official ideology includes the speeches and writings of the postwar political leadership, including President of the Republic Josip Broz-Tito and Edvard Kardelj, and the professors, publicists, and other intellectuals associated with the *Savez komunista* ('League of Communists' or LCY), such as Dr Najdan Pašić, professor at the Belgrade Political Science Faculty and editor of *Socijalizam*, and Dr Miroslav Pečujlić, professor at the same faculty and member of the Central Committee of the LCY.

To understand the official ideology of self-management, it is useful to know how it has evolved: what were the historical circumstances which compelled the Yugoslavs to formulate innovations in both theory and practice. Therefore a discussion of Yugoslav ideology should begin with an analysis of its origin in 1948–9 and its development since then. With that background, it is possible to examine several alternative ideological positions which have confronted the official ideology as it has evolved. The analysis of rejected ideological alternatives should clarify the theory of self-management — at least as it has been worked out by the Yugoslavs. Finally, no discussion of self-management would be complete without considering several inherent problems or contradictions that the official ideology has not yet resolved.

HISTORICAL EVOLUTION: 1948–71

Despite a willingness to seek precedent in the work of Marx, Lenin, and Gramsci, the Yugoslav ideology sprang primarily from the situation in which the new socialist regime found itself after the war. The success of the antifascist struggle, the need to unify mutually hostile social and ethnic elements, and the traumatic withdrawal of organized socialist support during the Cominform dispute — these factors comprise the background against which Yugoslavia inaugurated workers' self-management.[6] Once

6 An authoritative account of the decision to introduce workers' self-management has yet to appear. Indeed, it is shrouded in the mystique of Tito's leadership and the overcoming of severe internal stresses within the Party and the society. As a symbol of unity, it is presented as the fruit of the collective leadership of the time. Cf. Milovan Djilas's account of how he conceived of the workers' councils and how he and Kardelj worked out the idea and convinced Tito to support it. *The Unperfect Society: Beyond the New Class* (New York: Harcourt, Brace and World, 1969), pp. 221–3.

the seeds of innovation were sown with the introduction of workers' councils, continued economic and political isolation encouraged the Yugoslavs to adopt an increasingly pragmatic interest in
economic development and industrialization, as well as a willingness to experiment with new forms of organization and control. From 1948 to 1955, i.e. from the break with the Soviet bloc
until Khrushchev's state visit to Belgrade, the political situation
in Yugoslavia was tense.[7] Yugoslav political leaders saw the country as caught in the whirlpool between the Scylla of Soviet occupation and the Charybdis of American domination. They saw
themselves, no doubt, as balancing the ideals of a socialist revolution with American food and dollars. In this situation, the
political leadership was playing for support from three publics:
the socialist bloc, the United States and its allies, and the people
of Yugoslavia themselves. But this third public's support was no
more secure than that of the first two.[8]

Yugoslavia consists of a most heterogeneous assortment of
ethnic groups and national minorities who have been politically
united only since 1918. Furthermore, this political union had
been dissolved during the war, when Yugoslavia was shattered
along national–ethnic lines. The country was divided into two
zones of occupation (German and Italian), crossed — as the Yugoslavs say — by every major army, and fragmented by internal
fighting between various native armed forces (Partisans, Četniks,
Ustaše, Domobrani, Bela Garda, and others).[9] In addition to
ethnic hostility, the political leaders also had to surmount opposition to the regime from anticommunist elements ranging
from the Church (mainly the Roman Catholic Church in Croatia), to the rather small bourgeoisie, from the royalists who

7 For details on this period, see Milovan Djilas, *Conversations With
Stalin* (New York: Harcourt, Brace and World, 1962); Adam Ulam,
Titoism and the Cominform (Cambridge, Mass.: Harvard University
Press, 1952); and Robert Bass and Elizabeth Marbury, eds., *The Soviet-
Yugoslav Controversy 1948–1958: A Documentary Record* (New York:
Prospect Books, 1959). On the ideological aspects of this dispute, see
A. Ross Johnson, 'The Dynamics of Communist Ideological Change in
Yugoslavia: 1945–1953' (Ph.D. diss., Columbia University, 1967).

8 For a description of the leadership's attempts to placate the external
publics — although not in those terms, see John C. Campbell, *Tito's
Separate Road: America and Yugoslavia in World Politics* (New York:
Harper and Row, 1967).

9 See Jozo Tomasevich's chapter on World War II in Wayne S. Vucinich,
ed., *Contemporary Yugoslavia* (Berkeley and Los Angeles: University
of California Press, 1969).

wanted the return of King Peter, to the democratic Left. Also, the break with the Cominform created a hostile faction of Soviet sympathizers ('Stalinists') within the Party. Thus it is understandable that Yugoslavs perceived this period, especially 1948–50, as traumatic. Into this historical situation — provoked by the break with all other socialist countries — the Yugoslav leadership introduced workers' self-management. They wanted neither to provoke Soviet attack, nor to alienate American aid, but they did want to secure the support of their own people.

Moreover, the dispute with Stalin produced a curious ideological problem, for the Yugoslavs had to justify their revolution not only as socialist, but also as totally divorced from the leading exemplar of socialism at that time, i.e. the Soviet Union.[10] Thus, early in their history they were impelled to assume the dual role of both innovator and defender of an ideological tradition. Casting about in the annals of socialist practice, the Yugoslavs must have carefully examined the acts of the Paris Commune of 1871, Lenin in the Soviet Union, and Gramsci in Italy.

At least since the insurrection and reorganization of society attempted by the Paris Commune of 1871, the archetypal organizational form which seems to emerge in revolutionary situations when workers usurp the general organs of government is that of a mass-based council. Councils or *soviets* were established by Russian workers during the short-lived 1905 Revolution and again in 1917. Responding to this popular movement, and especially to the identification in most people's minds of Bolshevism and *soviets,* Lenin incorporated them into his revolutionary program just prior to the Bolshevik seizure of power in October 1917. At the conclusion of the World War, the idea of *soviets* swept through the entire European socialist movement. Similar councils were established in Germany and Hungary in 1918 and 1919. In 1919, also, Gramsci and the other Italian socialists around the journal *Ordine nuovo* publicized the idea of factory councils as organs of the working class which would operate differently from either the Socialist Party or the trade unions. As practical political thinkers, both Lenin and Gramsci saw the potential of these councils not only for solidifying the working class's support for the revolutionary movement, but also for educating the workers

10 For a similar analysis of early Yugoslav innovation as a response to Stalin's rejection, see M. George Zaninovich's chapter on 'The Yugoslav Variation on Marx', in Vuchinich, ed., *Contemporary Yugoslavia.*

to perform their leading role in a socialist society. In Gramsci's
opinion and, to some extent, in Lenin's, this type of council
could also act as a model for the new society's political and economic organization. Ideologically, too, councils of workers' and
peasants' deputies carried out Marx's ideas about self-government and direct democracy. At least in theory, the *soviets* and
the factory councils revived the perspective of the Paris Commune by giving workers the right and the organization to decide
the major problems of their life and work. In practice, however,
problems soon arose in implementing the theory behind the
councils. Although *soviets* and factory councils were introduced
under the rubric of 'Power to the Workers', the degree of autonomy that they were in fact permitted raised the question of
whether this meant Power *for* the Workers or Power *over* the
Workers.[11]

Because of their association with class struggle and socialist
experiments, *soviets* and factory councils suggested themselves as
a revolutionary institution which also fulfilled a practical political need. As such, they became a useful precedent to the Yugoslavs after 1948. When they were presented to the Yugoslav public in 1949, workers' councils were described as leading toward
'the complete realization of the constitutional principle of direct
participation by the workers in the administration of the economy and in the execution of economic control[s]' and also toward 'the most active involvement of workers in the struggle to
achieve the tasks of planning'. Thus, 'the task of the workers'

11 On the association between councils and revolutionary situations, see
Hannah Arendt, *On Revolution* (New York: Viking, 1965), ch. 6. The
intimate relationship between the appeal of *soviets* and the timing of
the October Revolution is documented by American historian Alex-
ander Rabinowitch (Columbia University Seminar on Communism, 14
February 1974). For documents on the significance of workers' councils in situations of revolution or class-based struggle, see Ernst
Mandel, ed., *Contrôle ouvrier, conseils ouvriers, autogestion antholo-
gie* (Paris: Maspéro, 1970).
  Barrington Moore, Jr., presents a suggestive discussion of *soviets* in
Lenin's pre-revolutionary thought and revolutionary practice. He emphasizes the dual problem in the use of *soviets* as it appeared to the
Russian leadership after 1917: to assure mass support for the revolution *through* the *soviets* as well as to consolidate Party control *over*
the *soviets*. *Soviet Politics: The Dilemma of Power* (1950; New York:
Harper and Row, 1965), pp. 41–2 and 128–38. On Gramsci's factory
councils, see John M. Cammett, *Antonio Gramsci and the Origins of
Italian Communism* (Stanford University Press, 1967), ch. 4.

council is to participate actively in the resolution of all the most important questions of the enterprise, to keep track vigilantly of the work, and to aid the progress of production and work in the enterprise'.[12] So the Yugoslav leadership offered their workers' councils as a step forward (in both theory and practice) toward the rule of the working class, as well as a means of mobilizing workers to work harder and to increase productivity.

Councils like these had appeared even before the war in Yugoslav workers' political demands, notably in the work of trade-unionist Filip Filopović, a contemporary of Gramsci's.[13] But wartime forms of political organization really prepared the citizens for popularly-elected and popularly-responsible councils in work as in government. One of the first liberated areas, the town of Krupanj in Serbia, established a committee of workers' control in the local antimony works. This elected committee ran the works, organized the work process, paid and provided food and housing for the workers. Similar workers' committees apparently existed in other industrial enterprises in Serbia also during the war.[14] From 1941 on, the Partisans set up local assemblies of loyal notables to administer the areas that they liberated from Nazi occupation or from Četnik control. During the first phase of the war these assemblies were called 'revolutionary organs of popular government'; later, as the Partisans tried to get the widest possible social support, their name was changed to 'people's committees'. As first described in October 1941, the duties of these local bodies were (1) to organize the population to supply the men at the front with necessities; (2) to guarantee order in the rear areas so that there would be no looting, speculation, or fifth-column activity; (3) to organize the provisioning and feeding of the people, especially the families of active Partisans; (4) to organize all forms of economic activity and communications in the area; and (5) to secure connections between the front and rear areas.[15] So besides performing vital functions for the military success of the Partisans, these people's committees also gave

12 Joint proclamation of Central Committee of League of Yugoslav Trade Unions, Federal Planning Commission, and Economic Council of the Yugoslav Federal Government, 29 December 1949, reprinted in Smiljković and Petrović, *Samoupravljanje*, p. 113.
13 *Workers' Management*, p. 9.   14 Ibid., pp. 10–11.
15 *Borba*, no. 1, 19 October 1941, reprinted in Smiljković and Petrović, *Samoupravljanje*, p. 109.

the population of liberated areas experience in governing, controlling, planning, and electing within the wartime parameters. After the war, the new socialist republic maintained people's committees as organs of local government. According to a 1946 law, these committees were redefined as 'the organs of state power by which the people carries out its power in administrative territorial units . . . the highest organs of state power of local significance on their territory . . . representative organs, elected on the basis of a general, equal, and direct electoral law with a secret ballot'.[16] Over the years, the representative organs gradually evolved into the parliamentary chambers, municipal and communal assemblies that Yugoslavia now has. On all territorial levels, from the commune up to the federation, the representative assembly is supposed to be the highest state organ. Thus the theory of territorial representation behind the legislative institutions of self-management does not differ in its federalism from that of Western parliamentary systems. But the continued reliance on people's committees and their assembly successors parallels the evolution of workers' councils.

While the wartime people's committees were still in power, the Antifascist Front led by Tito and the Communist Party instituted a form of workers' representation in all private, cooperative, and state enterprises employing more than five workers. The committees, called workers' representative councils, were intended 'to protect the interests of the liberation struggle'. Although the terms of their mandate were vague, the general purpose of the workers' deputies was 'to work on the defense of the social and economic interests of the workers and to help move production forward'.[17] The 1945 law which established these councils seems to be modeled on a Russian decree of 1917 which instituted 'workers' control over production, location, and buying and selling all products and raw materials'.[18] Just as Lenin had acted almost immediately to institutionalize the Bolshevik Revolution through 'workers' control', so the Yugoslav leadership — for similar motives — also instituted their workers' representative councils. However, propelled by circumstances, the

---

16 From the General Law on People's Committees, 28 May 1946, reprinted in Smiljković and Petrović, *Samoupravljanje,* p. 112.
17 From the Law on Workers' Representatives, *Borba,* 30 July 1945, reprinted in Smiljković and Petrović, *Samoupravljanje,* p. 111.
18 *Pravda,* 16 (3) November 1917, reprinted in Smiljković and Petrović, *Samoupravljanje,* p. 71–2.

Yugoslav workers' councils soon outstripped their Soviet precedent.

The 1950s

By the Law on Workers' Self-management of 26 June 1950, the power and the rights of management in all state-owned economic enterprises were given to the work collectives 'in the name of the social community'. The collectives — which signify the totality of employees — in all but the smallest enterprises were to 'manage' through both workers' councils elected by the workers and management committees elected by the workers' councils.[19] Furthermore, the management committee of the regional association of enterprises was to appoint the director of the enterprise. If the enterprise did not belong to an association like this, then the responsible state organ would appoint the director. In case the director proved unsatisfactory, the workers' council or the management committee of the enterprise could suggest his dismissal. In brief, the workers' council's role included these functions:

1. Approving the basic plans and the final accounting of the enterprise (within the framework of the state economic plan);[20]
2. Making decisions for the management of the enterprise and the fulfillment of the economic plan;
3. Electing the management committee;
4. Making enterprise regulations, subject to the approval of the management committee of the regional association of enterprises;
5. Discussing and judging the work of the management committee;
6. Discussing and approving individual actions of the management committee; and
7. Distributing that part of the enterprise's profit (*akumulacija*) which remained after taxes.[21]

19 According to industrial sociologist Josip Županov, the management committee, comprised of executives and directors, was intended at this time to be the dominant organ in decision-making in the enterprise. Županov, *Samoupravljanje i društvena moć*, p. 111.
20 Centralized state planning was eliminated during the first Yugoslav economic reform, 1950–54.
21 Law on Workers' Self-management, 26 June 1950, reprinted in Smiljković and Petrović, *Samoupravljanje*, pp. 114–15.

This 1950 law remains the formal basis of self-management. Successive pieces of legislation (including the 1963 Federal Constitution and a proposed Code of Self-Managers in 1971) have only amplified on these themes.

After three years of practice, the institutionalization of workers' self-management was reformulated. This seems to have represented not only a clarification of perhaps chaotically innovative practices, but also an affirmation of the leadership's commitment to the idea of self-management. However, the idea itself caused some confusion. According to Yugoslavs who discuss the initial period of self-management, many leading cadres — including directors, economic administrators, and Party officials — were puzzled by self-management and did not know how to implement it in their domains or enterprises. On the one hand, the prospect of real workers' control probably struck them as a threat — both as leaders and as communists who had believed in the Soviet model of Party control through a centralized state.[22] On the other hand, Lenin's turnabout, from 1918 to 1922, as the exigencies of government persuaded him of the indispensability of white-collar and managerial personnel, probably also influenced the Yugoslavs to avoid equating self-management with (manual) workers' control. In this sense we may note that the Yugoslavs' terminological innovation — self-*upravljanje* — neatly pushes aside the problems involved, for *upravljanje* refers more properly to 'administration', 'management', or 'direction' than to 'control'. The term thus fits in a continuum of related concepts which are distinguished by the degree to which they are inimical to the existing political and economic power structure: workers' control (the proletarian weapon), workers' self-management (including workers from all skill levels), workers' participation (as in Sweden, in France, and under discussion in the United States), consultation (as with trade union representatives), and co-determination or co-management (as in West Germany's *Mitbestimmung*).

As both the concept and its subsequent legal evolution indicate, Yugoslav self-management was intended as an integrative

22 The movie *The Role of my Family in the World Revolution* (1970) dramatizes this point very well. In one scene, an idealistic youth confronts an experienced Partisan colonel who has become an official of the new state and asks him about the (forgotten) issue of workers' power. 'I am workers' power', the colonel replies. The time is around 1948.

force rather than as a weapon of class struggle. Not only manual workers or other underprivileged strata, but all Yugoslavs who work for a living have a right to aspire to and to participate in workers' self-management. So, in the late 1940s, the Yugoslav leadership bid for the reconciliation of manual and white-collar workers, subordinates and supervisors, and communists and non-Party members. In these innovative circumstances, many of the leaders responsible for making changes either did not know what to do or showed reluctance to do it.[23]

During the initial years of self-management, also, the economists who advocated decentralization were gaining more influence among the leadership. According to their concepts, the economy would benefit by loosening state controls so that individual enterprises could manage their own production, sales, and expansion. Their analysis apparently made sense to the Yugoslavs, and it also complemented the ideological theme of self-management. Furthermore, the continued opposition of the socialist bloc, at least until Stalin's death in 1953, may have encouraged the Yugoslavs to depart even further from the Soviet model of socialism. So in 1953, during the process of overhauling the 1946 Federal Constitution, the government clarified the semi-autonomous status of enterprises as well as the rights and duties of the workers.

A federal government proclamation of that time stated officially that enterprise autonomy — as far as plans, profits, and wages were concerned — was an essential component of workers' self-management. Specifically, the government defined the rights of the enterprise 'to establish independently its economic plans . . . to distribute independently the organization's income [limited only by federal taxes and reinvestment of a federally-set minimum back into the enterprise] . . . and to set the workers' wages [above a state-established minimum] . . .' This formulation marked the most extreme decentralization attempted to that time in a socialist economy. However, the state maintained certain controls to ensure that the enterprise would fulfill its financial obligations to the government, to its workers, and to its own continued functioning. The 1953 proclamation also upheld 'the right of work collectives to manage economic organizations directly and through workers' councils, assemblies of agricultural

---

23 There are indications of this in the academic discussions of self-management, which tend to slough over the initial etatist period.

cooperatives and other representative organs which they themselves elect and recall'. Thus the management committees yielded, at least on paper, to the more popularly-based workers' council.[24]

By the mid-fifties, the first flush of workers' self-management may have faded. Yugoslavs today attribute this modified failure of self-management to limitations in its adoption. These were mostly limits imposed by the centralized state, the centralists in the Party leadership, and the central bureaucracy of the economic planning apparatus. Although a series of economic reforms enacted between 1950 and 1954 attempted to circumvent these limitations by placing more responsibility in the enterprises' hands, the state retained great power. Thus the state could still allot profits and decide on almost all investments in the enterprise.[25]

So it is not surprising that the First Congress of Self-Managers in June 1957 demanded greater autonomy for enterprises in production planning, spending, and development. On the whole, however, this Congress symbolized yet another affirmation of the leadership's commitment to self-management as the official ideology. Moreover, the Congress indicated that the leadership was coming more and more to elevate the model of workers' self-management above and beyond the level of the enterprise: to generalize workers' self-management in terms of the whole social system. At least one statement produced at the Congress documents this point, for it says: 'The process of the free association of producers is reflected in the workers' councils and in the communal system, beginning with the enterprise and the commune *all the way to the state entity which itself by degrees is becoming more and more a community of free socialist producers'.*[26] As

24 Decisions on the Proclamation of the Constitutional Law, *Službeni list FNRJ*, no. 3, 1953, reprinted in Smiljković and Petrović, *Samoupravljanje*, pp. 115–16.
25 On the economic reforms, see Deborah D. Milenkovitch, *Plan and Market in Yugoslav Economic Thought*, Yale University Russian and East European Studies, 9 (New Haven, 1971), chs. 4, 10, and Rudolf Bićanić, *Economic Policy in Socialist Yugoslavia* (Cambridge University Press, 1973).
26 Cited in Smiljković and Petrović, *Samoupravljanje*, p. 170. Emphasis added. In itself, this language appears to be a mystification. However, the formulation suggests that, at the time, the Yugoslav leaders connected the idea of self-management with some form of the withering away of the state. That view would also coincide with the 1958 Party program, which worked out the concept of an ideologically guiding, rather than a politically commanding, Party.

the First Congress's demand for greater enterprise autonomy indicates, this has been a significant factor in the development of workers' self-management. Thus it is practically impossible to speak of greater self-management within the enterprise, i.e. of the greater power of workers' councils, without also considering the enterprise's ever-growing latitude vis-à-vis the central state, the local commune, and other enterprises. The legitimation of enterprise autonomy again brings up the problem of the precise meaning of workers' self-management. Theoretically, at least, 'enterprise power' might instill the consciousness of collective capitalists rather than socialists. In that way it would seem to threaten workers' control, although it could be made compatible with workers' self-management.

The increasing autonomy of small units has also been the key to social self-government.[27] Since the state has not yet withered away, the political leadership has tried to shift more responsibilities and rights to the commune (*opština*). Like the enterprise, the commune raises its own funds, sets its own budget, and provides its residents with various social services. Furthermore, the partial equation of self-management with the autonomy of small units like the commune and the enterprise has shaped the development of two unique institutions: market socialism on the one hand and, on the other, a still inchoate form of national federation.

Besides the increased emphasis on enterprise and local autonomy which developed after the First Congress of Self-Managers (and the Seventh Congress of the LCY), the official ideology made another ideological innovation by stressing the self-interest of the individual producer. This step contrasts with the official ideologies of most communist states. According to the more usual communist ideology, the individual producer in a socialist state works for the good of the people and for the triumph of communism, not for his own material interest. So the Yugoslav ideology was the first to state explicitly that working to raise one's standard of living is legitimate under socialism. Furthermore, in line with the pragmatic urge to innovate which emerged during the dispute with the Cominform, the Yugoslav leadership recog-

27 This term (*društveno samoupravljanje*), in contrast to workers' self-management (*radničko samoupravljanje*), seems to have gained widespread use around the time of the 1965 economic reforms, perhaps after a germination period initiated by the 1957 Congress of Self-Managers and the Seventh Congress of the LCY (1958).

nized that this individualistic, material interest could be used as a rational means toward the societal goal of economic development. Thus the Yugoslavs introduced into socialist ideology not only a rationalization of self-interest but also the elevation of self-interest into a historical necessity in an underdeveloped socialist country. As the League of Communists' Program for 1958 says, 'Through [self-]management [producers] realize their personal interests every day: higher wages, a higher personal and general social standard of living.' Moreover, this program makes the Party's pragmatic orientation explicit once and for all by stating categorically, 'Socialism can not establish personal happiness for man by means of any "higher goals" because the highest goal of socialism is the personal happiness of man.' [28]

The 1960s

Throughout the following decade, the official ideology made its pragmatic emphasis on economic growth even stronger. Although the Yugoslavs originally associated self-management with the socialist goal of de-alienation, they eventually shifted its focus to the societal goal of economic development. At the same time, self-management became an increasingly important catch-phrase in the official ideology; thus, every social action and policy was expressed as a function of *samoupravljanje*. As Edvard Kardelj says, self-management is a value which exists independently of the social situation — a value which would have to be created if it did not exist. But Kardelj also signals the official ideology's

---

28 LCY Program, VII Congress LCY, 1958, reprinted in Smiljković and Petrović, *Samoupravljanje*, pp. 168–9.
   This orientation is shared by the Yugoslavs, the Czechs, the Hungarians, and the Poles and opposed by the Chinese. The Chinese prefer to build socialism through moral rather than material incentives, reinforced by group rather than individual pressures. According to the Chinese, a country cannot create socialism by appealing to pre-socialist, i.e. capitalist, modes of thought and behavior. Sooner or later, the contradictions between the base and the superstructure will reveal too wide a chasm to be bridged by slogans. Furthermore, the Chinese believe that moral exhortations and moral incentives counteract the tendency, as evidenced by the Soviet Union, for selfishness to develop its own rewards — notably, through the establishment of a class of bureaucrats and experts who disdain the masses. Finally, the Chinese hope that the use of moral rather than material incentives will enable underdeveloped countries to take off on the transition to communism without imitating the 'classical', i.e. the Soviet, model. See E. L. Wheelwright and Bruce McFarlane, *The Chinese Road to Socialism* (New York: Monthly Review Press, 1970), esp. ch. 8.

growing preoccupation with factors of economic development. Just as self-management means socialism, Kardelj says, so it also means economic growth. In his words,

the orientation of socialist forces and the socialist state toward varied and richer forms of social self-management and of direct democracy, toward the attainment of greater freedom for the creative initiative of personality and more democratic, more humane relations between people — must just as well be the essential element of the entire socialist construction *as it is the effort to attain greater labor productivity, that is, to develop more strongly the productive forces of society.*[29]

Thus on one level Kardelj's statement glorifies self-management in itself and in its direct relationship to socialism, while on another it asserts the priority of economic development.

The material source of this pragmatic emphasis in the official ideology was the economic situation, particularly a declining growth rate, in the early 1960s.[30] So the political leadership decided to stimulate the productivity of both the individual worker and the enterprise by material incentives. Implementing this decision, the economic reforms of 1965 released enterprises from many financial obligations vis-à-vis the federal government. Moreover, these reforms replaced the 'firm hand' ('*čvrsta ruka*') of the central government with the 'invisible hand' of the market. According to the Yugoslav conception of market socialism, success on the market rather than government subsidies was to determine whether enterprises survived. The implication of these reforms was that enterprise funds, now freed from government intervention, could be invested in whatever way the workers saw fit, preferably in the enterprise's expansion and in material stimuli to the workers. At this time also, the slogan 'Reward according to

29 Edvard Kardelj, 'Novi ustav socijalističke Jugoslavije' [Socialist Yugoslavia's new constitution] (Report delivered at the Combined Meeting of the Federal People's Assembly and the Federal Committee of the Socialist Alliance of Working People of Yugoslavia), *Prednacrt ustava Federativne Socijalističke Republike Jugoslavije* (Belgrade: Komunist, 1962), p. 82, cited in Silvano Bolčić, 'Samoupravljanje — cilj ili sredstvo' [Self-management — end or means], *Gledišta* 9, no. 2 (February 1968): 226. Emphasis added.
30 See Milenkovitch, *Plan and Market*, pp. 174ff.; Bićanić, *Economic Policy*, ch. 7; and Ljubomir Madžar, Miodrag Ostračanin, and Mladjen Kovačević, 'Economic Development: 1947–1968', *Yugoslav Survey* 11, no. 1 (February 1970): 23–42.

the results of work' began to express the leadership's new criterion for the distribution of social rewards and income.

By the time the Ninth Party Congress met in 1969, the leadership had proceeded toward defining the role of LCY members more in terms of cybernetics than traditional Marxism. Consonant with the official priority of economic growth, the Party member's task is

> to fight for the completion of existing and the development of new forms of self-managing decision-making in work organizations; for the *modernization* of the process of preparing, making and carrying out decisions; for the development of *contemporary information systems;* for the *scientifically-analytically based plans,* programs, and decisions; for the continual perfection of cadres and their affirmation on the basis of *creativity and the results of work.*[31]

A Yugoslav social scientist has also studied this Party Congress as the official incubator of recent trends in Yugoslav ideology. Dunja Rihtman-Auguštin of the Economics Institute in Zagreb has analyzed the resolutions of the Ninth Party Congress, and her findings show that the official ideology is closer in spirit to Henry Ford and Elton Mayo than to Karl Marx. According to Rihtman's analysis of the Congress resolutions,

> the culture of a self-managing enterprise must presuppose an orientation to production for the market along with self-managing planning, agreeing, and harmonizing the interests of all participants in the production process. A business orientation in this context is based on scientific results, desires modernization and the introduction of modern technology, and its final goal is raising the standard of living, the personal and social security of the producers. The economic content of self-management is in an income system which hastens the development of human capability and creativity. The culture of a self-managing enterprise should be an inherent socialist solidarity as the prime element of integration and a struggle against everything which leads to social inequalities.[32]

31 Resolutions of the IX Congress of the LCY, reprinted in Smiljković and Petrović, *Samoupravljanje,* pp. 183–4, at 183. Emphasis added.
32 Dunja Rihtman-Auguštin, 'Samoupravljanje kao kulturno-antropološki fenomen' [Self-management as a cultural-anthropological phenomenon], *Naše teme* 14, no. 1 (January 1970): 44–5.

Historical evolution: 1948–71

Thus the Congress resolutions promote an orientation toward business, the standard of living, and modern technology on the cultural side, material incentives on the economic side, and a wish for 'inherent socialist solidarity' on the side of the angels.

During the 1960s the Yugoslavs carried further the institutionalization of self-management in both enterprise and commune. According to the Federal Constitution framed in 1963, divers organizational forms of self-management cover the landscape of social activity. These forms include

> the self-management of working people in work organizations; the free association of working people, work and other organizations and social-political communities for the sake of satisfying mutual needs and interests; self-government in the commune and other social-political communities for the sake of even more direct participation of citizens in directing social development, in the carrying out of power and decision-making about different social matters; democratic political relations, which enable man to realize his interests, the right of self-management, and other rights and guaranteed relationships, to develop his personality through direct activity in social life, but especially in the organs of self-management, social-political organizations, and associations, which he himself creates and through which he exerts influence on the development of social consciousness and on the broadening of conditions for his own activity and for the realization of his interests and rights.[33]

Besides this all-inclusive enumeration of organizational forms which work on the principle of *samoupravljanje* or self-management, the 1963 Constitution also explains the functions that the worker has come to assume under the rubric of workers' self-management. There are eight such functions:

1. to manage the enterprise directly or through the councils that the workers elect;
2. to organize production, development, and planning;
3. to decide all business matters, including changes in the product;
4. to decide how profits will be used (bearing in mind the

33 From the Constitution of the SFRJ, 1963, reprinted in Smiljković and Petrović, *Samoupravljanje*, pp. 116–17, at 117.

societal goal of achieving the greatest effectiveness of work);

5. to distribute the enterprise's income so that the enterprise pays its own way;

6. to make all decisions on work relations, controls, and working time;

7. to organize work conditions and vacations, guaranteeing conditions for self-improvement through education and raising the personal and social standard of living;

8. to make all decisions regarding the enterprise's division into various units as well as the enterprise's possible amalgamation with other work units.[34]

Thus, in comparison with the 1950 law which established workers' councils, the 1963 Constitution bears witness to the greater autonomy of both councils and enterprises.

Since the 1963 Constitution, the official ideology's concept of self-management has remained stable. However, prior to and during the Second Congress of Self-Managers (not held until May 1971), there was much discussion among experts, in the trade unions and workers' councils, and in the mass media about a proposed Code of Self-Managers. This code was supposed to embody all the rights and duties which have evolved during the twenty years of workers' self-management. Because the committee of experts had not drawn up the Code by the time the Congress convened, the Code has not yet been accepted by a constituent assembly representing all the workers of Yugoslavia. One reason that the Code was not completed by the deadline was that it included a controversial provision for legalizing work stoppages or strikes. Thus Yugoslavia may be the first socialist country to legalize strikes. Until now, these work stoppages have been considered illegitimate, for workers in that situation have been regarded as striking against themselves, or at least against their representatives in the workers' council. Yet for the last fifteen years Yugoslav workers have participated in strikes, often in the form of work stoppages called for limited periods like half a day, but sometimes lasting as long as several months. In anticipation, perhaps, of legitimacy to be conferred by the federal leadership, a workers' council in Slovenia legalized the right to strike at the beginning of 1971. In their new statute, the railroad workers in

34 Ibid., pp. 171–2, at 171.

Jesenice defined the roles appropriate to all parties — mainly the workers' council and the striking workers — in a strike.[35]

Over two decades, the official ideology of self-management, which began in the ideal of the Paris Commune and the Yugoslav Partisans' need to secure and govern liberated territory during World War II, has evolved toward an increasingly pragmatic concern with economic growth through industrialization and a tendency to promote the values supposedly borne by technological cadres. Thrown on the defensive by the Cominform dispute of 1948, the Yugoslavs launched their own offensive in 1949–50 with the introduction of workers' councils, the epitome of 'the Yugoslav way'. From the mid-1950s, economic problems and a willingness to innovate made the political leadership develop an increasingly pragmatic interest in economic development. This pragmatism resulted in the legitimization of self-interest and hence the introduction of material incentives to both workers and enterprises. Moreover, the 1960s have seen a continued emphasis on economic priorities and technological development, as well as a new stress on the role of the market in setting social and financial rewards. Perhaps a significant innovation in the official ideology in the 1970s will be the legitimization of the right to strike, favored by many workers and leaders. In sum, *self-management* remains the most important clause in the official ideology and, as such, the major societal goal in Yugoslavia.

'ANTI-SAMOUPRAVLJANJE CONCEPTS'

It helps to highlight distinctive points in the evolution of self-management's official ideology by showing how the Yugoslav leadership has explicitly rejected certain concepts associated not only with 'Stalinism', but also both parliamentary and socialist democracy. As with many other countries, especially those dominated by one political party, we can assume that ideological principles which call forth the political leadership's criticism —

35 Several Yugoslav sociologists have made proposals to institutionalize strikes, e.g. Josip Županov, 'Upravljanje industrijskim konfliktom u samoupravnom sistemu' [The management of industrial conflict in a self-managing society], *Sociologija* 13 (1971): 427–47 and 'Two Patterns of Conflict Management in Industry', *Industrial Relations* 12, no. 2 (1973): 213–23. On a lengthy strike which affected a whole town, see Vuk Drašković, 'Društvo: Štrajk koji ne prestaje' [Society: strike that doesn't end], *NIN*, 5 September 1971, pp. 15–18.

and even their explicit negation — bear some resemblance to phenomena and orientations current in society. These criticized ideological concepts may in fact be proposals that the leadership has discussed but rejected or proposals that the citizens have discussed but the leadership has not yet accepted. Thus we may regard concepts which the official ideology of self-management labels as 'anti-*samoupravljanje*' or 'misconceptions' of *samoupravljanje* as representing orientations within the Yugoslav public that the leadership wants to combat. According to Professor Pašić, there are three major misconceptions of self-management, which he terms etatist, representative, and liberal, respectively. They are based on the predominance of institutions such as the state, the legislature, and interest groups, and thus call for negation in the name of social self-management.[36]

Etatism

The official ideology's attack on 'bureaucratic etatism', or the omnipotence of the centralized state and its apparatus, developed during the Cominform dispute. At that time, Yugoslavia responded to ostracism from the socialist bloc first by establishing and then by emphasizing differences between its 'way' and the Soviet model of socialism. But although, since then, the etatist orientation within Yugoslavia has had little support, it apparently has never died, for the official ideology continues to belabor and belittle this opponent. So there are still Yugoslav citizens and politicians who believe that the Party and a strong state must protect the working class by exerting control over political and economic life. Thus this line of thought counters the official ideology as it has evolved since the early 1950s, especially on the development of economic and political decentralization and the intended transformation of the Party into an 'ideologically' guiding force. Despite its continued attack on etatism, the official ideology makes it clear that some organization linking political units and enterprises is necessary, for otherwise there would be anarchy. What the official ideology objects to, in short, is the imposition of Party and state *over* self-management and *between* the self-manager and his work.

As part of their attack on 'Stalinist' etatism, the Yugoslavs have maintained a critique of 'egalitarianism' in the mistaken as-

36 Pašić, *Političko organizovanje*, pp. 61ff.

sumption that this was part of Stalin's economic policy.[37] They define egalitarianism as a fallacious interpretation of socialism, according to which everyone earns the same salary and receives the same or equivalent social rewards. As *uravnilovka* ('leveling'), egalitarianism takes on the connotation — for Yugoslavs — of thought-processing and brainwashing so that everyone's personality is reduced to the same gray shade of mediocrity, without distinguishing characteristics. Thus egalitarianism is opposed to the Yugoslav adoption of market socialism and distribution 'according to the results of work'. Moreover, Yugoslavs castigate the whole mentality that they associate with egalitarianism, a mentality that, as we have seen, the Belgrade philosopher Svetozar Stojanović calls 'primitive communism'. In contrast to this 'primitive' ideology of 'collectivistic and ascetic egalitarianism', 'developed communism' should show greater concern for the individual and his needs. Thus 'developed communism' should negate 'etatism' and 'egalitarianism'.[38]

Representative government

After etatism, a second challenge to the official ideology apparently comes from the representative system of assemblies and workers' councils, both of which are based on hierarchically-arranged, territorial units. Some critics charge, on the one hand, that even this degree of representation — hence, indirect participation — reduces self-management to merely another form of bourgeois parliamentary democracy. On the other hand, some Yugoslavs think that there should be even more reliance on representative government. To the first charge Pašić replies that only the current organizational forms of self-management make direct democracy possible in the future. The representative system socializes the greatest number of citizens into the norms of participatory democracy. According to Pašić, the present system enables Yugoslavs to achieve 'the social position which makes them capable of direct and decisive influence on the management of the general affairs of the society'. Thus self-management with its attendant representative forms, like workers' councils, will continue to be necessary during the indefinitely long transition to direct democracy. In response to the criticism that the organs of

37 See Alec Nove, *The Soviet Economy*, 3rd rev. ed. (London: Allen and Unwin, 1968), ch. 4.
38 Svetozar Stojanović, *Izmedju ideala i stvarnosti*, pp. 204–9.

self-management are neither sufficiently representative nor sufficiently powerful, Pašić cautions against placing too much belief in any form of representative government. In his view, every representative government — no matter how freely elected or how broadly representative — tends consciously or unconsciously to encroach upon the functions of the self-managers, i.e. the citizens. If, despite its predominance, such a government perpetuates the 'myth of direct democracy', then it is guilty of having elevated itself into an elite. According to Pašić, this political elite justifies its rule by the claim that it alone can guide the self-managers toward some future democracy.[39] Thus Pašić intends his argument to quash both utopian socialists and those who admire Western parliamentary systems.

Interest groups

The third major concept that the leadership has attacked is that of self-management through interest groups. Despite official encouragement of market competition since 1965, the leadership frowns upon the ability — and the determination — of many enterprises to create monopolies in trade and production, to utilize their advantageous position to eliminate other enterprises, and to exercise a dominant interest in political decision-making in the commune — if not also attempted in the republic and in the federation. The official ideology regards such competition as illegitimate because it destroys socialist unity, according to which all parts of the social system recognize their interdependence. Furthermore, Pašić says, this kind of economic competition revives classical liberalism, except that here 'social property is actually treated as the group property of those collectivities which manage it in society's name'. Thus he castigates the idea of individual enterprises and whole economic sectors advancing their own interests, even to the extent of pressuring the political leadership. These self-managing interest groups are pernicious, for they combine 'the greatest social means with the least social responsibility and control'.[40]

39 Pašić, *Političko organizovanje*, pp. 65–7.
40 Ibid., pp. 71–2. This is a real problem for Yugoslavs. For example, during 1971 the government severely criticized the larger banks for their monopolistic control over investment and credit. Also, a large oil company was accused of making deals with retail outlets such as gas stations and automobile companies so that they would sell or recommend only its products. During 1972, political leaders continued to criticize these and similar abuses of 'socialist' market competition.

Problems inherent in the ideology

These three bogeys of the official ideology — etatism (including bureaucratism and egalitarianism), representativism, and interest groups — express threats posed by political circumstances and economic choices to the Yugoslav conception of self-management. There is yet another type of 'anti-*samoupravljanje*', of misconception which negates the essence of self-management as the official ideology sees it. This is socialist elitism, which takes either an idealist and or an 'instrumentalist' form. Both of these hold that a 'tutor' is necessary to mediate between the society (the working class) and its goal (self-management). According to the idealists, the society needs experts like technocrats and economists so that it can create the material base and the cultural values which are conducive to the 'true' realization of self-management. The instrumentalists also support the technocracy because that insures the pursuit of their primary goal, which is not self-management but economic development and industrialization. They are called 'instrumentalists' because they regard self-management as a means — not necessarily the most efficient means — toward economic development. Similarly, the 'idealists' derive their name from their view of self-management as an ideal social state located in the far future. The political leadership perceives in their shared reliance on 'tutors' for self-managers a tendency for both idealists and instrumentalists to contribute to the growth of a technocratic elite. Thus, like the other three 'anti-*samoupravljanje*' concepts, idealism and instrumentalism also draw a rebuttal from the official ideology and from concerned intellectuals.[41]

PROBLEMS INHERENT IN THE IDEOLOGY

To summarize without being repetitive, I shall briefly mention four problems which are inherent in the formulation of the official ideology as it has evolved over the past twenty years. These are simply unresolved issues in the thinking-out of the ideology which seem to involve, if they are followed to their logical conclusions, contradictions with classical socialist assumptions. The

41 Two Belgrade sociologists have written interesting essays on instrumentalism and idealism. See Bolčić, 'Samoupravljanje'; and Jagoš Djuretić, 'Dileme proleterskog konstituisanja vlasti' [Dilemmas of the proletarian constitution of power], *Gledišta* 9, no. 4 (April 1968): 521–30.

problems concern pragmatism, elitism, solidarity, and — in capitalist systems — private ownership.

Pragmatism

As I have tried to show in this and the previous chapter, the official ideology has become increasingly preoccupied with issues of economic modernization on the model of the advanced post-industrial societies. The official emphasis on technology, science, and material stimuli has influenced an instrumental orientation toward self-management, that is, one which treats self-management as a means to economic development rather than a socio-political end in itself.[42] Stated in terms of a dichotomy, the Yugoslavs have opted for 'practical' over 'pure' ideology. They have tried to combine the pure and the practical aspects of their ideology because of their concern about whether socialism can successfully take root in an economically underdeveloped country. Their experience thus far makes them optimistic. However, in their assumption that economic modernization through industrialization will provide a base for political development toward self-management, they seem to have given priority to economic over socialist development, or, in Mao Tse-tung's terms, to have let economics — rather than politics — take command.

This pragmatic emphasis has intensified over the years into a strain on the pure ideology. According to a Slovenian psychologist who has studied workers' attitudes toward self-management, this strain is evidenced by a latent demand for the 'economization of self-management'. Moreover, he goes on to say, the present balance of what I have called the pure and practical aspects of the official ideology is not viable, for ' "self-management" as an "ideological subsystem" is incompatible with the enterprise as a technical-economic subsystem'.[43]

Elitism

The emphasis on economic over socialist development could also lead — if it has not already led — to the political predominance of a technocracy which both visibly and symbolically 'bears' the central values of the official ideology of self-management. Be-

42 According to Bolčić, 'Samoupravljanje' (p. 224), many Yugoslavs believe and act with the idea that the basic, if not the only, motivation is to increase personal income. Surely this attitude is an unanticipated consequence of the direction that the official ideology has taken.
43 Arzenšek, 'Samoupravljanje', p. 31.

cause an elite like a technocracy performs 'specialist' functions based on 'specialized' knowledge, it can attract a multitude of functions in the political sphere. In fact, this appears to be happening in the Yugoslav political leadership. Contrary to the views of some observers who find the Yugoslav technocratic elite apolitical, the technical specialists are replacing the political generalists in making policy.[44] As a Yugoslav sociologist told me, 'Ten years ago we saw the economization of the political elite, but now we are seeing the politicization of the technocratic elite.' The official ideology has made no attempt to combat the political monopoly of either Party-based leaders, which has obtained until recent years (perhaps until the late 1960s), or economy-based leaders, which the emphasis on economic development portends. As Djuretić says in a broader context, the official ideology has not yet resolved whether socialist democracy means that everyone makes political decisions — or only a single political class.[45]

Solidarity

The third problem in the official ideology concerns the contradiction between the desire for social integration and the distribution norm of market competition. The norm of 'reward according to success on the market' would seem to promote a separate group consciousness in each enterprise, industry, profession, commune, and republic, which would in turn threaten socialist unity or solidarity. Moreover, there is a problem of definition here: whom does 'socialist solidarity' include? For example, does it include only manual workers (the real working class), or managers and other professionals too? Does solidarity end at the borders of the commune — or of the city, the republic, or the federation? This question has important practical consequences, also, for 'solidarity' implies a willingness to share financial obligations as well as resources. For example, citizens of the rich agricultural region of the Vojvodina may not feel morally responsible — though they are legally bound — to send part of their taxes to the underdeveloped region of Kosovo, which is also part of the greater Serbian republic. However, the economic in-

44 Djuretić, 'Dileme', p. 527, says, 'It is hard to imagine a more real bearer of this process [of economic development] than the technical and economic-political bureaucracy.' See also Albert Meister, *Où va l'autogestion yougoslave?* (Paris: Editions Anthropos, 1970), pp. 203ff.
45 Djuretić, 'Dileme', p. 524.

73

terests and the predominant ethnic origin of the Vojvodina's population differ from those of Kosovo's. So there may be little basis for solidarity between them except the paying and receiving of tax money. Within the city of Belgrade, which contains a relatively homogeneous population, the tax monies of the richer communes are shared with the poorer communes. Even here the more prosperous citizens may not be satisfied with this degree of solidarity. Perhaps an ideological clarification of solidarity — especially the kind of solidarity expected under market socialism — would help resolve this problem.

Private ownership

The fourth and final problem is more relevant to capitalist countries which propound some organizational variant of workers' self-management within the framework of private ownership of the means of production. However, there are at least three arguments against the compatibility of private ownership and self-management. First, as Pašić argues, the economic system fully and rationally knows what resources it can mobilize only when it controls — through public ownership — the means of production. Second, as Pašić also indicates, if institutions and persons are not ultimately responsible to the society as a whole, then either a political class will come to dominate social life or conditions will be anarchic.[46] But a third, psychological argument may be more salient to technological conditions in advanced capitalist society. According to the psychological point of view, self-management is meaningful only if the workers know that they have full legal, social, and moral control. Thus they can develop a self-concept consonant with their autonomy and control in decision-making. Proponents of splitting up the functions of ownership, so that big capitalists still legally own the industry and the profits and workers 'control' their working lives, ignore the psychological aspects of self-management.[47] This criticism is especially relevant because such writers often claim that their motivation for proposing the introduction of self-management is to alleviate the psychological malaise of the blue-collar worker. Finally, it seems a travesty of the ideals of socialist humanism,

46 Pašić, *Političko organizovanje*, pp. 61–2.
47 See Dahl, *After the Revolution?*, pp. 121ff.; and Gunnar Adler-Karlsson, *Functional Socialism: A Swedish Theory for Democratic Socialization* (Stockholm: Prisma, 1969).

a mockery of claims to 'democracy' and 'equality', to appropriate the concept of self-management to patch up a capitalist system.

At any rate, I have tried only to suggest several problems of the official ideology of self-management, not to solve them. This chapter has opened the study of politics in one socialist country by examining its official ideology, which centers on the concept of self-management in work and in social life. I have shown how the historical evolution of this ideology embodies responses to the political environment, both domestic and international, predominantly in a pragmatic form which emphasizes the priority of economic development. I have also tried to clarify the official ideology by considering several concepts which it tries to negate as 'anti-*samoupravljanje*' propositions or misconceptions of self-management. Finally, we have looked at several problems that the official ideology has not yet resolved. As an expression of the formal norms and values fostered by today's historical situation and its political leadership, the official ideology is both a continuation of and a counterpart to collective experiences of the recent and the remote past. In the next chapter I shall move directly into this area, by looking at how some citizens relate their lives to the societal changes of war, revolution, and socialist self-management. It will be interesting to see how far ordinary citizens accept and use the ideological prongs for handling social reality that their leaders have offered them.

3

PERCEPTIONS OF SOCIETY
AND POLITICS

But for too long we have had an atmosphere of easy 'success',
a deluge of paraders, a certain equality crashing through the
spirit of expert mediocrity. Maestros are sprouting up all over
with the help of the cane and the cushion: one time they
crop up as 'businessmen', another time as 'revolutionaries',
sometimes they are 'writers' or 'idea throwers' . . . There are
more vociferous leaders than methodical political work, more
writers than real books, more so-called doctors than discoveries,
more 'successful' businessmen than factories whose accounts
are in the black. Too often we greet serious orientations and
methodical efforts with a snide smile, as something old fashioned;
they are easily belittled, meeting with our skepticism or indifference.

> Života Djordjević,
> 'Zrelo i zeleno grožđe'

The official ideology does not prepare us for a depiction of Yugoslav society as one of 'easy "success", . . . paraders . . . equality
. . . in mediocrity'.[1] Still, the official ideology bears some resemblance to the social reality that ordinary citizens know, if
only because it provides a scenario, a codification of norms, of
which all citizens are conscious. This scenario is the substance of
social learning outside the home. As such, it exists in a dialectical
relationship with the social reality that citizens know from personal experience. Thus its incongruence with this social reality
is axiomatic. Realizing this, we can compare the nature of social
change as revealed both in individual lives and in the official
ideology.

While chapter 2 examined the interrelationship of social
change and the official ideology of self-management, this chapter
will investigate the reflection of both social change and official
ideology in the lives of Yugoslav citizens. We begin with their
perceptions of 'socialism', or the form of their society. I wanted
the Yugoslavs to describe what socialism has meant for them

---

1 Života Djordjević, 'Zrelo i zeleno grožđe' [Ripe and green grapes], *NIN*,
15 August 1971, p. 15.

personally: the changes which have occurred in their lives in the past quarter century that they associate with socialism. Extending this line of questioning to ascertain what have been the collective experiences which have most impressed ordinary Yugoslavs, I found that concepts from the official ideology have less relevance than the historical events of war, the reconstruction, and the break with the Cominform. Furthermore, Yugoslavs' perceptions of socialism are related to their standard of living, relative to their previous experience, on the one hand, and, on the other, to the kinds of lives they see their neighbors and relatives enjoying.

Because the purpose of this chapter is to use the experiences of representative Yugoslavs to understand how they 'make sense' of self-management and other social changes, we shall look mostly at data from life stories and personal statements. We will get well acquainted with several of the Belgrade families whom I interviewed.[2] The quotations from these interviews are lengthy so that perceptions and attitudes may be presented in as complete a context as possible, thus eliminating some distortion. The major topics of the chapter emerged during the interviews: the respondents' upward social mobility, the subsequent 'struggle for a dinar', the horrors of World War II, the social joy of reconstruction, the Cominform trauma. It is no accident that the introduction of self-management is not part of this list, for most of the respondents have a dualistic, perhaps even a contradictory, perception of self-management as both an ideological goal and a set of economic rights. Moreover, neither as ideology nor as institution does self-management appear as salient to ordinary citizens as other formative experiences.

EVALUATION OF SOCIALISM

The historical circumstances under which socialism was introduced to the mass of the population have probably affected the way that people originally understood and perhaps still perceive it. In recent Yugoslav history, socialism appeared to most of the people in several successive guises. First, during the war, it appeared as the organizational ethos of the victorious Partisan movement. Second, from the proclamation of 21 November 1944 in which the Antifascist Front announced the confiscation of

2 See chapter 1 and appendix.

traitors', i.e. Germans' and collaborators', property, socialism appeared as an ideology which promised a redistribution of wealth to the 'little man'. Third, from 1945–6, socialism became the ideological basis of the state, the official ideology from which deviance was punishable. Historical conditions also helped to establish the revolutionary equation, paraphrasing Lenin: Socialism = Land + Bread. During the war and the reconstruction which followed, 'socialism' and 'revolution' seem to have taken on the meaning which was most significant to Yugoslavs in those times: first, liberating the country from the occupying Nazis, Italians, and Bulgars; then, building up the country's equipment and facilities; finally, improving one's own life chances within the given conditions.

The war and other collective experiences of deprivation that Yugoslavs know and remember have influenced a basic preoccupation with the standard of living. This preoccupation is in turn reflected in all expressions of the common good, including the official ideology and personal ideologies. Thus, both the official ideology and personal philosophy equate the common good with individual betterment. Just as individual Yugoslavs tend to describe socialism in terms of a higher standard of living, so the official ideology imparts the lesson that 'Progress is our most important product'.

Several collective experiences have created this mentality. First, before World War II, almost all Yugoslavs were peasants whose perspectives began at one end of the village and ended at the other. Second is the experience of war itself — devastation and occupation — and the hope held out by the Partisan movement. Third, when the postwar period of reconstruction emerged in a frenzy of community- and country-building, it was interrupted by the trauma of the break with the Cominform. This was a shock felt even by ordinary citizens.

Yugoslavs who came to consciousness during these collective experiences are now middle-aged. They are the pillars of the official ideology, the political and economic leaders, the writers, the parents and teachers. Through all the media that they control they impart a remembered sense of relative deprivation and a great relief at having survived various national crises. During the past twenty-five years, while peasants have moved to the towns, while families have atomized from the condensed *zadruga* (cooperative) toward the nuclear unit, while industries and houses have been built, and while a four-plane airline has evolved into three competing airline companies, one constant has remained: the perception that this is 'socialism'. In summary, the social learning undergone by the middle-aged generation which has left the village, built the industries, and developed the official ideology has evolved into what all Yugoslavs 'know' as socialism. What the middle-aged generation knows best is the tremendous change in lifestyle that the past twenty-five years have brought.

This is the approach to socialism, for example, of one middle-aged, working-class couple. Rade Popović, a highly-skilled machinist, and his wife Branka are trying to compare life before the war and now. Branka is not very clear about some facts of political life, but she does know that 'earlier a Yugoslav may have had some money, he may have had some chances, but he wasn't informed, it wasn't organized . . .' 'Today's society and before the war', Rade starts to say, and Branka interrupts, 'Today it's socialism!'

> You can't compare them nohow [Rade continues]. Before the rich were only rich and today the conditions are different. Today you can, take me, for example. I can get credit to get on an airplane and fly to Korčula [an island in the Adriatic Sea]. And before the war it wasn't like that. If you were rich, if you had money, if you had land or factories, then you go, you get on a train, you have your limousine, whatever you want. But today it isn't like that. They take some pocket money, or nothing even, and off they go. Company credits, airplanes, buses, trains, credit for anyone who works. The workers in a big trading company, for example, they get credit for clothing. Three or four hundred dinars, just for clothing.

Janko Vuković, a Montenegrin pensioner who was in the Partisans, humorously makes the same connection between socialism and prosperity. Pointing to his sister, a hefty woman who takes in ironing and a boarder to supplement her pension, he says, 'Look at Dušica. Under capitalism she weighed around 55 [kilograms, or 120 pounds], but under socialism she weighs 125!' But he proceeds seriously enough to the social level. Janko says,

> We never had anything. Socialism is very good here. It isn't a 'spectre' for society. Socialism doesn't drive anybody

to the poorhouse. Socialism can only bring prosperity to the majority of the people, and it can make the people secure. That percentage, that maybe top 20 percent — it doesn't hurt them . . .

It was always like that here: poverty. You know what, it was like Harlem. But now it's changing. Today a peasant's thinking about where he's going to put the refrigerator, where he's going to put the electric oven . . . Maybe we still don't live the way we should, but if we look at this one twenty-year period — you can't deny it. A kid doesn't have to live the same life that we did. Maybe we slept three to a bed, but they — let them sleep, in twenty years every one of them should only have his own bed to sleep in . . . If you'd've come twenty years ago, if you'd've seen how it was here and how it is now, now it's like paradise.

Furthermore, Josip Djordjević, a retired army officer and current political activist, says that now the peasants in his native village in Dalmatia are completely different from what they were before the war: newly accustomed to stoves, electric lights, and newspapers.

They have electrification in the villages now and everything [according to Djordjević], stoves, ovens, televisions, schools. I used to have to walk thirteen kilometers to school every day . . . The peasants watch television, they read the newspaper. Talking with them is just like talking to a city person.

Dušica from Montenegro also emphasizes the changed lifestyle of Serbian peasants, especially the ones around the outskirts of the city who make their 'lettuce' by selling fruit and vegetables in Belgrade's markets.

Did you see on television [Dušica says], women are at home in the village, the wives of two brothers. For twelve years they've been together, they get along so well together that they built a house together. They built it just so, they got steam heat — they got everything in the village in Serbia. What don't the people have?! Why, they live better — they got furniture — better than in town. You can't give away, you can't give them anything, they

won't take it. They have money. Because they make money
off pears, say, off apples and potatoes. Here there's plenty
to live off of.

So to Dušica, Djordjević, and Rade and Branka Popović, the
period of their lives marked by the advent of socialism represents
economic development and upward social mobility. Indeed, a
glance at the intergenerational mobility of most of the ten sample
families (summarized in table 3) indicates that they advanced
occupationally from peasants to skilled workers and clerks in
the postwar years. Their view from the new urban height is under-
standably proud. Of course, as one of my acquaintances from the
prewar aristocracy points out, there is a question of the standard
of comparison. If his family never lived in the city before the
war, then a man will say that life is better now. For my well-
born acquaintance — whose family before the war had two houses
in Belgrade and a week-end villa — the standard of living is
high but not so high as it once was. However, the upward social
mobility of most of my respondents' families appears representative of the major part of the society, for it is substantiated by
economic and social indicators for the country as a whole. All
the data available for the past half-century, especially for the
twenty-five years that socialist Yugoslavia has existed, indicate
that the country's industrial production, labor force, and cities
have experienced tremendous growth in the transition from an
agrarian to a semi-industrial economy. Moreover, economic and
social policy after the war both broadened the class origins of the
higher social strata, at least for the middle-aged generation, and
increased the goods available for general consumption.[3]
Aside from the experience of upward social mobility, there
are certain other events and processes which may also have affected Yugoslavs' perceptions of politics and social change. The
collective experiences which seem to have been most formative in
this regard are events connected with national liberation. Indeed,
these events appear to have left a more indelible impression on
the ordinary Yugoslav than those related to the introduction of
socialism and self-management. As my respondents recall them
today, the key events of their lives were war, reconstruction, and
the break with the Cominform. They seem to view the introduc-

3 For a model relating social mobility, economic growth, and birth-order
within the family in Yugoslavia, see Hammel, *Pink Yo-Yo.*

81

Table 3 *Social mobility of ten Belgrade families*

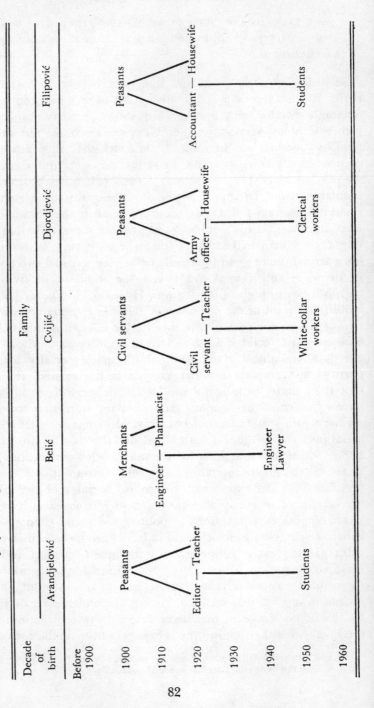

Decade of birth	Family				
	Arandjelović	Belić	Cvijić	Djordjević	Filipović
Before 1900					
1900	Peasants		Civil servants	Peasants	Peasants
1910		Merchants			
1920	Editor — Teacher	Engineer — Pharmacist	Civil servant — Teacher	Army officer — Housewife	Accountant — Housewife
1930					
1940		Engineer Lawyer			
1950	Students		White-collar workers	Clerical workers	Students
1960					

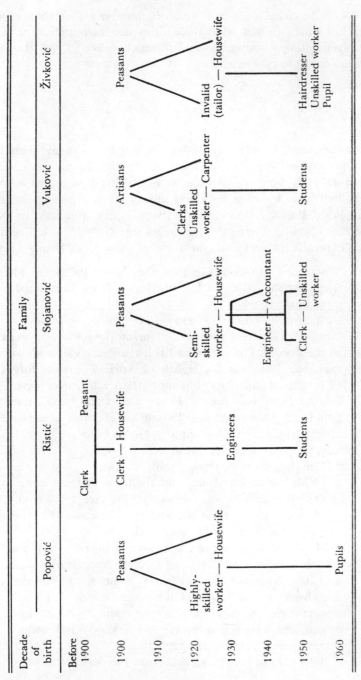

Decade of birth	Family					
	Popović	Ristić	Stojanović	Vuković	Živković	
Before 1900		Clerk — Peasant				
1900	Peasants	Clerk — Housewife	Peasants	Artisans	Peasants	
1910						
1920	Highly-skilled worker — Housewife		Semi-skilled worker — Housewife	Clerks Unskilled worker — Carpenter	Invalid (tailor) — Housewife	
1930		Engineers	Engineer — Accountant			
1940			Clerk — Unskilled worker		Hairdresser Unskilled worker Pupil	
1950		Students		Students		
1960	Pupils					

83

tion of self-management as a given parameter rather than as an event in which they participated. Thus the introduction of self-management is a rather neutral memory, good in the abstract but unrelated to everyday life.

FORMATIVE EXPERIENCES

War

To understand the effect of war on the Yugoslavs' social memory and present orientation, we must relive part of the actual experience with them. From their accounts today, war was a constant hell of occupation, fear, and misery. Even a non-combatant like Rade Popović, working in the machine industry in Niš (southern Serbia) during the war, who 'just kept my mouth shut', vividly recalls the fear and confusion of those days. Popović says,

> When they killed one German, they killed 100 Serbs. Then they shot the gypsies a lot, the Jews — they liquidated them immediately . . .
>
> April 8 they came, seventy-eight Stukas, and they bombed. The army pulled out during the night and went to the border. Here they had the army, the railroad, some materiel. That was the eighth of April, I'll never forget it. It was a small place, but more than 100 people were killed. It was very tough. There wasn't any bread, they took it all. They took away livestock and grain; whatever they needed they took. People got by in every conceivable way. Shops didn't exist any more.
>
> The Bulgars came trooping in; it's near the border. We didn't have anything, and then the Bulgars came in as Occupiers, and they sent everything away: the iron, the bridges, they sent it off, and the Germans were there as masters of course, they commanded.
>
> Maybe in my area the war wasn't so horrible as it was elsewhere, like in western Serbia, Kruševac, Kraljevo there, and then Kuzmanovo, Paraćin, Svetozarevo, to Belgrade, then back toward Bosnia. They made an army out of the *šiptars* there, the Albanians. Nobody knew who was killing whom, and who was in power — everybody and nobody was in power. It was very tough.
>
> This part of Serbia, to here, and the Serbs in Kosovo

84

Formative experiences

suffered terribly, and the Serbs in Bosnia, and in Croatia. There were already Partisans, and there were Četniks. One guy would go to the Četniks, one guy would go to the Partisans. And the Četniks stole, they burned houses, they shot children . . . That's the way it was . . . Everyone who lived through the war can only tell his own little story.

Another non-combatant, journalist Danilo Arandjelović, recounts how the war affected him and his family in western Serbia. According to Arandjelović,

> Not one youth or girl from my village strayed by collaborating with the Occupier. In general they stayed on our side, some working directly with the Partisans, some remaining to the end sympathizers with the National Liberation Movement. I had quite a few difficulties because of that. I was jailed several times and I was sent on forced labor. I had some troubles. The Četniks killed my uncle. They came looking for me and a friend who they thought was there, and I escaped just in time. So wartime was very difficult. Because my parents were old, and my uncle and my aunt, all four of them depended on me, so I wasn't able to go off in '41 and I stayed there, I suffered a lot of troubles in those years. When the Liberation came, some Četniks attacked me, I got a blow here [pointing to his temple], killing one nerve, and causing my eye to be taken out. Liberation found me in Belgrade in the hospital.

Meanwhile, former Partisans like Janko Vuković's brother Milovan remember bravery under impossible odds. Milovan talks about

> kids of twelve, of ten, they simply go as messengers, and they come right up to the guns and they won't cry, they don't start weeping and wailing, they stay in the brigade, kids of ten. They were in battle with us.

To ex-Partisans like Josip Djordjević, the experience of living in the woods for four years and fighting the Germans seems almost unbelievable from the comfort of an apartment in New Belgrade. Despite his subsequent career in the army, Djordjević's

85

Partisan life remains his most severe emotional experience. On the other hand, Janko and Milovan Vuković relive their Partisan experiences with joyous excitement. Janko tells apocryphal stories about the time that he led a Partisan squad in Italy and about how the Montenegrin warrior tradition helped make the Partisans victorious. Janko says,

> All of us, us Montenegrins especially, we fought in the National Liberation War. In the war, out of the political commissars 50 percent were Montenegrins, 50 percent — and we're pretty few. And sixty-three generals were Montenegrins, well, sixty-one. Eh, what about the case of the Božević family? All the Boževićes went into the Partisans, nine brothers, one sister, and the father and mother. He went into the Partisans when he was seventy years old, seventy or seventy-five. His sons left, his wife left him. He was seventy years old and he was in the Partisans all four years. And now he died last year at the age of ninety-nine.

These still vivid memories, aided by official ceremonies and symbols, indicate that the horror and fear of war significantly affect Yugoslavs' social orientations. Having fought or resisted the enemy on native soil, they developed great pride in the state which emerged from their sacrifices.

Reconstruction

Just as the fear of wartime was transformed into the construction of the post-Liberation period, so the heroism of the Partisan troops evolved into the more widespread self-sacrifice of voluntary work brigades. Because of this mass self-sacrifice, the postwar reconstruction period has taken on the aura of a golden age, at least to the middle-aged generation.[4]

4 Judging from the comments of some Serbs who remained in their villages after the war and who either stayed poor or — losing some land in the 1945 redistribution — became poorer, this feeling of postwar euphoria may have been limited to the urban population. Furthermore, the happiest people at that time were probably peasants who had just migrated to town. For example, Zora Filipović, the 42-year-old wife of an accountant, was still living with her parents in a Serbian village when war ended. Her view of that time is essentially negative. She says, 'Supplies were destroyed. Those who had more had to give to the state; they fed the country a long time. The situation was difficult.'

Formative experiences

The engineer Steva Ristić, for example, recalls the general norm of hard work which prevailed after the war. At that time, he says, every effort was social, and no one thought of personal rewards. Ristić says,

> The director got the task of making an iron, I don't know from where, the Federal Commission for Industry, I guess. So then he gave out the assignments. And he called me because I was working on electrical constructions. So then you find some old model and you see how it's put together, and then you change it a little so it'll be nicer, right, so that it could be exported. And then you make two or three items and you see which is the best and this one or that one is accepted for production, and that's how it was at that time.
>
> We worked from morning through to the following morning. No one asked any questions. At that time it was considered absolutely normal, normal working conditions. I learned to make sacrifices, to work together with others for no pay. It was a normal task for that period to create without material goods. That was the time, that's the way people were.
>
> Today it looks different. To the younger generation, it's absolutely unnatural, peculiar: How was that possible? Nevertheless, if you had been in that generation you would have done just the same. If you would have been in that situation, there's no yes or no about it.
>
> At that time the theaters weren't open, movies were rare. Everything was restricted, services were thinned out, everything was poured into a superhuman effort. You have to work if you want to realize something, right, and that whole generation knew that. No one forced them. If someone says 'I won't' then you couldn't do anything. Maybe the Party organization or SKOJ [the Communist Youth League] would talk to him. Today it's a different situation. Everyone has his own life that he puts on a pedestal above everything else. People think more about their personal lives than about social life. That's the situation.

Thus the postwar period lives in memory as an extraordinary time. Perhaps that was a form of social revolution in Yugoslavia

— when individuals molded themselves into a community. Today, according to Ristić, people, especially young people, prefer to work for their own advancement instead of for societal goals.

The Vuković brothers like to talk about the self-sacrifice of Partisan-generation youths. Milovan says, 'Those youth brigades — this was young people going off, leaving the villages, this was a poem', and Janko goes on,

> Lissen, we got things on a card [rationing]. There was hunger, there was all sorts of things. But do you think that no one was looking out for the people? Here at the Slavija [a big intersection in the center of town], on Terazije [the center of downtown], at the National Theater, they danced till midnight, the *kola* [folk dancing] every day, and they sang. They didn't think anything at all about — if help was needed somewhere, for example, if they were looking for 5,000 young people for a project, why, 50,000 turned up. Voluntarily.
>
> There were work projects on all sides. Only now there aren't so many. You never had — this was work brigades that were working for free, this wasn't some economic calculation, ya know. If you built the country in the normal way, then you'd have to work three years in the normal way to do what they accomplished in six months with the work brigades. And that means a lot.
>
> They worked without pay but they got apartments and clothes, uniforms, and food, and so on. Lookit, it would cost as much, I think, to build the normal way . . . And they even sent foreign workers to Yugoslavia. They made three or four good railroads and the Belgrade-Zagreb highway. If they had been working normally on that highway, it wouldn't even be finished today.

Ristić and the Vuković brothers indicate that this was a period of extraordinary exertion, of work with no thought of personal reward. Nevertheless, extraordinary work *was* rewarded. Through the Partisan-cum-Party network, peasants and workers were rushed through school to become leaders and executives. The postwar period saw tremendous social mobility not only as peasants moved to the towns but also as Partisans became social leaders. Milovan and Janko Vuković describe the rapid promotion from peasant to leader in terms of the need for reliable cadres who would be loyal to the new state. First Milovan:

> After the end of the revolution, after the liberation of the country, it was the majority of the nation who had taken part in the struggle.[5] These were *borci* [fighters] from 1941 —

> Janko: — tested men.

> Milovan: — men who've been tested. Now, they went to Belgrade, right, but you didn't fight, so they didn't trust you, understand, as much as him. Then they simply placed him, like a *borac* from 1941, with that credential, and he was responsible . . . And those *borci,* they even went to night-school to get some education. After the Liberation — you want to go to school, you simply have to — if you didn't finish school, you go to college. They give you money to study —

> Janko: They give you everything — leave from work, and they pay you your salary if you'll only go to accomplish something.

> Milovan: And in the Party organizations, a guy says, 'Well, I don't have four years of school' [the prewar elementary education, which is now eight years]. And they say, 'You have to finish high school'. 'Why?' he says. 'No,' they say, 'you have to finish night-school and high school'. So he goes after work or he gets off to go. If an exam comes along, then you get fifteen days off to pass the exam.
> And every man accomplished something. Anyway, they got some diploma, they got educated. And that's the way these people went higher and higher.

This is precisely the way that Steva Ristić went to technical school. This is also how the journalist Danilo Arandjelović left a Belgrade hospital for a job on a newspaper and a simultaneous high-school and college education. In fact, Arandjelović's first

5 According to one foreign scholar, the Partisans included about 100,000 men and women by the end of 1942, 300,000 a year later, and, as they claimed, 800,000 by the end of the war in 1945. Phyllis Auty, *Yugoslavia* (New York: Walker, 1965), pp. 89, 91, 104. The population in March 1941 is estimated at 15,970,000 and in 1945 at 14,270,000.

steps up the social ladder indicate both how important the Partisan-cum-Party network was after the war and how rewarded hard work could be. Arandjelović recalls,

> While I was lying here in the hospital I sent word to the government at that time. They didn't know who I was, but they got my data from my area and I had the luck to be immediately taken care of, sent to an enterprise that published a newspaper. I came, of course, without any kind of qualifications, just as a man, even though I was fairly literate — my degree of literacy was somewhere on the junior-high level, not in all areas, but in general — I had read quite a few books, been involved in things [like setting up the first public library in my village] . . .
>
> I advanced quickly because I had a lot of interest in the work and it was very flattering for me as a man from the village, without any schooling, to be in an educated milieu with highly educated people. And when I gave the old editors my articles, they liked them, so I let them know [that I was willing] several times, and they stood behind me. . . .
>
> Then they started a paper called *The Peasant Struggle*. And because I was from the country, I knew the country well, they invited me to join the editorial board and write about the countryside . . . I was rather successful, people noticed me. I was pretty active at work, in the union. Then an organization of the National Front existed, I was quickly elected to some of its organs, and I was accepted as a member of the Communist Party in 1945.
>
> Then I knew that I couldn't go any further because I didn't have any education. They had opened up evening schools for people whose lives had been disrupted by the war, and as soon as they set up these schools I enrolled and I started to go . . . In two years I completed four years of high school, and I was working regularly, and I had other social [i.e. political] functions too . . .
>
> That school of journalism and diplomacy, since it was just opened, allowed people to enroll in the first year who hadn't completely finished their secondary education because of war factors but who were involved in journalism and showed some talent for it. They were allowed to

register on the condition that in the course of their studies, during the first two years, they would finish high school. I took this opportunity and I registered, that is, I persuaded those people who were in charge of permitting registration to let me enroll. That was the 1948–9 school year. Well, they allowed me to register, then they gave me a leave from work and a scholarship equivalent to my salary. They were very proper in this regard. I remember that my salary at that time was 4,500 dinars [or 450 dinars a month by today's currency valuation], which for that time was very, very high, a very large fellowship.

So I enrolled and began to attend high school [the fifth of high school's eight years] and college. To go back a little, I had a great deal of difficulty convincing those officials, the director of my newspaper and the Party secretary and the ones who accepted students at the school to take me because I was a rather good — what at that time was called a *masovik* [mass worker]. I had some kind of communication with people. In those days the [newspaper] enterprise had about 500 employees, it was pretty large. I was at that time secretary of the Party organization, which had around 100 members. And of those 500 people employed in the enterprise I knew every one. Somehow I succeeded in making contact with people, so they didn't want to let me go. So I persisted . . .

I wanted to take all the exams at once: the seventh and eighth years of high school, the graduation exam, and nine subjects from the first year of college. And I passed eight of them at the regular time, and my average grade was over 8.0 [out of 10.0] . . . I studied full time for three years, I was one of the better students, not one of the best, but still . . . I was in the top twenty . . . I finished college in 1952.

For Arandjelović as for others of his generation, those six years (1946–52) represent a golden age which today is almost a dream. 'You know', he says,

after the war there was a certain dynamism, a certain movement. A man practically didn't have any other kind of life, not even a private life, or a personal life, he was always in the enterprise where he worked or in school, in courses,

or in various seminars, Party and union seminars. There
was that energy, that enthusiasm, those projects . . .
Almost everybody was caught up by this huge enthusiasm
so that today when a man looks at that period, even to us
who lived through it, it looks like a dream, like some
kind of special romanticism, really.

Cominform dispute

Into this whirlpool of enthusiasm and energy the break with the
socialist camp intruded abruptly, to the masses unexpectedly,
and — for a time — disastrously. Yugoslavs of all ages almost
visibly shudder when they recall the Cominform dispute of 1948.
Contrary to the outsiders' impression of that crisis, the confrontation between Stalin and Tito reached down to ordinary Yugoslavs in everyday life. To them this was a domestic crisis, not
primarily a question of foreign policy. Because of their stands
at that time, some political leaders were discredited as traitors
and some citizens, also discredited, lost their Party affiliations
and their jobs. The people as a whole was traumatized, for the
break with the Cominform ruptured their newly-won identity
both as socialists and as a unified nation.

To someone who lived through that period, the break with
the Cominform must have been a rude awakening from the
dream that any feat was possible for Yugoslavia. Janko Vuković
indicates the rapid and complete disillusionment that the Cominform dispute brought. He says,

> We're too optimistic about building our state . . . but
> we don't have any kind of illusions. Ya know, when the
> Soviet Union left us high and dry, and the Americans
> themselves thought, they thought that we were going to
> run away, that the people would die off right away —
> Tempo [Svetozar Vukmanović-Tempo, a political leader],
> when he went, when the U.S.A. had to give wheat so they
> could feed the people that much, he says, 'No, we learned,
> we ate grass, our people learned to eat grass, and we'll eat
> grass again if we have to'. We've already learned to live in
> trouble. For us it isn't hard, for a while.

His brother Milovan goes on to sketch the sources of insecurity
in 1948. He says,

There were two years when we came to such a situation that we didn't have anything to eat. Then — the Russians on the borders. They sent the army already to Yugoslavia. Then we had to look for some way out; we had to go to America. When they simply start to enter Yugoslavia, when they start, understand — our people didn't allow the Germans, we didn't allow anyone . . .

Because of the Cominform dispute, the engineer Steva Ristić who 'worked from morning through to the following morning' lost his job. Describing the effect of the crisis on his life, he says,

In that enterprise I was planning director. Then later I became technical director. I was technical director for a year and a half, then 1948 began. In 1948 I spoke out for — I was for the resolution [against the Cominform's stand] only I didn't come out strongly enough on the modifications for the letters [the exchange of letters with the Cominform]. So I made some mistakes, and they expelled me from the Party, right, and after that they removed me from the position of technical director, but they made me director of development. They had to do this because I was an expert, highly valued regardless of everything else. An expert. The questions on which I deviated were of a, a sporadic nature; they weren't the major questions or dilemmas, but sporadic. So I wasn't in that group which was working against the state, against the people. I was in that enterprise up to the middle of 1952.

Thus Ristić lost something because of his political position in the Cominform crisis, but the societal need for expertise may have modified his punishment. The experience of one generation, the Cominform dispute provided a lesson that following generations have learned. An 18-year-old high school student like Vera Filipović, who was born several years after the crisis, knows that

1948 was a very big crisis. Yugoslavia wanted an independent position. It wasn't only that: Yugoslavia was split — the country itself, the society — those who were for Stalin and those who were against him. Now it's much better.

Furthermore, a Belgrade University student who participated in the October 1970 strike described to me the 'tremendous fear' among her colleagues for

> these are students whose parents for the most part made the revolution. They remember very well the situation in 1948, with the Cominform. One day we were saying 'The Russians are our brothers', and the next — People remember what happened then. What would happen to me if my father were arrested, to my mother, my brother? People have dependents, so they are afraid.

Despite the fact that these three collective experiences have concrete and personal substance for all Yugoslavs, there is a difference between those who have directly experienced and those who have learned about these events. The generation now in their twenties and late teens have learned about the war and its aftermath from stories at home, lessons at school, books, and movies. However, current events, particularly the daily ebb-and-flow within their own frequently apolitical lives, are most relevant to them. Like 24-year-old Miša Cvijić, whose parents were both in the Partisans, they probably fantasized as children that they were fighting that war. Thus when they talk about war, reconstruction, and the Cominform, their accounts are detailed. However, other historical events, e.g. World War I, the Great Depression, the Spanish Civil War, and — during their lifetimes — the introduction of workers' self-management, the end of forced collectivization in the countryside, the Soviet invasion of Hungary, these events stirred almost no response from the younger respondents. When they did say something about any of these events, they expressed themselves in formal, textbook, sometimes even propagandistic phrases. Obviously these other collective experiences have come through a different mode of social learning. But even the middle-aged generation has vague recollections about these events. Even very recent events, like the 1968 uprisings of students and some workers and the 1971–2 amending of the Federal Constitution, fail to excite much interest. Except for the external threat that they still perceive in situations like the Soviet invasions of Hungary in 1956 and Czechoslovakia in 1968, they do not seem to regard any of the societal changes of the past twenty years as highly relevant to their lives.

Formative experiences

Self-management

Nor does the official key to societal change of the past two decades, i.e. the introduction of self-management, stir much self-expression among the respondents. When they talk about the historical event or phenomenon, they begin with assertions of the official ideology, go on to describe institutions, and eventually come to the conclusion that they themselves, albeit formally self-managers, do not do any self-managing either at work or in the society. This orientation to self-management is analogous to any citizen's attitude toward artifacts of his country's political past which remain sanctified by the official ideology but contradicted or even negated by practice. Citizens may identify positively with the intention or the principle of an historical act or a political institution, but not with its ultimate consequences and the way things have worked out.

The Yugoslavs who tend to perceive themselves as real self-managers are those who hold offices in self-managing, i.e. political, bodies, such as workers' councils and the League of Communists. For others, at least in my small acquaintanceship and smaller sample, the introduction of self-management has become just a given condition of life. The two self-concepts of self-manager and non-self-manager occur within the Djordjević family. Josip Djordjević, the retired army officer who is active in local politics, can talk for hours (and did, to me) about self-management. According to him, everyone is a real self-manager, or will be as soon as material conditions permit consciousness to be raised to that level. Yet his personal experience in self-management is limited to political organizations rather than workers' self-management. As he says, 'There's no self-management in the army; there can't be, in an army.'

Josip's 21-year-old daughter Vesna admits to being completely bored by politics and so does not attend any kind of self-management meetings, either in her enterprise or in the commune where her father is so active. She indicates that she has gained her knowledge of self-management through formal lessons, as in a school civics course, rather than through practice. Vesna says,

> I wondered and worried a lot over that, what is self-management? What is it that a man is made more intense, he's not just one man, a passive person, but he takes part in the direction of the factory. And the wage-earners

95

get their right to vote, the right to a vacation, and profit, and trade, and all that. I know that. That's the way the system is. It's not a bourgeoisie but socialism.

Eighteen-year-old Vera Filipović also describes self-management vicariously. According to Vera,

> they talk a lot about the introduction of self-management. From society the workers took everything into their own hands. It's something more than what the Soviet Union has. In the Soviet Union they have state ownership. Here we have social ownership: the workers themselves have a higher position in society than in the Soviet Union. But the Soviet Union was the first socialist country. Here there wasn't any revolution — we didn't have that here. Here everything is social, and they say that it's all the workers'. In capitalist countries the worker works only to fulfill his own needs, but here he works both for himself and for society.

However, when personal desires and motivations enter the discussion, the concept of self-management appears quite remote from personal experience. Vera, for example, thinks only about finishing high school, going to college, and getting a good job. 'I'm not interested in politics', she says, 'everything's fine with me . . . I talk very little. I withdraw: I do what I have to, and I have to finish my education.' Nor does another young Yugoslav, Vesna Djordjević, enjoy the political avocation which occupies her father. 'We never talk about politics', she says of herself and her acquaintances. 'You work and you only think about how you're going to get your salary on the first of the month.'[6]

Somehow, in the crush of finishing school, getting the monthly pay envelope, and other personal matters, self-management be-

6 Surveys of Yugoslav and Croatian college students, as well as free association tests of Slovenian students, also illustrate that the concept of self-management is remote from many young people. See Milosav Janićijević et al., *Jugoslovenski studenti i socijalizam* [Yugoslav students and socialism] (Belgrade: Institut društvenih nauka, 1966), pp. 22, 17; Mirko Martić, *Studenti Zagrebačkog sveučilišta: Sociološka ispitivanja, 1959–1965* [Students of Zagreb University: Sociological Research, 1959–1965] (Zagreb: Institut za društvena istraživanja, 1967), appendix, tables 30A and 32; and Vid Pečjak, 'The Cognitive Structure of the Concepts Communism, Socialism, and Capitalism' [in Slovenian], *Teorija in praksa* 7, (1970): 1022–34.

comes a rather remote relevance. In this case, Yugoslavs may tend
to see self-management more in terms of economic benefits than
ideological goals. When Vesna Djordjević says that self-management includes the workers' 'right to vote, the right to a vacation,
and profit, and trade, and all that', she seems to be confusing
self-management with trade-unionism. The ideology of other
young Yugoslavs who have grown up under self-management —
a generation which has not experienced the trade union agitation
typical of prewar Yugoslavia — may also make this mistake. Actually, though, this 'economist' interpretation of the official ideology is not so different from that of the political leadership, for
the leaders have bridged postwar deprivation and foreign-policy
trauma by emphasizing economic development.

Vesna's and Vera's comments on self-management indicate a
dualistic view of self-management as both an ideological goal and
a set of economic rights, and other Yugoslavs may find this dual-
ism hard to swallow. Rade Popović, for example, the highly-
skilled machinist who formerly belonged to both the Party and
a workers' council, candidly says that he finds a contradiction
between ideological goals, on the one hand, and economic priorities, on the other. He muses,

> I don't remember what year it was, somewhere around the
> establishment of workers' councils, around 1950, or later,
> we propagated some kind of socialist democracy in the
> country. They wrote about it and they talked about it.
> I'm a living witness of all that, so I know. They propagated
> some kind of socialist democracy and through that 'democ-
> racy' all kinds of nonsense came out. And people are
> inclined, regardless of whether they're Yugoslavs or who
> they are, if they feel that they can come to some wealth,
> to money, to the good life, we're all ready to do that, to
> put aside our ideals. Because ideals only go a little way,
> only a few people live by an ideal, scientists maybe, but
> like this, with the society the way it is, it's 'Why does
> So-and-so live better than me?' and 'I want that.' So every-
> one runs so that we can live better, and some succeed.

Thus Popović sees some sort of connection between innovation
in the official ideology toward 'some kind of socialist democracy'
and the advent of consumer society. In Popović's interpretation

of Yugoslav norms and values, self-management has failed to affect the pursuit of self-interest, perhaps because 'ideals only go a little way'.[7]

In contrast to Popović, the journalist Danilo Arandjelović sees no contradiction in the evolution of self-management. For Arandjelović, the economic development of Yugoslavia is a prerequisite of the institutionalization of self-management. Thus Arandjelović's orientation parallels the official ideology. He says,

> You know, self-management without a material base isn't self-management. We can sit here all day discussing things and setting up theoretical forms, convincing ourselves, but if we don't have the basic material lever, if we don't have anything to distribute — You know, we used to say ironically that self-management in the enterprise was like throwing a bare bone to hungry dogs, and they're fighting over the bone and gnawing it. Maybe I'm painting too extreme a picture, but that's the way it was.

The Belgrade sample indicates that self-management as an ideological goal has little relevance to people's everyday lives. Instead, Yugoslavs appear preoccupied with the standard of living. In part this preoccupation is a response to social conditions, to the 'struggle for a dinar' which is waged with the tacit, if perhaps reluctant, approval of the political leadership. This mentality may also be related to the felt insecurity and relative deprivation of those experiences which still dominate the collective consciousness: the war, the reconstruction, and the break with the Cominform. In contrast to these experiences, the two decades of self-management are perceived as a given institution, a formalism, from which the ordinary Yugoslav derives only such benefits as he can see and spend. From this consciousness, within the scenario of the official ideology, arises a dualistic conception of self-management as both ideological goal and economic rights.

Through individual life stories we may be able to grasp more concretely the sources of this consciousness. If its roots lie in a past of relative deprivation, then the life story should reveal what forms this deprivation took and how it has been integrated

---

7 Similarly, a survey of workers in two Slovenian enterprises shows that their dominant attitude toward self-management is skepticism, that is, a belief that the concept is unrealizable. Arzenšek, 'Samoupravljanje', p. 29.

into the citizen's perceptions of society. We have already seen how personal experiences of war and its aftermath form the stock of social knowledge of both the middle-aged generation and their children. For the parents, particularly for those who left the village, war and reconstruction represent a tidal wave of change which has left them on the once distant shore of creature comforts and conveniences. Thus they are living better than ever before. As the very beginning of this chapter indicates, the change in their lives has been so fundamental a part of Yugoslavs' social reality that many of them have equated it with 'socialism'. Moreover, they have transmitted the experience of poverty, war, and rapid economic growth — especially the spread of consumer goods — to their children, whose direct experience, of course, conditions them to expect progress rather than impoverishment.

SOCIAL MOBILITY

Danilo Arandjelović, the middle-aged journalist who started his career and education simultaneously during the reconstruction period, provides the typical beginning for a life story of his generation: rural poverty. He recalls,

> I was born in a peasant family from the mountainous region of western Serbia near Užice, Zlatibor — It's beautiful there, half mountains — in a poor family. I worked there as a child in a cooperative (*zadruga*) we had, watching the stock and other physical labor; I didn't have the opportunity to go to school. Already when I was fourteen I began to earn my living, to work in various enterprises, with private owners and firms. I worked on roads, as a construction worker, and then at that time I had a friend, a work-mate, who had finished carpentry training, so I worked with him and so I gradually succeeded in getting various jobs. I learned — I'm not saying that I finished any school in — the carpentry trade. I learned it, but I never passed any examination of skills. So during the winter I worked as a carpenter.

However, Arandjelović, a youth who 'meanwhile . . . had the desire to learn', has been more successful than the average peasant who left the village after the war. Through his hard work

as a reporter and perhaps also through his good political credentials, he is now on the editorial board of a prestigious news organ
in Belgrade. His salary of 4,500 dinars a month ($300) and his
Peugeot 504 place him in what the city calls the new middle
class under socialism: 'the Peugeoisie'. Married to a teacher
since 1954 (he waited until he finished high school and college),
he owns a new single home in a semisurburban area inhabited
by the Peugeoisie. He has also traveled around Europe and America. Because he knows that I am interested in this view of his
life, Arandjelović says,

> I don't know whether I'm what's called in America a
> 'self-made man'. I don't think I am, although my life
> story may have some of those elements in it. But you can
> find self-made men in Yugoslavia, about 100,000 of them,
> because Yugoslavia is an economically undeveloped coun-
> try and it lags behind . . . Therefore, all of us more
> or less come, maybe 90 percent of today's intellectuals
> and employees come from the village. Either the first
> generation was born in the village or the second genera-
> tion has direct contact with the village.

Indeed, Arandjelović's lifestyle does not approach the upper
limit of villas, Mercedes, and expense accounts represented by
directors and importers. But his is the highest salary reported
in my sample: twice as much as an accountant the same age
makes, two-and-a-half times the salary of a highly-skilled worker,
five times the pension of a retired clerk.

Nevertheless, Arandjelović's origins are no different from those
of other former peasants who have not made it so far up the
social ladder. The highly-skilled machinist Rade Popović, who
earns 1,800 dinars ($120) a month in a good year, also begins his
story in a poor village. Popović says,

> My area, it's a pretty passive area, agriculturally unde-
> veloped. In fact, there's no place *to* develop because it's a
> valley surrounded by mountains on one side, then the
> river from Niš on the other. There's a[n old] road that
> goes from London to India there. There's almost no in-
> dustry. Before, there wasn't any at all. There were crafts,
> small crafts, with a master, a landlord, or whatever. Some
> masters kept a few men with them and some big masters
> sold land. There wasn't any industry at all.

Social mobility

And people were leaving even before the war, going
to Belgrade as the main center. They all left during the
summer, to work for six months and make some money and
then come back to the village. Otherwise, life was pretty
hard for the peasant. Furthermore, the house was always
crowded, then he had to pay the tax, and make a living,
so it was very hard to get ahead . . . There was a lot of
livestock, that's how you lived: you worked the land,
you had a little livestock, to get some cheese, some wool,
and to sell it, to live that way, to pay the tax.

It was very hard to get a job. No one dared to make
up his mind. They went but you had to be a big adven-
turer, he even had to be a little of a thief, to tell you the
truth, to get along in all possible ways, to live . . . I
only remember, when I finished school, I went to a trade,
to learn a trade. I listened to the older ones, the ones who
had experience, and the ones who had their own shops,
and it was pretty hard. They only lived to earn a little.
A very small number, a doctor maybe, was able to go to
the shore for a vacation, to have fun, maybe go to France
or Germany. But today that isn't the case. Today whoever
has a little money in his pocket goes. Then it was completely different.

There in my area I left home to learn a trade at fifteen.
I worked there at a master's, forty hours a week. As a kid
— eleven or twelve years old — you worked with a master
for a little while, that was the practice, to clean out the
workshop, to take care of the pigs. He had a tiny workshop, he had a saw mill, I remember, and a pillow-maker's,
this was very small, not even industry, but he got along.
He was very able.

My classmates almost all left there. They're in Belgrade, Novi Sad, Niš. In general, you can find us every-
where. Some died, some were killed, but almost all
left.

My father was a worker in a cigarette factory in Niš.
My mother was a housewife. I have a brother and a sister;
he's a worker today and the sister is a teacher. My family
was in an average situation, as we say, 'in middling sorrow'.
They had their own little house and a little patch of
land and they helped their children as much as they

101

could. Then the war came. When the war was over, I
was twenty . . .

> After the war it was pretty simple to leave. I was then
> a young man, twenty years old, so I went to Niš, and
> there I worked till 1950. And then it bothered me there,
> you know how young people are, I wanted to see the
> world, I wanted to go and to see it all, I didn't have any
> peace, I wanted something better, something more, so
> that's how I came here in 1950. I worked on the railroad
> and lived on the edge of town . . . And I went to school
> here to be a machinist. And we had a lot of free time
> every day, so we were always saying, 'What'll we do now?'
> so we would hop a train and come in to Belgrade.

Just as his youth embodied problems common to many prewar
rural families, so the more recent half of his life seems to indicate
the current preoccupations of most Yugoslavs: a better life, but
still not the good life. Today Popović, his wife, and two children
live in a comfortable apartment owned by his enterprise in the
countryside north of Belgrade. Having bought a piece of land
four years ago for 40,000 dinars (about $2,666), Popović has also
recently erected a two-room week-end 'cottage' on the edge of
Belgrade, rather far from his home. Although this little cottage
is 'illegal', i.e. it was put up without a building permit, Popović
wanted it. 'When you put your money in the bank', he says,
'you don't get anything out of it.' He owns a bicycle rather than
a car, worries that he can't afford to send his wife and daughter
to the seashore, and has a Japanese camera and tape recorder.
His enterprise sent him to head a construction crew in the Middle
East, where he remained for a year and a half. His private travel
is limited to a car trip to Rumania with his brother. As Popović
himself says, 'I get along pretty well. I don't work too hard, that
is, I don't do any work except my job in the enterprise, then in
my free time I stroll a little, I sit around the house, I rest a
little. Otherwise I love to go fishing.'

But as Popović's living standard has risen, his family's needs
and wants have also expanded. His wife's injury in a recent
automobile accident, for example, resulted in a doctor's recom-
mendation that she spend a month on the Adriatic coast. However, Popović has neither the money for this nor the motivation
to 'make up my mind to take credit, to go to some agency to get

102

the money from there, to pay 1,000 dinars or whatever it costs'. Lurking behind the good years when he earns a 400-dinar bonus every month is the spectre of economic insecurity. 'Compared to others I'm satisfied', Popović says,

> but I don't know how it's going to turn out this year. It's been tough and it looks like it's going to be even a little tougher. According to some prognoses, according to the analyses of our economic experts, we're going to have to tighten the belt, but we pulled in the belt after the war. That had to be experienced, I don't have the words to describe how we pulled in the belt. After the war till 1955 . . .

Moreover, Popović is aware that families like the Arandjelo-vićes and other professionals live much better than he does. He compares their lifestyle with his, and he is puzzled about the degree of social differentiation that this comparison indicates. The official ideology, especially the classical Marxism in which he believes, does not prepare him for this social inequality. Popović says,

> My director makes half a million every month and I make 140,000 [8] [he says, and we both laugh] . . . The general director has a car and a chauffeur. The technical director has a company car and a chauffeur, too. The director of my workshop has a car but no chauffeur. Then there are various commercial people, different directors, I couldn't even explain it all to you. They've been with the company a long time, there are a lot of directors, they all have college educations — I haven't got anything against edu-cated people, competent people, who serve, but our income differences, our system in general, socialism — I don't know how to explain it all so you'll understand, it doesn't allow a story [i.e. theory] like this and a practice like that . . . It's come to the point where workers who are working directly in production, who are creating the economic goods, are paid very little.

Nevertheless, both Arandjelović and Popović are better off than ever before. They have come to Belgrade from poor villages

8 Figures are in old dinars. Since 1965, one new dinar is equivalent to 100 old dinars.

in western and southern Serbia, respectively, and they have never gone back to the standard of living that they knew before the war. Furthermore, many poorer families who have also come to the city are also living better than ever before. Perhaps those Yugoslavs are as conscious as Arandjelović and Popović of an ascent from the village to relative comfort. Jovan Živković, for example, Popović's neighbor in the 'wild settlement' where Popović built his cottage, is similarly content with the improvement in his living conditions. A man in his late forties, Živković lost one leg in the battle on the Srem front just before Liberation in 1945. He walks with a wooden leg that he puts on every morning when he gets up, around six o'clock. Trained as a tailor after convalescing in various hospitals following the war, he has found it too difficult to leave his home and walk to work. So for almost all of his adult life he has supported his family (a wife and three children) on his invalid's pension of 1,400 dinars ($93) a month. Živković remains a fervid Partisan in spirit. He likes to talk about his war experiences, to identify various political leaders and minor figures as his Partisan comrades even though he did not know them personally. He speaks favorably of the political and social education that he received in the Partisans, most of it from the political commissars who served with the troops.

The little house that Živković and his family built in the 'wild settlement' four years ago has a garden with flowers, salad greens, and even young trees. Inside, they have a television and several electrical appliances that they have bought on credit. It is easy for them to get credit by showing proof that a member of the family gets a state pension. They also plan to build an indoor toilet soon, but their plan depends on the street's getting water pipes. Because the city wants to destroy 'wild settlements' like theirs, the laying of water pipes is problematic. Last year the settlement's inhabitants were able to devise an illegal strategem to get access to electrical power. They paid an electrician to 'cut them into' the main power source nearest their houses, thus tapping electricity for their stoves and lights. So their hopes for bringing a water pipe up to the highest part of the settlement, where the Živkovićes live, remain bright. Twice a day now Živković's wife Slavka takes a couple of pails part way down the unpaved, sometimes muddy path to the nearest water supply.

Slavka does not work outside the home. Nor do any of the

children contribute to the family's maintenance. The eldest child, a hairdresser's assistant, lives with her parents-in-law in the Vojvodina; the middle child has quit two unskilled jobs since he finished elementary (eight-year) school and now bums around; and the youngest is still a pupil. Nevertheless, this little house in a 'wild settlement' that the city would like to destroy is the best home that the Živkovićes have known. The parents say, for example, that it is incomparably better than the conditions in which they grew up, when children slept three to a pad on the hard earth floor.[9]

Before the war, both Jovan Živković and Slavka lived in the same area in southern Serbia, near the town of Vranje. Like the other respondents, Živković contrasts the poverty of those days with current prosperity on the national level and improvement in personal life. He says,

> At that time, before the establishment of socialist Yugoslavia, the leaders of the country only looked out for their own initiatives, understand, they didn't pay any attention to the common people. But people still have to live, except that incomes were small from the little pieces of land that people had . . . Today we have everything, even to the farthest region; people are producing very nicely, they have forests, and goats, they raise plums, and apples, and all these are produced beautifully, understand . . .
>
> Then, for example, when Yugoslavia fell, when Hitler attacked our country, then our people was, how shall I

9 Since 1945, an estimated 300,000 dwellings have been constructed in 'wild settlements' on the edges of major cities. Today, for example, Belgrade has seventy-eight such settlements, each of which contains from ten to 300 houses. Zagreb now has about 10,000 dwellings in 'wild settlements'. The homeowners here are usually recent migrants from the village, like the Živkovićes, and also predominantly workers, like Popović. According to a Yugoslav sociologist, these migrants feel a strong sense of anomie vis-à-vis the city which promises much but delivers very little in concrete social benefits. Stipe Šuvar, 'Urbanizacija, socijalna diferencijacija i socijalna segregacija u našem društvu' [Urbanization, social differentiation and social segregation in our society] (Paper delivered at the Fifth Annual Meeting of the Yugoslav Sociological Association, Dubrovnik, February 11, 1971), p. 10. See also Djuro Djurović, 'Bespravna stambena izgradnja — jedna od karakteristika urbanog razvoja Beograda' [Illegal housing construction — one of the characteristics of Belgrade's urban development], *Sociologija* 12, no. 3–4 (1970): 499–507.

say it, our people was left without any support, from the government, and so on . . . Then the Communist Party raised the banner, and then people got together . . . By 1944 we were already successful at cleaning out the Bulgars, the Četniks, the Albanians there in southern Serbia. When we had already liberated ourselves, we were there on the Srem Front, and we only know that the enemy is before us. Belgrade was already liberated . . . I was wounded near Vinkovci and there I lost my leg. That's the way it goes. Then I was in and out of hospitals . . .

Before the war I was young, I herded the stock. My family lives in the Vojvodina, in Bačka. They got land there, a plot, you know because of the confiscation of German property . . . My brother died in the war, and I was left without a leg. We were all in the Partisans . . . In that moment when the Partisans were starting up, my oldest brother was told by the Bulgars to give them grain, or wheat, and he said, 'I won't do it', and they said, 'We'll kill you'. He left home for the Partisans in '42 and in '45 he was killed, by the Bulgars.

Thus Jovan Živković's early life was shaped by deprivation and war.

Like many other families, the Živkovićes moved to Belgrade for their children's sake, so that they would be able to find good jobs in the city. Similarly, the Filipović family moved to Belgrade so that their two children, when the time came, could go to Belgrade University. They would not have been able to afford the extra expense of a dormitory or a rented room. The Zivković and Filipović children are even more delighted with city life than their parents. For them there is 'no comparison, this is a big city', as Dragan Živković, the 18-year-old unemployed son says. Belgrade offers him unlimited vistas of tall apartment houses and small homes, which he can look down upon from the height of the 'wild settlement' where he lives, and which he can tour with his good friend, the son of rich peasants, who owns a car. Nevertheless, the children take the move to the city and their parents' improved living standard in their stride. Thus the relevance of the city to their lives is not, as it is to their parents', that it is a step upward, but that it is simply there.

A young woman who seems to have internalized many norms

of contemporary Belgrade life is Vesna Djordjević, the daughter
of local activist Josip, who was born in 1950 and moved to Belgrade during her adolescence. Vesna's experiences and ideas contrast — if they do not collide — with those of the Partisan generation. Indeed, Vesna explains the divergence between the Partisans,
of whom her father was one, and her contemporaries in this way:

> We studied about them [i.e. the Partisans] in school and
> then my parents told me about it. I was younger then and
> interested . . . But when I started to go out with the
> crowd, to discoclubs and dances, it didn't interest me any
> more, I went off in another direction, what can I do,
> right? You saw how my father and I went off to London
> [on a charter flight] with that actress, with a fine group of
> people — It's normal that you set yourself up differently.

In her desire to keep pace with social developments, especially
through increased consumption, Vesna is far from atypical of
many young Yugoslavs. 'It's normal that you set yourself up
differently', she says, thus establishing her distance from the
Partisan generation and the self-sacrifice that they represent.

The grand-daughter of peasants, the daughter of a retired army
officer, Vesna is a clerk-typist who earns 1,200 dinars ($80) a
month. She has managed to save $1,600 *in dollars,* 300 German
marks, and some Greek drachmae in her bank account. Even
though her mother asserts that one can buy whatever imported
clothes or objects one desires in Belgrade shops, Vesna, like
many young Yugoslavs, makes the frequent trek to Trieste and
other Italian cities to buy all her clothes. However, she bought
her wig in Germany where they are, she says, better and cheaper.
Her lifestyle amply bears out her father's statement, 'Now you
can buy everything in Yugoslavia and no one is hungry. Everyone has bread, although some people are looking for meat.'
Vesna is one of those who look for meat.

Vesna goes out almost every night, especially to the new,
luxury-class Hotel Jugoslavija. In its discoclub, really a supper
club, a husband-and-wife duo sing the latest European hits. Only
their dark hair and complexions suggest that they, like all cabaret
singers in Serbia, are gypsies. Vesna says that her idea of entertainment differs from the average Yugoslav's: 'I don't like to
sit in a hotel and drink and listen to folk music'. This preference
is shared by many of her contemporaries who flock to Belgrade's

ten flourishing discoclubs.[10] Vesna indicates her other relevances
in the following conversation, which we held after she came
back from a week in London, her first visit there. She says,

> You've been to a discoclub here. Everyone's dressed so that
> you think you've gone into a clothing store. You know
> what they wear in London? Usually 'shorts', with a blouse
> and a belt, but the belt's nothing; here the belts are really
> fancy. So people travel, they buy stuff on credit, they go
> to London to buy clothes. You see how the girls look here
> — well dressed, good hairdo and make-up . . .
>
> You know what I need? First I need a car. Second, it's
> expensive to go out. Going into a discoclub costs thirty
> [dinars, or $2], so I can't go every night. Aside from that,
> living in New Belgrade I need a car, I need this and that,
> and a wardrobe. Everybody looks you over to see how
> you're dressed; I can't go around with some funky dress
> on or something from three years ago. That could be
> unpleasant for you because today this world looks espe-
> cially at how you dress, that's number one, and second is
> whether you've got anything. If you haven't got anything,
> then nobody will look at you. Well, that's the way it is
> all over . . .

Thus Vesna couches her relevances in terms of personal needs,
not societal needs, and her needs are those consumer goods which
will establish her social status in the eyes of other Yugoslavs. This
is, at first glance, a drastically different social reality from that
of the Partisan generation and the official ideology. As Vesna
continues her description of the social reality that she sees in
Yugoslavia, her mother Milica interrupts, protests that this is not
the way things really are. The ensuing dialogue between Vesna
and Milica indicates an incongruity between the two generations'
views of the world. Vesna says,

> I'm telling you, here people look at everything with dollar
> signs in their eyes [literally, they look at everything
> through a dinar]. They look you over to see if you're
> going to be a success only so they'll be able to use you in
> some way, whether you're male or female.

10 See Bogdan Tirnanić, 'Zabava: Nije za "tatine sinove"' [Entertain-
ment: Not for 'daddy's sons'], *NIN*, 16 January 1972, p. 23.

Social mobility

Her mother Milica interrupts: That's nowadays . . .

Vesna: If you go to a friend's place he'll say, 'Bring this and that', you know, so you buy the things, and then he'll never say thank you. He wants to make a fool out of you . . . Well, now people travel more, they see the world more, you know, and everyone wants what he can't have, he always envies the man who has something. If he sees that you have money he says, 'Come on, buy this or that', if you have clothes, 'Come on, give me something'.

What kind of self-managing society is this where, according to Vesna, 'everyone looks at you through a dinar'? Like all Yugoslavs Vesna says, 'I don't love money but today you can't do anything without it. You're nothing without money — no one, nothing'. But how do the 'self-managers' make the money for high consumption in an underdeveloped, half-agrarian country? On this seemingly factual question, Vesna's view of social reality again clashes with Milica's. Vesna says,

People are involved in trade, they make contracts right and left, what do I know. All our little people, understand, they have two cars apiece, two or three apartments, they have villas — they don't get that off their salaries. They steal from society — who knows what they do?

This last assertion, which I have heard just as categorically from other young Yugoslavs, shocks Vesna's mother Milica. 'They don't steal!' she says. 'Well', Vesna concedes, 'they don't steal directly.' This mollifies Milica slightly. She says, 'At least in Yugoslavia there are very few of such people', but Vesna interrupts, 'Wait'll I tell you! A manager who works with us, who takes money directly, himself, who sends money to the banks himself — he can live for a whole year on those profits!'

To negate Vesna's implication that stealing from society, or embezzlement, is widespread, Milica tries three separate arguments. First, she says that embezzlers are sent to prison and duly punished; 'Like hell!' her daughter says. Then Milica says that people make money by legitimate investment, such as buying land cheap and selling it high. For example, Milica says, 'My brother bought a vineyard for a million old dinars and now it's worth ten million. Prices jump.' When Vesna tries to counter this argument by asking, 'Then how was Lena able to buy a Renault 16? From her father!' Milica uses her third line of argument. This is that Lena's family, one of the prewar bourgeoisie, has held on to their land and money. When the argument tones down, Milica presents two more legitimate ways in which Yugoslavs make money: moonlighting from their regular jobs to earn 'honoraria' and receiving money from relatives abroad. Thus, this little exchange between mother and daughter suggests five ways, besides embezzlement, that self-managers make money over and above their salaries.

Yet Vesna's social reality is not so diametrically opposed to that of the Partisan generation as we had thought — at least, while it is far from the wartime deprivation and prewar poverty that the Partisan generation experienced, it is the same social reality in which both generations now live. Even Milica, when she is alone with me, admits that money is important and that relevances have changed. She says,

> Today the dinar is your means of living. Here you have, as Vesna says, a 'struggle for the dinar', as they say. Naturally people work for that and struggle to make more money, to set themselves up. As I've been saying, when we were poverty-stricken after the war, then both our wants were different and the opportunities were different, because nothing was even the least bit possible, and we were reconciled then with the fact that we couldn't do anything. For a while we had those 'imported points' [i.e. the Stalinist model], and under those points everything was identical, the same goods, then we started to trade with all the foreign countries . . .
>
> So with such a rich market already the opportunities are different. This means that a person is never satisfied, he has his personal desires, so he looks for dinars, and everything else . . . Because a person can never be completely satisfied.

This is an interesting assertion for a woman who has been a member of the Party since the end of the war. Indeed, Milica's comments indicate that Vesna's relevances are not such an illogical outgrowth of the scenario of the official ideology. Milica herself not only condones working for one's personal advancement, investing in real estate for speculation, and moonlighting, but she regards such activities as natural. Similarly, we have seen (in chapter 2) that the official ideology condones and legitimizes these activities in the name of productivity and historical necessity.

Furthermore, another Party member of Milica's generation, Milovan Vuković, corroborates Vesna's assertion that there is much embezzlement or 'stealing from society'. Like Milica's account of the 'struggle for a dinar', Milovan's explanation of 'stealing' hinges on the rapid transition from poverty to economic opportunity of a large number of persons. Milovan tells how the Partisan veterans, who were mostly peasants turned guerrillas, became the only postwar cadres whose loyalty to the state could not be doubted. There were many cases in which uneducated Partisans were made directors of factories and, according to Milovan, the temptation of personal riches proved too much. 'They simply put him', Milovan says,

> like a *borac* [fighter] from 1941, with that credential —
> and he was responsible. He kept account of everything.
> But as soon as all the money started going from pocket
> to pocket — he was a peasant, a peasant, he was a *borac* —
> he never had so much money in his life! And someone
> comes along, someone who's just as strong, and he says,
> 'Lissen here, c'mon, throw something our way and here's
> 100,000 in your pocket'.
>
> So then he takes it. If he doesn't, well anyhow, it's a
> lot of money, and he has to buy his wife a dress, he has
> to buy furniture, and this and that. And it starts slowly:
> he thinks that no one will know. So then those people
> started taking bribes, bribes, and more bribes. And they'd
> give [one of these *borci*] something on the level and then
> they'd go away. But some individuals stayed on — *borci*
> naturally — and afterwards they went to school. They
> went with only four years of schooling, they went right
> into college, they were directors because they trusted these
> people.

What Vesna says about widespread 'stealing from society', what Milovan adds about the peasants who overnight became directors — this is part of the stock of social knowledge which fleshes out the official ideology. Probably all Yugoslavs know that 'stealing from society', albeit a violation of one kind of social norm, is just part of the 'struggle for a dinar'. Moreover, people who do it seem to enjoy social rewards like money, houses, cars, and prestige. The machinist Rade Popović, for example, says, 'We all know in this country that there are rich people, that's the truth. They have a couple of apartments here in Belgrade, then they have a cottage in the mountains somewhere, on the sea — that's known, that's a public secret.' But when he tries to connect this phenomenon with the official ideology of self-management, Popović finds only contradictions. He goes on in exasperation and bewilderment,

> In this kind of a system, with this 'jam', how can it be self-managing? Who's managing whom? It's understood that people worked full time, so they earned a lot of money, and they built several houses while many people didn't have apartments; that's the most basic thing in life. No one can understand this. I don't like it. Everyone talks about it, it's public, nothing's hidden. That people live like that, enjoying life, it's really something.
>   And it happens with those leaders who are 'idealists'. Let's say, their children, at their own expense, go to school in France or Switzerland. Where do they get the money from? Or a limousine? And they say, 'We're not America, we're far from that'. Wait a minute, buddy: Where are we?

Where the self-managers seem to be, a generation after the revolution, is in the midst of the 'struggle for a dinar'. Earning money, getting along: this is the social lesson that parents teach their children and that the official emphasis on economic development reinforces. This is also the social reality that the journalist quoted at the beginning of the chapter condemns: a social reality of 'easy "success", a deluge of paraders, a certain equality crashing through the spirit of expert mediocrity'. Although the younger generation is much more secure economically than their parents ever were, the 'struggle for a dinar' and the status of high consumption represent relevances for Yugoslavs of all ages. Despite the official ideology's legitimization of self-interest, the goal of mastery of self and social problems that self-management implies seems to recede further and further into the future.

The poet Matija Bećković describes this predominant mental

ity with incisive humor in his short piece 'On Yugoslavs'. Bećković starts with a problem that we have already considered: 'Yugoslavs make more than they produce, and spend more than they make. How?!' And he answers: 'Pretty nicely! With magic wands they pull out of soldiers' caps, crocheted beanies, hats, and cylinders that which the modest possibilities of the current stage cannot offer them'. He goes on, like Rade Popović, to point out the contradiction between the state's chronic impoverishment and the individual's often illicit gain. Moreover, he ironically describes the replacement of the traditional struggle for national liberation with the struggle for a dinar:

> Thus on this volcanic ground of great uprisings and illegality there has quickly spread a new illegal movement for happiness, for flowered cottages, for tiled bathrooms, for coaches and deodorants.
> What there's less of — there's more of, what's given less — is taken more!

Bećković concludes his treatise on Yugoslavs with an enumeration of the miraculous and multifarious ways in which the self-managers manage to earn their dinars. He asks, 'Off what *do* you live, faithful reader?'

> Per diems, separate maintenance, bribery, graft, contests, kitchen gardens, hens, a half to you — and a half to me? A little renting out an empty room, a little Trieste, a little Sofia? Councils, commissions, analyses, interpretations, extra lessons, supplemental supplements? You rewrite, you rearrange, you recommend? You do a favor so they pay you back, hmmm? . . . Confess! . . . You have an aunt in America, an uncle in Australia, a sister-in-law in Sweden? You save on food? You turn the old one over so it looks like new? . . . Wow! You resell a house they're going to tear down, a crypt, a chauffeur's license? . . . You sold your house and you got an apartment from your enterprise? . . . In wholesale trade you steal a little retail? Or vice versa? . . . You put away cigarettes before the price goes up? . . . You auction off the land of your former work cooperative? . . .
> You surely do something! . . . What would you live off, both you, and your little canary, and your piano

tuner, and your maid, and your cosmetician, and your
dog, and all the others that you carry on your back?!
Whatever you do to work, that's your thing. It's important that you live, that you somehow make ends meet! [11]

From the stories of the Belgrade respondents, as well as from
satirical social essays like Bećković's, the struggle to build a
socialist Yugoslavia appears to have evolved for its citizens into
the struggle to make ends meet. The lives of the middle-aged
members of ten Belgrade families suggest some generalizations
about the nature of social change there. Like the working classes
of those countries which industrialized during the nineteenth
century, many Yugoslavs have been thrust into a new life whose
time and space are delineated by factories, cities, money wages,
and, increasingly, consumer credit and long-term installment
buying. At first, during the golden age of reconstruction and
perhaps even through the 1950s, socialism and industrialism
acted as both mutual incentives and mutual palliatives. That is,
leaders and masses alike saw socialism as a part of industrialism
and hence of collective and personal improvement. Similarly,
they were able to view their material sacrifices and hard work
through the prism of socialist ideology, so they were able to feel
that they were making their contribution to the greater good
of their nation and of mankind. Then, as the official ideology
shows, they came to perceive industrialism as the immediate goal
and socialism as the ultimate goal. In other words, they now
believe that once the material base of a highly industrialized
society is set up, Yugoslavs will be able to develop socialist consciousness. The rationale behind this development is pragmatic,
as we have seen in chapter 2. Furthermore, the political leadership has shown a practical recognition that attitudes have
changed. That is, the leaders have recognized that the transition
from peasant society to industrial labor force involves a new kind
of mentality built around the struggle for a dinar.

In opting for this kind of industrialization and in accepting
this change of attitude, the leadership feels that it has bowed to
the historical forces of the epoch. However, as Rade Popović
points out, the degree of social inequality that Yugoslav leaders

11 Matija Bećković, 'O Jugoslovenima' [On Yugoslavs], in *Dr Janez Paćuka o medjuvremenu* [Dr Janez Paćuka on the meantime] (Novi Sad:
Matica Srpska, Biblioteka Danas, 1969), pp. 81–4.

Social mobility

have so far tolerated has led to disillusionment, confusion about means and ends, and the dissociation of everyday life from the struggle for socialism. As Popović says of the social reality which is called *self-management,* 'Who's managing whom?' Perhaps a comparison of social experiences with political attitudes could help us answer this query.

4

POLITICAL GENERATIONS AND
POLITICAL ATTITUDES

> Being young does not mean just starting out, it also means
> continuing; it does not mean being rootless, it means growing
> further . . . The philosophers say that the sense of such
> stability is the continuity of generations . . . By their own
> social nature, by their social being, by their legitimate desires,
> young people — as a whole — can not be anything but front-
> trench fighters: for democratic, self-managing relations, for the
> full equality of nations.
>
> Dragan Marković, *NIN* editorial
> on Tito's birthday, 23 May 1971

The collective experiences that the Belgrade respondents still
find significant — the mass base of support that the Partisans
were able to build during the war, the numerous volunteer brigades of the postwar reconstruction, and the solidarity that the
break with the Cominform reinforced — created a revolutionary
dynamic that self-management was intended both to utilize and
to perpetuate. By institutionalizing the almost spontaneous social activism of the war and the reconstruction, the leadership
probably hoped to make their revolution permanent in at least
three senses. First, in order to legitimate the new political system, they created self-management organs in the image of political organizations which enjoyed widespread support from their
population. These organizational models were the National Liberation committees of local government that the Partisans had
instituted during the war and the workers' councils (like Lenin's
soviets and Gramsci's factory councils) which had attracted support from Russian workers in 1905 and 1917. The second way
in which the leadership probably hoped to make their revolution permanent was through the continual raising of consciousness that participation in these organizations implied. Under the
'ideological guidance' of Communist Party members, continuing
the work of wartime political commissars among the Partisan
troops, citizens would be able to keep their discussion of local
problems in the perspective of larger social issues.

Finally, the activism that Yugoslavs showed during the 1940s indicated that the reserve of peasant energy could be tapped for social purposes, perhaps even for building the polity. Peasants who traditionally did not take part in activities organized by the state (except where they could not escape an obligation, as in paying taxes or serving in the army) had fought in the Partisans, moved to the towns, and joined work brigades. Their enthusiasm, combined with the leadership's need for support, also resulted in a mass influx into the Communist Party. It is estimated, for example, that peasants constituted about ninety percent of the Partisan forces and over half of the 1946 Party membership.[1] If the reminiscences of the Belgrade respondents give some indication of the social atmosphere during the 1940s, then the thousands of former peasants milling around the cities, dancing the *kola* till midnight, working from morning straight through to the following morning, formed an energy source that the political leadership could utilize. Thus legitimate organizations, socialization through enthusiastic raising of consciousness in community-building projects, and the population's availability for mobilization comprised the base on which self-management was to build.

Today, more than twenty years after the founding of the first workers' councils, we may well ask how much of the support, the energy, and the social consciousness remains. As the Belgrade respondents indicate to an outsider, support for the social system which has evolved under the rubric of 'socialism' is still defensively high. However, many groups and individuals who feel that they have been disenfranchised in effect by socialist policy — particularly by distribution norms — admit to more general dissatisfaction. Individually, Yugoslavs seem to have exhausted their energy in the market place rather than in political participation. So pursuit of the dinar (*trka za dinarom*) has replaced pursuit of social equality. Generally, Yugoslavia's urbanizing, industri-

1 By the end of the war the Partisans claimed an army of 800,000; in 1946 Communist Party membership totaled 258,000. Ruth Trouton, *Peasant Renaissance in Yugoslavia: 1900–1950* (London: Routledge and Kegan Paul, 1952), p. 208; and Slavko Filipi, 'Statistički pregled razvoja KPJ-SKJ u periodu 1946–1966 i struktura članstva' [A statistical survey of the development of the KPJ-SKJ in the period 1946–1966 and the membership structure] in Miloš Nikolić, ed., *Savez komunista Jugoslavije u uslovima samoupravljanja* [The League of Communists of Yugoslavia in conditions of self-management] (Belgrade: Kultura, 1967), p. 755.

alizing society has created sharp differences between various occupational and income groups. Just as this has disappointed some Yugoslavs who believed that socialism would eradicate class differences, so it has encouraged others who are enjoying consumer comforts. In this way, social differentiation has contributed to differences in political attitudes and demands.

As we saw with their positive evaluations of 'socialism', many Yugoslavs' response to social change has been influenced by perceptions of their own social mobility. However, the tenuous unity of support for 'socialism' breaks down into divergent orientations toward key political problems, such as the state's role in regulating the economy and the polity. In many cases political orientations seem to be related to a sense of relative social deprivation or satisfaction. Like citizens in other societies, for example, Yugoslavs who have 'made it' up the social ladder tend to be more supportive of the existing situation and to express belief in the official ideology as it now stands. This is especially true of the post-Reform ideology (1965–72) which seemed to sanction almost unlimited economic gains by both individuals and enterprises. But persons or groups who feel that their interests have not been satisfied through the political processes of self-management, or that their personal goal of upward social mobility has been frustrated by the rise of other social groups, generally express some dissent from the official line. Reacting against the system's neglect, they translate their grievances into a critique resembling a political platform. Among Yugoslav national-ethnic groups, nonfulfillment of aspirations has resulted in the increasing tendency toward formulating an Opposition platform. Similarly, those few republics which are relatively satisfied with the distributive status quo, or which stand to lose the most from a reorganization of the federal lines of responsibility, are most supportive of the current, modified decentralist official line. It is significant that this tendency toward systematic opposition has developed parallel with the leadership's increasing attempts over the past decade to placate discontent. On both individual and group levels, the leadership's policy has focused on redistribution of material rewards. Their policy has been symbolized by such formulas as *'Raspodela prema rezultatima rada'* (Distribution according to the results of work) and *'Čisti računi'* (Clear accounts). Because the goal of this policy has been a vague conception of equality, an unfortunate consequence of this policy has been that all of the people want more, all of the time, and the scales of influence and wealth have hardly been tipped.

The nonfulfillment of aspirations toward a higher social status also indicates another reason for the emergence of political differences. Those citizens who deplore the 'keeping up with the Jovanovićes' that such aspirations have inspired feel that the revolution has not lived up to their ideals. In their disillusionment, former egalitarians perceive a discrepancy between the promises of the official ideology and their implementation. Similarly, those who joined the revolution to destroy the authoritarianism of Yugoslavia's past decry visible Party discipline and signs of etatism. These idealists usually turn to alternative interpretations of socialist ideology which their leaders call utopian. In other words, the very unrolling of policy which, for various reasons, has satisfied some Yugoslavs and irked others, spawns disagreement which, as a more or less systematic orientation, take the shape of alternative interpretations of socialist ideology. These orientations could easily take the form of rival political platforms within a general socialist framework. So far, at least until the 1971 purges of the Croatian Party leadership and the resultant tremors within the Serbian Party, the national-ethnic groups have provided a base for the republican leaderships to unfurl embryonic platforms of this type. To this end they have made alliances with various economic cadres such as enterprise directors and students of technological development.

But our interest is in mass attitudes rather than elite competition, and among the ordinary citizens another significant factor in the emergence of political differences appears to be generational change. Today's young Yugoslavs, born in the era of industrialization, urbanization, and decentralization, must assimilate a vastly different social world from that in which their Partisan parents grew up. Just as the two generations differ in social experiences, so they also differ in perceptions of society and of their role in society. Respondents Vesna Djordjević and her mother Milica exemplify these contrasts. What Vesna sees as a social norm of opportunism and chicanery, her mother explains away as aberration. But when Milica was Vesna's age, after the war, she did a brief stint on a highway work brigade, married a young army officer, and joined the Party. Twenty-five years later her daughter defines social activity in terms of frequenting discoclubs and dining in good restaurants.

Yet some continuity joins the early idealism and mass activism of Milica's generation with the cynicism and apathy of Vesna's. An important source of the younger generation's political attitudes and behavior has been change within the Partisan generation itself. Responding not only to shifts in policies and institutions but also to their own relative social mobility, the older generation has adopted a different approach to political life from that of their young adulthood. Thus in many cases idealism has evolved into disillusionment with their limited social role as citizens and workers. With the industrialization of the economy and the professionalization of political activism, these Yugoslavs have withdrawn from the larger social world. This evolution in attitudes and behavior has taken place within and despite the framework of self-management.

To work, the self-management system requires that all citizens and workers be at least minimally interested and active in political life. But this ideal does not correspond to the reality in which Yugoslavs live. Behaviorally, Yugoslavs' activism has turned into their withdrawal and their children's privatism; attitudinally, the idealism of the Partisan generation has ceded to disillusionment on their part and to cynicism on the part of their children. The fracturing of the voluntarism and egalitarianism of the early postwar period has also led to the emergence of divergent political orientations which cross generational bounds. Let us consider each of these areas of change in turn.[2]

DECLINE OF REVOLUTIONARY ACTIVISM

During the Belgrade interviews, I tried to provoke the respondents' feelings about the decline of mass activism by telling them a certain hypothetical story. The story concerns an elderly woman's withdrawal from public life into a private realm of consumer comforts and parochial concerns. In the words of the Ljubljana sociologist who made up this story to dramatize his

2 Despite the resurgence of Yugoslav nationality conflicts, this analysis will not deal specifically with ethnic politics. For one thing, they do not directly influence a general understanding of socialism; for another, the Belgrade respondents did not initiate discussion of this problem. Perhaps they were reluctant to talk about it with a foreigner, or they may have tried to avoid a psychologically threatening area. Or they may tend to accept Belgrade's traditional view of the country as a rather centralized entity.

survey findings, the woman's political orientation exemplifies that of

> Slovenian consumer-producer civilization. Although she lives very modestly, she still pretty much saves her small pension; *a new type of socialism interests her, various household appliances, new garden shears, a kitchen fan, wall tapestries,* with special enjoyment she arranges her room. World political events are only a neutral background on which real human interest is drawn . . .
>
> She does not attend Party meetings any more, but she is active in the wider management of the household, that is, of the block — but only insofar as she is directly concerned. *Although twenty years ago she was a fanatic activist, this hasn't left any trace in her;* everything has dropped off like a husk *and her psyche continues where it would have been if there had been no war and no nation-wide ideological 'activism'* (the 'mania' of moral activity). It is clear that she is nationally oriented toward Slovenia, but without any special sharpness toward the 'south'; but the thought of danger from workers from the south [who have migrated to Ljubljana from Bosnia and the other underdeveloped republics in search of jobs] is more compelling. That's why she mostly stays home in the evening . . . She is much more interested in locking the doors than in changes in the federation [i.e. the constitutional amendments], so she also does not know who the commune president is, but she is greatly disturbed about the question of construction near her home. *Voters' meetings she does not attend because she does not believe that this would in any way influence the government's decision-making (as she herself was in it, she knows the relationships in a 'directed' democracy . . .)*[3]

Identifying with this protagonist as with a successful projective technique, the Belgrade respondents recognize in her the rundown of their own initial enthusiasm for volunteer brigades, limitless working hours, and political meetings. In addition, they offer two reasons for her — and their — change of heart. First,

---

3 Taras Kermanuer, 'Kultura, umjetnost i prosječni gradjanin' [Culture, art and the average citizen] (Paper delivered at the Fifth Annual Meeting of the Yugoslav Sociological Association, Dubrovnik, February 11–13, 1971), p. 2. Emphasis added.

the Belgrade respondents explain that they have been prematurely aged by the struggles that they have experienced. On the individual level, they have engaged in the struggle to make a dinar; on the collective level, they have worked in the struggles for Yugoslavia's political and economic independence. The second reason that these ordinary citizens give for their withdrawal from public life is that, as they saw their socialist ideals not being realized, they decided that the emotional and physical strain of political participation was too great a sacrifice. From my observations of Yugoslav political life, I would add only one other consideration. As the need for mass mobilization of unskilled or inexperienced cadres has decreased, all areas of social life have become more rigidly defined. Tasks of nation- and industry-building have become more specialized. Just as economic cadres have become more professionalized, so political leaders on all levels have shaped their activism into an occupation. To some extent the recruitment of political activists has become a function of self-selection. It is perceived as such by ordinary citizens, who respond by leaving the field.[4]

Rade Popović, the highly-skilled machinist and former workers' council member, discusses how continued economic insecurity and the struggle for a dinar have made people withdraw from social life. Explaining why he no longer attends workers' council meetings, Popović says,

> I have the time but you know how it is. That's the way people are. They're not interested much because you know what the mood is — the economic situation is such that people aren't in the mood to live. They're not very interested. Before there was much more interest. There was something in the atmosphere so that people felt that they wanted to participate, they had the will to do it. Today we're already all dead. I don't know how you're going to understand our

4 My journalist-respondent Danilo Arandjelović also suggested a fourth reason for the disappearance of revolutionary activism and enthusiasm after the reconstruction period. According to Arandjelović, the political leadership had no long-range program which would utilize the already-mobilized population. At that time Yugoslavia obviously lacked the resources to sustain a large public-works program, and there was probably not enough industrial work to employ the willing labor force. Furthermore, mass political activism may have been blocked by the postwar political elite in either confusion with or negation of their conception of the Stalinist model.

system, but in my personal opinion you have to think about
the economic situation, where we are.

Although Popović implies that the futility of a perennial struggle to make a living has exhausted people's will for activism, another respondent emphasizes two other aspects of the collective
struggle. Marko Ristić, a 71-year-old, retired foreman, refers to
the strain of fighting in the Partisans. However, Ristić goes on,
Partisan veterans have their compensations, that is, their hefty
pensions, which also influence a withdrawal from political life.
Ristić says,

> Above all, we're talking about masses of people who fought,
> who gave their all in the war, for various reasons. These
> weren't people who sat home during the war; they got up
> and joined the Partisans in the woods. Then there were
> people who went into the woods with guns, who fought the
> uprising, who were killed. Then you have those people
> who from their youth were not used to such ideas [as the
> Partisans']. Now it's my personal opinion that people who
> haven't experienced those things can't have any idea about
> what it's like under those conditions . . .
> [But some people], through the force of circumstances, by
> taking part in the war, got to high positions, they got a nice
> pension, they received a good apartment. Then they
> changed it for another one, and maybe for a third one for
> all I know, and now their family is assured of a good apart-
> ment and a nice pension. What reason do they have to do
> more for society? They don't even think about society any
> more. And they might have hoped from their youth on to
> take part in the struggle of the working class! They shared
> certain ideas. Now they sit at home and listen to the radio.

Another respondent, 25-year-old Miša Cvijić, talks about people's withdrawal from political life as a result of disillusionment
with socialist practice. According to Miša, ex-Partisans like his
parents 'didn't get any satisfaction of what they were fighting
for, so they pulled out. It's a frame of mind, I think.' He continues by citing his own father's experience. The elder Cvijić
had been in the civil service

> and after that he wanted, when he came back to Belgrade,
> to be a deputy in the Federal Assembly. He had, I think,

tremendous support from the people in his area, a village
100 kilometers [south of] Belgrade. And he also had this
terrific desire to be a deputy. He went around, he was active. But meanwhile there was another candidate who was
put up by the Socialist Alliance. He was the official candidate, my father was more the people's candidate, the other
guy was a political personality. The election was in the
spring, and my father thought he couldn't lose. In any case,
he did lose. And now he's out of it. He lives in the country
to get away from it all. He follows it passively, he reads —
about the situation, that is. He entered the civil service in
1948, now he's retired, and now he follows the whole situation but passively and keeps on living there in the country . . .

People feel injustice, disillusionment I think, in their
surroundings — these people were full of ideals: when war
began, those ideals, that confidence, that human confidence, and so on. Meanwhile, later, it's different. There's a
terrific struggle in every individual these days . . . Regardless of whether or not we're socialist, man is a social
being, he's only one unit, and in that sense, to live to be
able to fight for something — he sacrificed everything, but
the results I think were such that — *about that story you
told, it's that what she fought for hasn't been realized.*

The opponent to whom Miša Cvijić's father lost the election —
the 'political personality' — was evidently one of a corps of professional political activists. These leaders seem to occupy a level
above that of merely 'active' citizens or Party members. For example, respondent Milica Djordjević, a member of the League of
Communists since after the war, perceives her husband Josip —
but not herself — as an activist. In Milica's estimation, activists
like her husband have a special knowledge about society, a particular interest in politics, and an aptitude for surviving in political life. She explains,

Josip studied sociology . . . that's exclusively sociological
questions, that's 'Society' like a sociologist knows it, like
someone who works with those problems. *Because no ordinary man can get to know society like 'Society', even though
a man is a member of the Party and everything.*

I don't bother much with politics — very little. I, well,
I'm not thinking about going to meetings but about some
policy — I don't like to mix in. Whoever used to be in politics — his time is past, because *politics is hell. Today it's
one way, tomorrow it's another.* Except only if it's some
concrete question that concerns you personally. *Like Party
members, I think, we have a guaranteed right to raise questions, only that.* [Emphasis added.]

In contrast to our expectations about the self-concept of Party
members, Milica reveals that she regards herself as relatively incompetent in political matters — relative, that is, to a professional activist. She says,

Otherwise, as far as politics goes, I'm not going to get into
that — that doesn't interest me at all. Give my opinion —
me, think? — when They are competent?! So then what can
I do, what can *I* accomplish, as one measly individual? I'm
not a politician, what do I know?
  And me, I'm not a scientist, and I'm not fully involved
in politics. I'm telling you, Josip knows the society. Maybe
he got involved because he studied classical history, how society acted through the ages. As for me, I only studied history when I was in high school. I said good-by to it
then . . . Even so, as I was telling you, you have to know
society as 'Society' — how it developed and how it's moving
and where it's heading. Informed. A person either has to
have studied or read . . .
  You know, to be in politics you need a good brain, you
have to know everything, and I don't know what. Politics
moves this way today, another way tomorrow: it picks your
brains. So that's why people, if it's not their profession,
figure, Why do I have to bother about politics, why should
I care about politics?

Nevertheless, Milica seems to regret having confined her social
activism to the Red Cross, or what she calls 'social questions from
the humanitarian point of view'. Involved in these more traditional women's relevances, Milica sometimes thinks that she
could have chosen the activist's life. Telling me that all Party
members after the war could get a free political education and
attend lectures on Marxism, she says,

If I hadn't had children, maybe I would have gone, as a
Party member. They had schools free of charge, and today
I'd be some kind of political leader, who knows. Aside from
that, I'm plenty sorry that I stayed in the kitchen, but
that's the way it all goes. Because of the children, because
of the house, and all that. And I even had a talent for —
and I loved to — even today — I loved studying, and, what
do I know, I had ambitions. Only I didn't have time for
that.

Another woman who has stayed at home is Milutin Filipović's
wife Zora. Zora is a quiet woman who does not contradict her
husband. She takes in sewing to supplement his salary as an accountant. When I ask about her non-involvement in political
life, she says,

I'm just a little fish (*sitna riba*). I don't mix in . . . [But
an activist] takes part in conferences, holds talks. There are
too many of those — more than necessary. The thing is, not
to talk: you have to work more and talk less. I'm more interested in the house, the family, the children. I don't talk
much. As far as work goes, I'm first in line, but as for conversation I'm in last place . . .

When I was growing up no one was concerned with politics. Everyone was interested in his own problems. My
father didn't bring me up to have an interest in politics.
*The ones who are interested in politics are the ones who
have a desire for power.*
[Her daughter Vera says, 'You can't say that about all
politicians.']
They have some job to do that doesn't satisfy them, they
try to make use of it to gain some position. [Emphasis
added.]

Like Zora Filipović, Rade Popović also sees professional political activists as different from though not better than himself.
Popović thinks that activism has been tarnished by the lack of
democratic practices in political organizations and the full-time
activists' monopoly on political office. Although Popović, a
highly-skilled machinist, was once a member of a workers' council, he has rejected political activism. He says, 'To tell you the
truth, I was a Party member after the war, till 1955. But then I
couldn't allow myself to be [railroaded] that way — as a man,

first off, to do something that went against my grain. So that's why I left the Party. I didn't want to go again even though they called me.' [5]

The generation of young adults seems to have adjusted to the professionalization of political activism as their parents have: by either choosing this vocation or rejecting political life. Like their parents, those who choose the latter course perceive a great difference between themselves and the activists. In these days of specialization, professional political activists can be distinguished as early as their teen years. An acquaintance, a 25-year-old woman administrator, describes the activist's career as he

> starts out by being president of his class political organization in school. Then he goes to college and becomes president of FOSS (*Fakultetska organizacija Saveza studenata*), the student organization. Then he gets a job and he works in the commune, and on he goes. Those people are very ambitious. They're always careful, always watching themselves, saying, 'What will So-and-so say?' They're always going to meetings, to conferences . . . At work, those people keep apart from everyone else; they keep their distance.

As this statement implies, young people still choose political activism as a means of upward social mobility. Miša Cvijić points up the differences between his contemporaries of that type and himself. He says,

> There are differences between, well, my generation that lives in the city and those from the countryside who came to study here and to find themselves a job, and they're struggling. With them it's really completely different. At college they all live off their activities, either with the LC [the League of Communists] or with the Student Association (*Savez studenata*) or the Vacation Club (*Ferijalni savez*) . . . These students who come to the city, now, they feel a little insecure. Surely one factor is the pace of life. In ad-

5 In interviews conducted by the journal *Kulturni radnik*, Zagreb workers say that the Party has become the purview of professional politicians and administrators. They also perceive the self-management organs as dominated by a clique of Party leaders and enterprise directors. Thus, like Popović, they no longer regard either the Party or its members as authoritative. Vjekoslav Mikecin, *Socijalizam i revolucionarni subjekt* [Socialism and the revolutionary subject] (Zagreb: Kulturni radnik, 1970), pp. 91–120, esp. pp. 101ff., and 121–46, esp. pp. 134ff.

dition, maybe they even have an inferiority complex which
develops when they move to the city and increases when
they start to work. They try to resolve this complex
through being active in various activities, and they're also
improving their social position a little . . .

In some cases political activism may be an adjunct to another
sort of professional training, but it still serves as a social ladder.
Eighteen-year-old Vera Filipović says, 'I have a friend, he's my age,
and he's politically active. As much as politics interests him, it
doesn't interest me. He's part of the LC, in the school committee.
He wants to study medicine, he's a big mover. He's really going to
go places.' [6] Similarly, young college professors, particularly in
the social sciences, frequently become active in city-level Party
committees. We must assume that, just as their political credentials help their academic careers, so their growing academic publications contribute to their political careers.

The observations of the Belgrade respondents suggest that political organizations like the League of Communists and self-
management organs such as the workers' council have become restricted, in effect, to professional activists and their dependents.
We have seen how a Party member like Milica, who attends
meetings but never holds office, keeps on thinking that she is
different from, even incompetent vis-à-vis the professionals. We
have also seen how a politically inactive person like Zora believes
that the professional activists are different from though not more
diligent than herself. Meanwhile, a former Party member like
Rade Popović comes to perceive a widening gap of both influence and morality between the professional activists and questioning laymen like himself. Milica, Zora, Popović, and the others indicate that, despite feelings of economic security and general competence as compared to their pre-war situations, many
Yugoslavs suffer from a low sense of political efficacy. Obviously,
this negates the self-management ideal. Widespread feelings of
political uselessness under the domination of professional activists denote elitism, not self-management. Moreover, the barriers

6 A Belgrade sociologist also finds a relation between upward social mobility and political aspirations. In a survey of over 500 young Serbs,
she finds that the lower their social strata, the more parents seem to
motivate children toward political activism. Olivera Burić, 'Family,
Education and Socialization' (Paper delivered at the International
Symposium on the Educational Functions of the Family in the Contemporary World, Warsaw, November 23–7, 1970), pp. 11–13.

of political stratification may be rising even higher, at least in the opinion of one Yugoslav sociologist. According to Josip Županov, the mystique of 'greater social democratization' veils the fact that very few — in fact, a decreasing number of — 'professional political workers' actually control Yugoslav political life.[7]

FROM VOLUNTARISM TO INVESTMENT

Another area of political life affected by the professionalization of some workers and the withdrawal of others is that of voluntary action. In the collective memories shared by middle-aged respondents like engineer Steva Ristić and the Vuković brothers, volunteer work brigades of youths and even of foreign workers accomplished Yugoslavia's postwar regeneration. However, current construction projects rely on professional workers rather than volunteers. Indeed, the manner in which they are conducted, particularly in the soliciting of funds, suggests that the dominant mode of social action has shifted from voluntarism to investment. Two of today's major building projects — the Belgrade–Bar (Serbian) railway and the Zagreb–Split (Croatian) highway — offer Yugoslavs long-term financial investment with a guaranteed return. Although many older people are freely donating money to the Belgrade–Bar project, which for years has been an uncompleted national, i.e. Serbian, dream, most of them are looking forward to the return of their investment with interest. Moreover, the younger generation has generally thought of their participation in Belgrade–Bar as investment rather than donation.

Nevertheless, the older generation still perceives these projects in terms of voluntarism and cooperative nation-building. Milica Djordjević, for example, who once took part in a brigade which built the highway from Belgrade to Novi Sad, talks about the Belgrade–Bar railway as

> a purely humanitarian thing where help is needed. It's a question here of building our country, which will be useful to us, for all I know. You see that people are clearly delighted to give even their extra pay. Why, this soccer match

7 Josip Županov, 'Društvena pokretljivost i razvojne perspektive jugoslovenskog društva' [Social mobility and the developmental prospects of Yugoslav society], *Gledišta* 12, no. 11–12 (November–December 1971), p. 1497. This theme — the stratification of political activists — will be continued in the next chapter.

— Red Flag [the Belgrade team] is going to give 25,000,000
dinars [old dinars, i.e. 250,000 new dinars or about $16,666]
to the Railroad Association, they said so today on the radio, right? Enterprises, even schools, even the Pioneers —
you see that, how humanitarian it is? One kid will bring
100 dinars [one new dinar] or 500 and this way there'll be
hundreds of thousands of children who'll bring something.
It's nothing, 100 dinars, what do I know, but I'm thinking
about the hundreds of thousands — 100,000,000 [dinars] —
so then you have nothing you have to *persuade* people to
do, people are delighted to do this.

And when they had that collection after the earthquake
[in Skoplje in 1964], people subscribed so much money to
that collection, they wanted to give more and more. It went
from enterprise to enterprise, from school to school, from
house to house, where women work. It was exactly like I'm
telling you, a humanitarian thing that we figure this way:
*You do something for me today, maybe I'll do something
for you tomorrow.* You don't know what life has in store
for you.

Although the middle-aged generation no longer has to form
work brigades, some feeling of voluntarism has apparently survived. When I explain to the Vuković brothers the way that
investment works in America, pointing out the similarity to 'sub-
scribing to the loan for Belgrade–Bar', Milovan and Janko protest at my capitalist's view. Janko points out first that many people, particularly pensioners, are giving 'whole pensions, 1,000
dinars' as a gift. Then he posits an economic difference between
socialist and capitalist investment: the lack of a profit motive in
socialism. Janko says, 'If you give some money to the bank, you
have 7 percent annually in the bank, but the railroad, you lose
7 percent of what you give. You're not gaining but you're losing,
really. The loan won't be returned till '75'. So according to
Janko, Belgrade–Bar represents socialist investment.

Volunteer youth brigades still exist, at least during the summer months, to help areas which have been destroyed by natural
disasters, e.g. flood and earthquake, and to construct community
facilities, such as roads and buildings, in underdeveloped regions.
However, Yugoslav press reports indicate that these summer
youth programs have eroded into small, dispirited projects. In
1971, for example, twenty-five years after their appearance in

socialist Yugoslavia, a work project in Banja Luka lost an estimated 740,000 dinars ($50,000) because only half as many youth
brigades showed up as had been expected. According to the engineers and the youth organization leaders who planned 'Banja
Luka '71', the regional youth leaderships were responsible for
this failure. Many of these committees did not inform the project's organizers in advance that the brigades they promised would
not materialize. The engineer who headed the work project leveled this charge, for instance, at the Rijeka youth organization's
leadership: 'Two days before their arrival they let us know that
the brigade will be there on time. On Sunday, instead of the
brigade, we get a telephone call that they don't have a brigade,
without any kind of an excuse or a serious explanation.' But the
major point of the 'Banja Luka '71' fiasco is that the regional
youth organizations were either unwilling or unable to mobilize
their followers for volunteer work.[8]

Young Yugoslavs with whom I talked — like Vesna Djordević,
Miša Cvijić, and Vera Filipović — had no idea why anyone
would want to join such a work project. Perhaps these young
people are somewhat jaded by their urban life for, according to
a friend who took part in a summer work project in 1970, almost
all the brigadiers come from smaller towns and villages. They
apparently join the work project to get time off from their factory jobs or to travel away from their villages. Moreover, young
Serbs told me that it is most difficult to raise youth brigades from
Slovenia and Croatia, the two most economically developed republics. Thus the young Serbs imply that economic development
affects social consciousness.

Despite this special factor, the young adults' lack of activism
suggests, in the words of 25-year-old respondent Miša Cvijić, that

> this is not a *political* generation. The ones born during the
> war are thirty now — I know, I have a cousin who's ten
> years older than I am, she's thirty-five. She took part in all
> the work projects, she was a Communist — sure, she's no
> more a communist than me — but she always showed up
> for some activity, taking part in work projects . . . I think
> that my cousin's generation lived in close contact with the
> generation that fought the war. From the very beginning
> they've been closer to the pressures, the slogans. They

8 Živorad Djordjević, 'Optuženi ćute' [The accused are silent], *NIN*, 29
August 1971, p. 19.

weren't yet grown up during the war but they remember it; in some ways you could say that they did experience it. Except that the state itself acted demagogically . . .

I'm now twenty-five years old. In my generation are people between twenty and thirty. The ones who are thirty were born in 1941. That means that they became conscious when they were eight or ten. The ones who are thirty-five bear something of the afterwar period, of those very different political trends. I can't remember any of those political events . . . I have more in common with the next generation than with the older generation.

The stratum of 30-year-olds to which Miša's cousin 'the Communist' belongs represents a half-step between the ex-Partisan generation and their children. As such, their reaction to the work brigades may help explain the transition from voluntarism to investment. Just about the time that Miša's cousin 'took part in all the work projects', Zagreb sociologist Rudi Supek examined the attitudes of youths working in brigades on the construction of the Zagreb–Ljubljana highway in 1958. Supek's findings are interesting because they document a general decline in 'public spirit' during the course of the summer project itself. This shift in attitude may parallel the overall rejection of social activism. According to Supek, the youths became disillusioned with the summer project because it did not meet their expectations. They also complained about communal life, expressing a preference for working alone. Finally, the initial group solidarity broke down as friendship cliques were formed within each brigade. As the brigadiers themselves perceived the situation, relationships within the project worsened over the summer. Despite these findings, Supek's follow-up survey six months later convinced him that few negative after-effects of the project had remained. Supek ended his study optimistically, but the failure of recent work projects like 'Banja Luka '71' indicates that many young Yugoslavs have grown up without a motivation for social voluntarism.[9]

9 Rudi Supek, 'Motivation and Evolution of Attitudes in Youth Movement Work-Groups', in *Sociologija: Selected Articles 1959–1969* (Belgrade: Yugoslav Sociological Association, 1970; translated and reprinted from *Sociologija* 2, no. 1 [1959]): 211–37.

More recent data from a comprehensive survey of college students in Zagreb show that motivation toward private objectives is increasing while motivation toward societal goals and values is decreasing. Martić, *Studenti*, pp. 102ff.

From disillusionment to cynicism

The experience of other young respondents in my sample justifies Miša's assertion that theirs 'is not a *political* generation'. Miša himself has never belonged to any political group and does not even remember having been in the Pioneers, the Boy Scout-like association in which every small child is enrolled. Vera Filipović, the 18-year-old high-school student, is also politically inactive. Like nearly all high-school students, she belongs to the *Savez omladine* or Youth League, but she says that 'it doesn't do anything. Oh yes, we have outings and dances, but I don't see the other members often.' Just as the Zagreb students' interests and aspirations center on personal advancement, so do Vera's. She expects the most fundamental change in her life to be a college education; 'after that', she says, 'it all depends'. When I ask her with which people or social groups she feels a common interest, she says that she doesn't feel that way about anyone. Finally, her assessment of her age-group agrees with Miša's. According to Vera, 'My generation isn't like youth after the war. We discuss problems very little. Our youth is alienated, but *that* generation helped to develop the country.'

FROM DISILLUSIONMENT TO CYNICISM

Parallel with the behavioral change from voluntarism to investment, or from activism to withdrawal, the Partisan generation's attitude toward their postwar political idealism has shifted from staunch belief to cautious retrenchment. Many of them admit to disillusionment, while others reject their earlier ideals as naively optimistic. The disillusionment of the Partisan generation has implicitly or explicitly communicated itself to their children, whose attitude toward politics can best be described as cynicism. These attitudes emerge in a recent Yugoslav poll of fifty members of both the middle-aged generation who were eighteen to twenty-five years old when the war ended and young adults who are now of that age.[10] Of its older subjects the survey asked: What were your social and personal ideals when you finished the war as a victor, and which of them have been realized? To the younger respondents it posed the question: Do you have ideals, and what do you think of the ideals of your parents' generation?

10 This section is based on Zvonko Simić et al., 'Velikova NIN-ova anketa o dve generacije: (Ne)ostvareni ideali' [*NIN's* big survey on two generations: (Un)fulfilled ideals], *NIN*, 28 November 1971, pp. 41–6. Emphasis added in passages quoted.

Political generations and political attitudes

The older respondents indicate that when they were young adults, i.e. at the war's end, they felt that there was a unity of personal and social ideals. Eventually a schism developed between these two kinds of ideals, mostly because of the discrepancy between the ideals and the reality. The middle-aged respondents mention several social phenomena which awakened them to the incongruity between ideals and reality: the Cominform dispute, the *diplomatski magazini* or special stores where politically-favored individuals could buy scarce foods and imported goods in the early postwar period, and the development of a consumption society. The single revolutionary goal that they feel has been accomplished is political, that of setting up the institutions of a socialist democracy. But the personal goals that they sought in the revolution — whether individualistic, like upward social mobility through new careers, or collectivistic, like the creation of a new social order — remain largely unfulfilled.

A well-known respondent in the *NIN* survey, Belgrade philosophy professor Mihailo Marković, expresses what seems to be today's 'official line' on Partisan and SKOJ (*Savez komunista omladine Jugoslavije*, the Communist youth organization) idealism. Marković underlines the naïveté of the earlier ideology, criticizes its faith in social planning as incipient Stalinism, and praises the gains that the Yugoslav leadership has recorded. Despite the leadership's later criticism of the political implications of Marković's scholarly work, here he takes a pragmatic view similar to that of the official ideology. Marković says,

> When we're talking about social ideals, we should run away from making a lament for 'paradise lost' and a projection of our present emotions into the past. *Surely there was in the SKOJ generation to which I belonged much naïveté and lack of criticism. We believed that over several five-year plans we would create abundance for everyone, that all social differences would disappear,* that we would come to a penetration and a merging of national cultures, that the countryside, thanks to collectivization, would experience a complete economic and cultural transformation. *We weren't the slightest bit conscious of the danger inherent in the kind of monolithic and hierarchical organization that the State and Party were at that time, or of the danger which arises as a result of the complete identification of the revolution with its leaders.*

From disillusionment to cynicism

With us, such as we were, some too naive and some not
naive enough, we had to come to a certain gap between
ideals and reality.

Another middle-aged respondent indicates that as she has aged,
so her ideals have changed: some of the original goals have been
realized while others have not. She is somewhat critical of the
society which has evolved. As Vida Kastrin, a member of the
Republican Chamber of the Slovenian Assembly and former in-
structor in the Central Committee of SKOJ in Slovenia, says,

In this quarter century my ideals from the revolution have
been fulfilled. We don't have a bourgeoisie any more, at
least not in its classical sense. We liberated the fatherland.
The working man became the main factor of movements
and events. Meanwhile, just as the revolution hasn't ended,
so all my ideals haven't been realized. Namely, the revolution was 'altered' by its permanence, so my ideals changed
with it. Today, meanwhile, calm folks can say — that upon
this whole complex of ideals a shadow has fallen, created
by contemporary human relationships. *These relationships
are not comradely, at least not in the sense that I dreamed
about them before and after the revolution. And I don't
like that.*

Zagreb sociologist Josip Županov, who also appears in the *NIN*
survey, reflects further personal disillusionment with the kind of
uncomradely relationships that Vida Kastrin mentions. He says,

For me, the revolution was a chance to find an authentic
human community and to integrate myself into it. But,
when this almost mystical community disappeared into the
prosaic hierarchy of ranks, positions, power, and privileges,
it's as if I have gone back to the starting-point.

Yet several of the original socialist goals have not been negated
by the leadership, and Županov, Kastrin, and Marković can remain comradely joined in aspirations for their fulfillment. In
Marković's words,

Those ideals [which still remain] are: social equality, full
national equality, the right to work (in one's own country)
and an honest reward for everyone's work — from the
worker to the highest leaders, full democracy on all levels,

135

bringing every citizen of this country into the world of genuine culture.

The younger generation finds no fault with these ideals of their parents, but they blame society for moving in the opposite direction.[11] Their cynicism extends to the point that a sizable minority of the younger respondents in the *NIN* survey express the opinion that their generation has no ideals at all. Perhaps the intergenerational disillusionment with social reality has made them pessimistic, or the limited job market within Yugoslavia (as Marković implies) may have made them distrust official promises. At any rate, these young adults admit that they have no desire to sacrifice themselves for any ideals. A 23-year-old lawyer gives vent to all these feelings. He says,

> As far as their ideals are concerned, I'm thinking here about my father's generation, *maybe they were as romantic and honorable as they tell us. What's happened in the meantime I don't know, but I wouldn't say that these ideals are still held.* For the most part I don't have them: I'm unemployed, I have no money, I don't even have a father any more.

In other words, this young lawyer feels so deprived — fatherless, jobless — that he cannot afford to have ideals. Is such cynicism widespread? A 20-year-old actress in the survey says, 'At least [our parents] had ideals. It seems to me that today no one has them any more.'

A young blue-collar respondent voices a less cynical lack of idealism. This metalworker focuses his criticism on political activists within his enterprise and the general lack of employment. He says,

> The ideals of [my parents'] time are near to me, but I am today's child. My ideal is faith in my generation. Everyone points a finger at the one-tenth who steal people's cars, but no one shows the tens of thousands of young people who work in factories like me, and study in their spare time like me. I don't really have that much time to think about ideals, but, during breaks at the factory, I talk with the other guys. *We all think that there are few of us in the management*

11 See similar comments by young Croatian workers, especially the reiteration of their parents' disillusionment with social and economic inequality, in Mikecin, *Socijalizam,* pp. 107ff.

organs. On the management-committee-union circuit the
same people are constantly moving back and forth. I had
good luck: I've got a job. But my ideal is that every young
man who finishes school gets employment.

So on the whole the *NIN* respondents, like my sample, indicate
that the disillusionment of many of the Partisan generation has
spawned a cynicism among their children.

A major discontinuity between the two generations shows up
when younger Yugoslavs appear unwilling to sacrifice themselves
for ideals. Perhaps this is related to the difference between the
two generations' life-experiences. First, the Partisan generation
fought a simultaneously international and internecine, guerrilla
war. After the war, there were tremendous chances for employment and career advancement in building a new society. Compared to prewar and wartime deprivation, the standard of living
soared. By now, however, economic growth has leveled off so that
the job prospects of younger workers are not favorable. Many
workers of all occupational categories — from professionals to
unskilled laborers — have temporarily migrated to Western Europe and the U.S. to find higher wages and better jobs. A sense
of futility about 'making it' in Yugoslavia seems to pervade the
attitudes of many young people. For example, in a survey of
volunteer youth brigades on the work project 'Sava' in 1971, 60
percent of the respondents said that it was very hard for talented
young people to get ahead in Yugoslavia today. According to sociologist Josip Županov,

> The opinion that our society is closed to young people is
> present more and more with an increasing number of
> youths regardless of their future occupation and school-
> ing . . . Thus a young man just cannot be sure of a single
> one of the existing recognized and known channels of mo-
> bility; cannot have confidence in a formal diploma, even
> less in knowledge and ability; cannot have confidence in
> political activism; cannot have confidence in personal con-
> nections. He finds himself in a situation of maximum un-
> predictability, of total uncertainty.[12]

The resulting sense of futility probably turns the younger generation off from Partisan-like struggle and volunteer work bri-

12 Županov, 'Društvena pokretljivost', pp. 1493, 1502.

gades. However, the generational discontinuity that this implies may not be so great as it seems. Although the Partisan generation engaged in social struggle as young adults, their political activism has declined from that point. Just as the hypothetical woman from Ljubljana withdrew from political activity, so my older respondents have also deflected their social motivation to personal goal-seeking. Furthermore, parental indulgence of children takes on the added connotation of insuring that children should not have to undergo the same deprivations and struggles that they, the Partisan generation, did. From this perspective we should speak of the decline of political activism both between and within generations.

The three members of the Djordjević family provide a neat recapitulation of attitudes toward political activism. Josip, a retired army officer who holds the presidency of two local political organs and belongs to the executive board of two others, says that every Yugoslav citizen is interested in politics. Because they are interested, they come to meetings. His wife Milica, a Party member since after the war, says that 'no ordinary man can get to know society like "Society" . . . Whoever used to be in politics — his time is past, because politics is hell.' Finally, their daughter Vesna, born at the same time as workers' self-management, says, 'As far as politics goes, I'm not interested. It's boring. I don't keep track of that.'

SUBSTANTIVE POLITICAL DIFFERENCES

When they make up their minds on questions of substantive policy — weighing official ideology against personal ideals — the Belgrade respondents reveal a combination of attitudes. Elements of egalitarianism mix with feelings of relative social and economic deprivation. Just as there is concern about political repression and wage and price controls so, too, there is worry about what will happen if such measures disappear. In short, Yugoslavs show a diversity of opinions about authority and equality similar to that which we find in other industrialized societies. As individuals and as groups they show at least as much complexity in their political ideology as their foreign contemporaries. Indeed, delving into the ideology of ordinary men and women — in any society — suggests the possibility that most people today do not derive consistent political orientations which can be cate-

Substantive political differences

gorized simply, particularly by labels such as 'liberal' and 'conservative'. These two terms, and the orientations that they represent, explain very little about Yugoslav socialism, on the one hand, and political orientations in general, on the other. That foreign scholars have used these terms to categorize Yugoslav political orientations, mostly of elite groups, indicates a lack of understanding of certain complex relationships.[13]

In most societies, 'conservative' orientations look toward the past with the intention of keeping or reasserting elements of an earlier political model. In contrast to conservatism, 'liberal' orientations face the present by straddling both past and future; we might say that 'liberals' seek to correct the evils of the past by making moderate structural innovations. As opposed to both conservatism and liberalism, 'utopianism' seeks to command the future. Utopians make a clean break with both past and present in order to pursue the fulfillment of social goals which have not previously been satisfied, or perhaps not even set. In a sense, conservatives derive social satisfaction from the arrangements of the past, liberals derive social satisfaction from their relationship with the present, and utopians defer their social satisfaction until the future.[14]

As a socialist state, Yugoslavia's earliest meaningful political model was derived from Stalinism and its stringent political and economic controls (1945–7). In this context, the usual goal of

13 In her discussion of the debate over the Yugoslav economic system, Milenkovitch proposes a three-fold division of socialist humanists, conservative socialists, and the ruling Establishment. Milenkovitch, *Plan and Market*, pp. 281–9. In his discussion of the organizational models espoused by certain elite groups, Dunn makes a five-fold division of official ideologists, socialist humanists, conservative socialists, liberal socialists, and non-socialists. William N. Dunn, 'Ideology and Organization in Socialist Yugoslavia: Modernization and the Obsolescence of Praxis', *Newsletter on Comparative Studies of Communism* 5, no. 4 (1972): 30–44.

  However, such distinctions appear superficial beside the general relationship, as indicated in the following discussion, between political orientation and perception of time. Cf. Arno J. Mayer, *Dynamics of Counterrevolution in Europe, 1870–1956: An Analytic Framework* (New York: Harper and Row, 1971), pp. 48–55, and Michel Oksenberg's division of Chinese political orientations on the basis of their definitions of, 'the essence of China' and their approaches to modernization, 'Chinese Cultural Revolution: The New Phase' (Columbia University Seminar on Communism, 17 April 1974).

14 This terminology and these relationships with time are somewhat different from Mannheim's. Cf. Karl Mannheim, *Ideology and Utopia* (New York: Harcourt, Brace and World, 1966 [1936]), ch. 4.

conservatives — that is, keeping or going back to an earlier political model — raises the spectre, to Yugoslavs, of Stalinism and the assorted evils, e.g. the bureaucratism, the *'čvrsta ruka'* or strong hand, and the secret police, which threaten the self-management regime. So a 'conservative' orientation in Yugoslavia evokes the trauma of the past for masses as well as leaders.

Since the leaders' break with Stalinism, they have asserted their political orientation in terms of rejection of the past and all its evils. They have particularly castigated stringent forms of political and economic control. In contrast, then, to Stalinism, Titoism — or the official Yugoslav ideology — represents an orientation toward the present, rather than the past, and a corresponding moderation of control over politics and economics. Thus Titoism has stood for self-management over etatism, first in the economy and then in the polity. At each point in the recent past when the Yugoslav leaders have had to decide whether to strengthen or to loosen state controls — whether in the field of nationality policy or fiscal policy, in the forms of federation or taxation — they have generally opted for moderation. Moderation has enabled the official ideology to appeal consistently for support to the broadest possible constituency, overcoming extreme opposition from rival elite factions and disgruntled citizens. Foreign observers have termed this mode of behavior 'liberalization'; however, the Yugoslavs view this label as inconsistent with socialism, so they would not apply it to themselves. The Yugoslavs are completely correct in this regard, for 'liberalization' implies a continual weakening of the state's control over social life — to the point at which controls are no longer 'moderate' but 'weak', a state of affairs which can only be associated with utopianism. This logical progression suggests the possibility that, at some point, a present-oriented political ideology of moderate change, such as Titoism, becomes institutionalized: its *raison d'être* — a break with the past — becomes the orientation of the status quo. As such, it opposes both the 'conservative' forces which look toward the distant past and the 'utopians' who would move toward the future. In this context, the present-orientation seeks to defend and to maintain the very recent past over which it has held sway; in this sense, it becomes a sort of conservatism.

The Yugoslav leadership has not been oblivious to the dialectical relationship between past and present, according to which, at some point, an orientation toward moderate change takes on conservative functions. Indeed, a recent clarification of Titoism was sounded, interestingly enough, by Marko Nikezić before his resignation during the nationality disputes of 1972 from the presidency of the Serbian Party. At a conference on ideology in December 1971, Nikezić called for 'the liberation of our own communist conservatism'.[15] To the unaccustomed ear, this is a curious juxtaposition of terms. However, Nikezić's phrase only summarizes the 'platform' with which Titoism combats its diverse opponents. In contrast to conservatives looking toward the past, Titoism offers development, primarily economic; in opposition to utopians who look toward the future, Titoism offers achievement, stability, moderation. In short, as Nikezić indicates, Titoism now calls for retaining the 'best' of the very recent past. This orientation, which identifies itself as 'communist conservatism', could be expected to appeal to people who are generally satisfied with social arrangements and with their position within such arrangements.

Support for opposition demands is less easy to classify, except insofar as opposition to an official ideology derives from dissatisfaction, particularly from relative social deprivation. But social discontent may take the form of either conservatism, i.e. escape toward the past, or utopianism, i.e. escape toward the future. Even young people raised under socialism may be so bewildered by perennial social problems that they develop an orientation toward the past. According to Milorad Kozlovački, president of the Youth Committee in Zemun, a suburb of Belgrade, many of his peers would opt for the strict controls of the Stalinist past. Kozlovački told the 1971 Serbian Party conference on ideology,

> Even among the younger generation . . . there is the idea
> of a conflict-free society . . . there is the static conception
> of the national question . . . The justified demand of young
> people that some questions be quickly stricken from the
> agenda . . . is sometimes transformed into the demand that
> conflictful situations be resolved by fast action . . . Here it
> isn't difficult to recognize the ideology of the *'čvrsta ruka'*
> (firm hand).

15 This section is based on 'Savez komunista: Šta ne valje: norme ili život' [League of Communists: What doesn't matter: norms or life], *NIN*, 5 December 1971, pp. 10–12.

So, despite the traumatic relationship between Yugoslavs and the recent past, it seems as though some Yugoslavs still find their earlier political models compelling. For some reason, these Yugoslavs feel that state controls over social life would lessen the conflicts that they experience today. Perhaps they find a sense of security in the kind of well-known norms that state controls represent, or in the collective memory of the golden age of reconstruction which coincided with the 'Stalinist' period. At any rate, the political models of the early postwar period (1945–7) and immediately after that (1947–52) still exert great influence upon the political orientations of ordinary Yugoslavs and elite groups. Together, these two orientations toward the past comprise a sort of 'socialist backlash' which represents the greatest threat to the official ideology. The earlier, or Stalinist, orientation, which may be called, historically, Titoism I, differs from its successor, Titoism II, in at least one significant respect. Titoism II modified the strict degree of state controls over economic life with which Titoism I had begun. Similarly, Titoism II differed from its successor, Titoism III (1952–72), in that the later orientation modified the state's extensive controls over political life. Thus, as the official ideology evolved through Titoism I, II, and III, it reached a position in which the state exercised moderate controls over both economy and polity.

Although the official ideology and the two orientations of socialist backlash represent, numerically, the strongest ideological strains in Yugoslavia, there are two other orientations which depart somewhat from present and past political models. First, there is an orientation toward greater democracy, or fewer controls over political life, and continued, moderate controls over economic life. This orientation differs from Titoism III, the present official ideology, in the direction of what could be called socialist democracy. The second alternative to Titoism I, II, and III is the orientation that the Yugoslavs call 'utopianism'. According to this orientation, the state would reassert strong control over economic life in order to assure equality to a previously unrealized degree. These economic controls would be combined with a degree of democracy, or renunciation of the state's control over political life, also unrealized in the past. Thus the combination of strong state controls over the economy and weak state controls over the polity would not recreate any models of the Yugoslav past, but a new social situation. These five orientations,

Substantive political differences

found among Yugoslav elites and masses and represented in table 4 below, might suggest further analysis of the formation of political orientations under socialism, particularly along the lines of the complex relationship between past, present, and future; moderate change and institutionalization; and relative social deprivation.

Table 4 *Yugoslav political orientations*

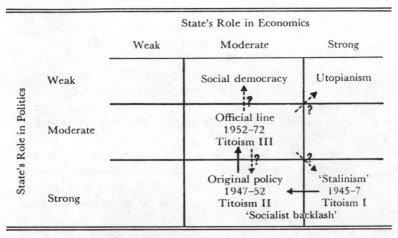

Insofar as individuals derive fairly structured, internally consistent, political ideologies, ordinary Yugoslavs exemplify all of these orientations (with the exception of 'Stalinism'). Among the Belgrade respondents, journalist Danilo Arandjelović and retired army officer Josip Djordjević verbalize an intelligent defense of the official line as it has evolved to this point. They are well informed about problems and options, perhaps because of their high degree of activism relative to the other respondents. Djordjević refuses to criticize any aspect of government policy to an outsider (and probably also within his family). Maybe because Arandjelović is more sophisticated than Djordjević and more used to speaking with foreigners, he is critical of the political leadership, for it has not yet instituted full political democracy. Indeed, the subjects and the institutions that Arandjelović has tackled during his journalistic career indicate that he has constantly battled injustice. At one point in an interview, when he is defending the 1971 Constitutional amendments, Arandjelović seems to summarize his — and the leadership's — political concerns. In this view, self-management and democracy are increasing, but certain difficulties remain to be overcome. As Arandje-lović puts it,

> The distance [from the workers' council to the federal government] is significantly shortened by the transfer of certain things to the republics and the transfer from the republics to the regions and the communes, so that *the material base comes closer and closer to the direct producer:* the direct producer, who will go on to finance many things that until now he didn't pay for. But at least he's going to ask himself — it's not going to be done outside his influence and outside his knowledge. If five or ten enterprises come to an agreement that this and that have to be done, then he's going to negotiate on how it's going to be financed, and how much who is going to give, for this object to be worked out. This is a little simplified but it's pretty much what is important for democratization.
>
> The most independent accent on the self-managing orientation is the strengthening, that is, the further degree of democratization in this society, and the transfer of these functions to lower organs may also be considered as a kind of democratization in its own way . . .
>
> *No one today would be able or would dare to curtail somebody else's rights to express his opinion.* Let him decide, let him weigh things. It's something else again that *there exists here, as everywhere, so-called manipulation,* that is, an orientation of both the masses and certain organs, but this is an orientation binding people together — maybe you have friends in the workers' council who are going to fight for some conception that you as a director or some official want to get enacted — you'll have this all over and always. But on the other hand, *the consciousness of self-management and of the real right of the self-manager, that is, the producer, is growing more and more . . .* [Emphasis added.]

In other words, the leadership has done and is continuing to do everything that is *possible,* given the present time and circumstances of economic development, to realize socialist democracy. Arandjelović cannot help but be optimistic about the current brand of socialism and self-management.

In contrast to Arandjelović and Djordjević, respondents such

as the Montenegrin brothers Janko and Milovan Vuković and
retired foreman Marko Ristić come closest to the orientation of
the second Yugoslav socialist period, 'Titoism II'. The Vuković
brothers and Ristić have been communists or close to communism since before the war.[16] When Janko Vuković talks about
socialism, he is likely to begin by reminiscing about the former
collective poverty. He says, 'We never had anything. Socialism
is very good here.' He sees that socialism has made the majority
of people secure and prosperous: 'Socialism never drove nobody
to the poor-house', he says. As far as market socialism goes, he is
all for it, because he believes it will help his country's economic
development and so make it strong. Thus his reasoning about
economic policy has a tinge of national pride.

But Janko does not believe that the society can withstand the
onslaught of disrespect and the lack of control that he connects
with democratization. No, for Janko the socialist order must be
protected like the cottage to which the peasant returns after a
day in the fields. Why else did he struggle? Janko defines the
limits of democracy in this way:

> [In America] you can't do this or that on the street, but
> here you can do anything — on the *pijaca* (market place),
> in the *kafana* (cafe) — curse your mother, or Tito and com-
> pany — no one can, only — Lissen, you have to let him,
> you have to forgive him once, twice — Wait a minute,
> lookit one thing: *There doesn't have to be such wide de-*
> *mocracy that you do whatever you want. That isn't neces-*
> *sary. Not even in your own house can you do whatever you*
> *want.* There's a certain order. If you think, it's good in
> your house, you must keep some order. But as soon as you
> let somebody get away with something today, you let him
> get away tomorrow, you let him get away the day after to-
> morrow without any punishment — They had a right —

16 Throughout the last few centuries Montenegro has been allied with
Russia, and so Montenegrins have felt strong sympathies, first national
and then political, with Russians. As Janko says, 'With a cry for help,
[aid] used to come from Russia. If Russia helps us then we're great,
you know. So we got help from this czarist Russia . . . When this 1917
Revolution came we worked on it, our people worked on it, I'm thinking about the communists and so on, so that almost every peasant was
caught up in it, that socialism exists, that this Russia is already a
fabulous country, that it's our friend . . .' Marko Ristić came to communism another way, by participating in union activities and strikes
during the 1920s.

They would have sent him away from society, at one time,
away from society to improve his mind.
  Democracy, democracy: but you shouldn't abuse it either.
Because if you abuse democracy, it goes to hurt the whole
community, the whole community. [Emphasis added.]

Like Janko, Marko Ristić looks around him, particularly at
young people, and comes to the conclusion,

Democracy is a beautiful thing, but it isn't for everyone.
Some individuals abuse it. What good do the police do?
We're still in a stage where we need 'em. D'you know what
kind of an Opposition there is? I'm not saying it's massive,
but it's expanding, and we need someone to put us on the
right path more often. Little by little we've been spoiled
rotten, like my grandson. There are models for their behavior. I know that we've had difficulties, political problems, for the past twenty-five years, and the people up at
the top, oh lord! They divide everything up among themselves and they don't do any work, but they tell everyone
else they have to work. The government organs, the Party
organs, they should find that out. Stricter — clean it up —
let them work without pay!

The attitude that 'you shouldn't abuse democracy' or 'democracy . . . isn't for everyone' is so widespread that it has inspired
parody. Matija Bećković ironically catches this orientation toward political rights, a belief that

Democracy is not for everyone.
  They consider that democracy should be alloted for holi-
days, jubilees, and special service.
  Democracy has to be saved, so that it isn't used up.
  Democracy is a place in books, programs, shopwindows,
and museums.
  Every use of such democracy is an abuse.[17]

Ironically, the political orientations that I have called 'social
democracy' and 'utopianism' seem to frighten the present leadership because they cling to tenets of classical Marxist ideology
with which the official line has dispensed. Citizens of these po-

17 Bećković, 'O zloupotrebi demokratije' [On the abuse of democracy], in
Dr Janez Paćuka, p. 12.

litical orientations are disillusioned with the degree of social inequality and political control which still exists. 'Social democrats' as well as 'utopians' believe that the state's control over political rights should decrease, but they differ in that 'social democrats' would not go so far as 'utopians' in placing economic life under increased state control. The machinist Rade Popović, former Party and workers'-council member, is disgusted by several social problems: the low wages that workers earn in contrast to directors' and politicians' benefits, the years that he has struggled as part of the labor force while the standard of living still lags behind that of the capitalist countries, and the limited sort of democracy that the leadership has instituted as 'socialist democracy'. These attitudes make Popović, in our terms, a 'social democrat'. He voices his wonder at the society in which he lives:

I don't know whether this is socialism. I don't know where we're at, whether it's semicapitalism where we're at, no one says and no one is going to say it, but we all see it because no one is covering our eyes. What's happening is really incomprehensible, what's happening now in society. *For me it isn't good; for me as an individual it isn't good. For the country it isn't good. Somewhere we went into some 'democracy', and it seems to me that that brought this on, what we have in the country today* . . .
Everyone's saying that it's going to be better, but — that economic rate of growth, that moves everything fast, it makes itself felt fast in the standard of living . . . Our system is the only one that's self-managing. While in the West, there are a hundred [kinds of] systems, and they've all gone much farther than us . . . Take a small Western country like Holland, or Norway up north there. It's a small country, which I believe hasn't had much industry before, but they're far from us. Maybe people work more, maybe there's some tradition of that, and literacy is probably high. There's a lot of progress, that's for sure, but I think — *as much as we've worked from the war to today, both the state and the people in general — there should be much more.* I'm thinking about the standard [of living], because that's where everything's set.
But this hasn't happened. *Maybe the state system [i.e. postwar etatism] was better, a stronger system, a tighter sys-*

> tem, so that we would have gone slow. We went fast, and
> what did we do? Where are we? [Emphasis added.]

Although Popović tentatively argues for the 'stronger system,
a tighter system' that he believes is part of Marxist economics,
he also speaks up for more participatory democracy. He has an
almost visceral reaction against what he describes as undemocratic voting procedures in the Party and in the polity. Popović
explains,

> Now we have one party, one system, and you vote only for
> one person. For a people's delegate, for example, you go to
> the election and you get a piece of paper and you put it in
> the box. You make your mark on the paper, or maybe you
> don't write anything at all. It's a secret ballot, but it doesn't
> matter. Ninety percent vote for the candidate, which means
> that there isn't, at least in my opinion — it bothers me, it
> bothers me as a personality, to vote for this guy and not for
> that guy . . .
> There are some things that just don't suit our mentality,
> especially us Serbs. *If this is democracy, we want to see de-*
> *mocracy. Then we all want to be equal so I can say every-*
> *thing I want to.* Now I don't dare say everything I want to.
> Let's say I want to go to some meeting, to say that some-
> thing's no good. Eh, that I don't dare do. [Emphasis added.]

Unlike the other political orientations, 'utopianism' usually
appears at universities rather than in the population at large.
Perhaps because, as students, they have no stake in the established order, or, as teachers, especially of philosophy or the other
liberal arts, they feel that they occupy precarious positions, 'utopians' criticize the leadership's failure to realize full democracy
and equality. As Dobrica Čošić, the famous novelist, has characterized these 'student revolutionaries and utopians', they 'want
for their country more freedom, social justice and equality, more
socialism than exists today'.[18] We can find the 'utopian' political
orientation in the demands of sporadic student protests (particularly at Belgrade University in 1968 and 1970), in the barbed
humor of the satirical magazine *Jež* (sometimes a thorn in the
leadership's flesh like the French *Le canard enchaîné*), and in the

18 Raymond H. Anderson, 'Yugoslavia Bans Serbian Journal', *New York
Times*, 17 September 1972.

Substantive political differences

New Leftish newspaper *Vidovci*. The Fall 1970 strike at Belgrade University, for example, centered on demands for democracy and egalitarianism. The students were protesting against the trial of one of their number on serious charges for his 'anti-state' activism the previous spring. At that time, the student, Vladimir Mijanović, had been president of the college chapter of the League of Students. As a student leader, he wrote several articles for college publications in which he criticized government policy. Mijanović also participated in a demonstration against the American invasion of Cambodia. These acts the political leadership found objectionable. Aside from the Mijanović case, the students were also protesting the banning of several issues of student publications for articles critical of the official line. Finally, they were striking in sympathy with Serbian miners who were out on strike at the time. Despite its broader social concerns, the 1970 student strike evoked much less interest than the 1968 demonstrations. At that time many workers and other citizens had supported the students on similar issues. The 1970 strike aroused mainly skepticism and suspicion around Belgrade. Although there was no press coverage, people said that the strike was being led — or manipulated — by Right and Left extremists and that the protest against poverty was merely a ploy for social support.

In general, student protests are a more active expression of the kind of social criticism that distinguishes *Praxis*, the Zagreb philosophical journal. The philosophers who write regularly for *Praxis* lambaste those characteristics of Yugoslav society which, they hold, are inconsistent with socialist morality. In the words of sociologist and philosopher Rudi Supek, these include 'an ideological vacuum . . . bourgeois habits, freshly-minted socialist merchants and speculators, embourgeoised socialist managers, a commercialized lifestyle'. For these societal defects Supek blames an underlying mentality of primitive Balkan competitiveness as well as an intelligentsia which has sold out to the standard of living.[19]

The political orientations that I have described in terms of the Belgrade sample are similar to the findings of Yugoslav survey researchers, who usually propose dichotomous schemas. For

19 Supek, 'Robno-novčani odnosi i socijalistička ideologija' [Goods-money relations and socialist ideology], *Praxis* 5, no. 1–2 (January–April, 1968) pp. 177–8.

example, a Ljubljana psychologist has described the dominant attitudes among workers in two Slovenian enterprises as 'etatism' and 'pragmatism'. Like Rade Popović's kind of 'social democrat', 'etatist' workers (40 percent of the respondents in one enterprise and 28 percent in the other) favor strong state action in the economy. Politically, they are skeptical about self-management for several reasons. First, they think it is an unrealizable ideal. Second, they do not believe, as the official ideology implicitly claims, that self-management is good for business. Finally, they say that self-management is subverted by Party and union officials who use its organs to further their own ends. The 'pragmatists' in the Slovenian sample are, in our terms, official liners. They say that self-management contributes to business success and that they want to take part in self-management activities. Thus they not only regard self-management instrumentally, i.e. as a means to the end of economic growth, but they also seem to connect the success of the official line with their own upward mobility.[20]

This point raises a final question in connection with political orientation and social background. Looking at the Belgrade respondents as well as Yugoslav survey research, it is possible to hypothesize a relationship between relative social deprivation and political orientation. If we may use this perhaps overextended concept, then it seems that those citizens who are most satisfied with the social rewards and material benefits that they have received for their struggles, relative to those of their fellow Yugoslavs, are most supportive of the current official line.[21] Of course, this line, or 'Titoism III', especially from 1965 on, has encouraged the distribution and the conspicuous consumption of material goods, so the haves' support for government policy may be provisional rather than static. Meanwhile, white-collar workers' wages were frozen in December 1972 as part of President Tito's campaign against gross social inequities, symbolized by the enemy whom he labels as 'socialist millionaires'. If this sort of wage control indicates the direction of 'Titoism IV', then some official liners may develop another political orientation. They would probably join a wing of the 'socialist backlash', i.e. they would revert to 'Titoism II'.

20 Arzenšek, 'Samoupravljanje', pp. 29–31.
21 Surveys of Yugoslav and Croatian college students in 1960 and 1964 show that individual identification with general social goals is positively related to self-confidence and self-satisfaction. See Janićijević et al., *Jugoslovenski studenti*, pp. 38ff and Martić, *Studenti*, pp. 111ff.

Substantive political differences

The division between those who now hold to a variation of 'Titoism II' and those who are 'social democrats' — between, say, the Vuković brothers and Rade Popović — is more difficult to conceptualize in terms of social background. It is possible that the Vuković brothers are more satisfied with what they have achieved in life both materially and experientially, as Partisan veterans and as Party members. Their twenty years of employment in the secret police, albeit in non-policy circles, must have also reinforced their sense of belonging to a favored group. Perhaps their earlier and deeper commitment to the Yugoslav Communist Party engendered loyalty to the first socialist model instituted on their country's soil rather than, as with Popović, loyalty to an as yet unrealized model of socialism.

In this chapter we have touched upon several burning issues and some factors of differentiation in Yugoslav political attitudes. First, we have examined intra- and inter-generational continuity and change. Yugoslavs indicate that social orientations have turned inward over the past twenty-five years despite the ideology — and ideology-making — of self-management. Personal life is now more relevant to them than social contributions. We can see this in the decline of revolutionary and postrevolutionary activism to the point where it becomes harder to mobilize Yugoslavs for political action. Furthermore, many of them convey the impression that political 'inputs' on their part are futile. Sources of this change within the middle-aged, Partisan generation have been general fatigue, the struggle for a dinar, disillusionment with contemporary social practice, and the growing restriction of creative political participation to a professional stratum of activists. But the Partisan generation is still more activist and more idealistic than their children. Reasons for the lack of revolutionary dynamism among the younger generation include conditions of economic prosperity and market choice, the decline in upward social mobility to the highest occupational strata, and, again, the professionalization of political activism. Moreover, in the on-going process of mutual learning between generations, the children who are now young adults have internalized their parents' disillusionment while the Partisan parents have accepted their children's priorities of personal over social concerns. Thus both generations have invested their energies in economic rather than political pursuits. This indicates that intergenerational learning is an important factor in postrevolutionary change.

Across the generations, at least four major political orientations hold sway. Ideologically, these are based on attitudes about the state's role in the economy and the polity. Socially, they may be related to perceptions of social mobility. Opting for the continuation of moderate state controls both economically and politically (Titoism III) are the official liners; choosing to continue this economic policy but to institute stronger political controls are citizens of a sort of socialist backlash who hark back to Titoism II. A third orientation is represented by the social democrats. These citizens would like to see a little more control over economic life, recalling classical Marxism's promise of equality, and a little less control over political rights. A fourth orientation, utopianism, joins demands for far fewer political controls and far greater economic restrictions.

In the last two chapters we have looked at Yugoslav attitudes about politics and society from the perspective of some representative statements. Now let us move directly to the scene of political behavior by watching the interaction of political participants. We shall see whether the perceptions and the attitudes that we have found are justified by practice.

5

THE STRUCTURE OF
POLITICAL PARTICIPATION

The sense of impotence in influencing the essential questions
which come up from time to time, to which the workers themselves admit, creates in general a sense of political impotence
and the futility of self-managing involvement.

NIN, 9 May 1971

The ideology of self-management insists that citizens participate
directly in determining their collective affairs. To provide a
forum for this sort of participation, the Yugoslav political leadership has created a sort of town meeting in each neighborhood
for all citizens of voting age (eighteen years). At the voters' meeting *(zbor birača)*, citizens are supposed to discuss their common
problems, to take action on them whenever possible and, when
direct action is not feasible, to refer their suggestions to higher,
elective bodies, such as the Commune and Municipal assemblies.
The problems to be considered form an agenda, which is drawn
up by commune and city-wide officials; the meeting is chaired
by the president of the 'local community' *(mesna zajednica)*,
elected by the voters.

The *mesna zajednica*'s primary function is to satisfy the needs
of its citizens and to regulate the services offered on the local
level. 'It is correct', a text on communal politics says in this
regard, 'that the *mesna zajednica* orient itself in the first order
to the resolution of those problems which are closest to the
citizens, i.e. [those] which concern the basic questions of life and
work of the working man, his family and household.'[1] Factors

1 Milivoje Kovačević, *Komunalni sistem i komunalna politika* [The
commune system and commune politics], 2nd ed. (Belgrade: Zavod za
izdavanje udžbenika S. R. Srbije, 1968), p. 177. See also Stalna konferencija gradova Jugoslavije, *Mesna zajednica u našem društveno-
političkom sistemu* [The local community in our socio-political sys-
tem] (Belgrade: Stalna konferencija gradova Jugoslavije, 1966); *Razvoj
mesne zajednice* [Development of the local community] (Zagreb-Bel-
grade: Porodica i domaćinstvo, 1968); and Marinković, *Ko odlučuje*,
pp. 219–25.

The structure of political participation

inherent in the *mesna zajednica*'s composition make for both the success and the failure of this task. On the one hand, the smallness of the *mesna zajednica* means that the proximity of its inhabitants assures some common interests. In relative size the *mesna zajednica* resembles an American election district or ward. As its name implies, it is the smallest unit of self-government, an atom within the social molecule of the commune. Its constituents — who generally number between 2,000 and 20,000 — represent only one-tenth to one-fifth of the commune population. Thus the metropolitan area of Belgrade is divided into fifteen communes, each of which contains from seven to eighteen *mesna zajednicas*. Six of these are rural communes, incorporating between thirteen and thirty-four village areas. On the other hand, the *mesna zajednica*'s size and position indicate that it remains subordinate to the larger units, such as the commune and the city, of which it constitutes one small part. It is the commune which provides most of the *mesna zajednica*'s funds and services.

The commune operates largely through an elected legislative organ and an administration appointed by the legislators.[2] The bicameral legislature (the Commune Assembly) has one chamber of delegates elected by voters living and meeting in the commune's *mesna zajednicas;* the other chamber is comprised of delegates elected by meetings of all the workers, as well as self-employed artisans and peasants, employed on the commune's territory. The Commune Assembly in turn selects the officials who run the commune's administrative offices and services. These are concerned mainly with housing construction and inspection; business and industry; health, education, and welfare; culture; recreation; transportation; and maintenance of public facilities such as streets, parks, market places, and cemeteries. In urban areas the commune services are often subsumed by municipal agencies, as in transportation and education. Like enterprises, communes are supposed to support themselves. So they get a share of various taxes: taxes on firms and on salaries of people working in the commune, and additional taxes, called 'contributions' (*doprinosi*), on residents.

The Commune Assembly's president and its advisory councils

2 On the organization, rights, and responsibilities of the commune, see Kovačević, *Komunalni sistem;* 'O ustavnoj koncepciji komune' [On the constitutional conception of the commune], *Socijalizam* 11 (1968): 893–958; Dragoljub Milivojević, *Yugoslav Commune;* and Marinković, *Ko odlučuje,* pp. 21–56.

154

of expert cadres (administrators, economists, and other professionals) evidently wield significant power in political decision-making, for together they formulate the options from which the commune delegates as a whole must choose. They are free to recommend programs and courses of action. Chosen by his or her peers in the assembly, the commune president makes up the assembly's agenda and calls the meetings. His or her position also carries general supervisory functions. The president has great responsibility in determining policy, for he or she must

> follow and continually be in the midst of problem-solving in all fields of social and economic activity in the commune; . . . *evaluate current problems, whose resolution he or she has to propose to the Commune Assembly and its chambers and . . . transfer these problems into a proposal* on the agenda of the sessions of these bodies; . . . *take proposals from the councils* and other communal organs . . . *and bring these proposals to the sessions . . .*[3]

The advisory councils also play a large role in governing the commune. Not only do they formulate laws and decrees for the assembly to pass, but they also supervise the day-to-day situation in their fields of competence. Although the number of these councils varies from commune to commune, they have to take charge of 'all fields of social activity and affairs of all administrative branches'. Thus the Commune Assembly usually creates councils in such areas as housing, the economy, education, culture, and recreation, depending on the variety of resources at the commune's disposal. By their composition, these councils are supposed to maintain a combined 'expert' and 'social' character, for they are chosen from among both expert cadres and representatives of the commune's social-political organizations.[4]

So the *mesna zajednica*'s position in the commune system limits its autonomy in several ways. First, its small size and corresponding share of financial resources such as the commune budget and taxes inhibit it from establishing many services and organs of its own. Second, it has to compete with other *mesna zajednicas*

3 Kovačević, *Komunalni sistem*, pp. 187–8. Emphasis added.
4 Ibid., p. 225. This text (p. 228) issues a double-barreled warning to both politicians from the mass organizations and expert cadres, that neither group should monopolize council appointments.

for commune funds and attention from municipal agencies. Although the *mesna zajednica* sends from one to five delegates, depending on its population, to the Commune Assembly and, in urban areas, to the Municipal Assembly, these delegates can only plead or argue on their constituents' behalf for the assembly's largesse. A third limitation is the same as that to which the Commune and Municipal assemblies are subject: the rule of experts and administrators. Finally, the *mesna zajednica* is limited because its scope of competence is extremely narrow. As the text on communal politics says, 'The *mesna zajednica* should always avoid an orientation on general questions; its tasks have to come out of the citizens' concrete, everyday needs.' So the citizens' initiatives from below are prescribed to fill any gaps which may exist between the functioning of public agencies and 'concrete, everyday needs', rather than to overhaul or to modify the commune system. Thus 'the *mesna zajednica* should not enter into the affairs of services and orientations already in existence, or undertake such business as is more normally organized by the responsible professional services or work organizations'.[5]

Nevertheless, the voters' meetings provide a focused situation in which citizens discuss the issues and problems confronting them in everyday life. This is the political situation where the formal rules of self-management, especially participation, are put into practice: where leaders meet followers, representatives meet constituents, and relatively rich citizens may meet their poorer neighbors. Furthermore, this is where each of these groups presents demands to, debates with, and perhaps even criticizes the others. Considered in this way, that is, as a situation in which actual norms of public life are worked out, the voters' meeting provides a Goffmanesque site for us to observe political participation.

According to what we can see and hear at voters' meetings around Belgrade, in the daily press, and in interviews, political participation under self-management has a definite structure which resembles that of other contemporary democratic polities. From that viewpoint, this analysis may evoke our own experiences with political participation. But here we are concerned with the experiences shared by Yugoslavs like the Belgrade respondents. Thus we should examine in detail the participatory

5 Ibid., p. 177.

structure through which they must enter political life. As part of Yugoslav social reality, this structure affects the perceptions and behavior of all citizens. Furthermore, the way the Yugoslav situation is put together indicates several dangerous practices — as familiar as the fallacies of our democratic politics — that self-management has not avoided. From this point of view, the information that we get from observing political life in Yugoslavia is essential.

A significant aspect of the participatory structure under self-management is that political actors are stratified into several levels. The highest echelon of political actors is that of the office-holders in representative bodies and mass organizations. This group appears to have solidified around 1946 so that circulation between elite positions is limited to the top ranks of Party and mass organization leaders.[6] Cadres with technical educations and skills are drawn into the Party organization and the commune administration, but this merely changes rather than broadens the base of political participation. According to one's position within the structure of participation, possible lines of action are restricted. Thus the scope of 'initiatives from below' is hierarchically determined. Because of the distance between the theory and the practice of political participation, citizens who try to participate creatively are thwarted. They may make 'input', but the 'output' that they get back is strictly standardized. Consequently, they perceive that their efforts are being frustrated. Not only do they become dissatisfied with their lack of influence, but they may also become cynical about politics and refuse to participate at all.

This structure of political participation shapes both the content and the style of argumentation at voters' meetings. By the same token, four motifs which emerge at the voters' meetings help us to define the structure of participation: first, the stratification of activists and masses; second, the attempt and its failure to affix personal responsibility for social problems; third, the absence of feedback or follow-through on previous decisions; and, related to this, the emphasis on form over content of decision-making.

6 See Vojin Milić, 'Osvrt na društvenu pokretljivost u Jugoslaviji' [A review of social mobility in Yugoslavia], *Statistička revija* 10, no. 3–4 (1960): 223.

The structure of political participation

Even though voters' meetings could be expected to bring out citizens who are not mobilized by other means, i.e. the Party, it appears that mere attendance at these meetings separates activists from the majority of the population. Moreover, the pattern of participation in the meeting itself graphically distinguishes between strata of political actors, from those who hold elective political office to ordinary citizens. Looking particularly at both the argumentation used by various participants and the fluctuating attendance over time, we can differentiate four strata of political actors. From most to least active, these include the 'Establishment' activists, the issue activists, the citizen-partisans, and the unmobilized masses.

The first three of these groups comprise the participants in voters' meetings. However, they are greatly outnumbered by the unmobilized masses. For example, while the territorial unit of the *mesna zajednica* or ward includes from 2,000 to 20,000 inhabitants, perhaps a third to a half of whom are above voting age, the corresponding voters' meetings may not bring out more than eighty-five citizens. In my experience, that maximum was reached in a *mesna zajednica* with a high population (20,000). In the *mesna zajednica* where I lived, an area including almost 10,000 persons, 4,000 of whom are of voting age, about forty — usually the same persons — attend each meeting.[7] Regardless of the total number, from five to seven women always attend. During the course of the meeting, several persons usually leave, larger numbers leaving larger meetings.

We may use the term 'Establishment' to denote the most active stratum of political actors — the office-holders — who attend most if not all meetings, hold elective positions which entail their reporting back to these meetings, and use argumentation which is based on acceptance of the status quo. Thus this group is basically the same as those citizens whose political orientations exemplify the official line of Titoism III (as described in chap-

7 As of 31 March 1971. [Belgrade,] Skupština grada Beograda, Gradska popisna komisija, *Informacija o izvršenju popisa stanovništva i stanova* [Information on carrying out the census of population and apartments] (Belgrade, 1971); remarks of the president of the *mesna zajednica* branch of the Socialist Alliance at the voters' meeting of Svetog Save, Commune of Vračar, 9 March 1971.

ter 4). A respondent whose attitudes cast him as an official liner
— Josip Djordjević — also holds such Establishment positions
as the presidencies of a *mesna zajednica* and a tenants' council.
Taking the Establishment view of political participation, Djordjević says that 'voters' meetings provide a chance for everyone
in the neighborhood to get together and decide the important
problems. Sometimes we have 1,000 people at the meetings.' On
the other hand, unmobilized citizens and some others describe
the participants in voters' meetings as 'only pensioners and Party
members'. They emphasize that Party members are supposed to
go to these meetings although the members themselves, like
Djordjević, may prefer to ascribe attendance to interest.

Probably members are encouraged to attend by Party leaders,
in line with the members' formal role-definition as 'actively and
creatively participating in the building and the actualization of
the internal and foreign policy of the League of Communists: in
the work organization and its associations, the *mesna zajednica,*
the commune and the wider social community'.[8] However, the
League of Communists has relaxed its members' obligation to be
active in other organizations, permitting personal and professional responsibilities to take priority over political mobilization. For example, Djordjević's wife Milica, a Party member since
the reconstruction period, says,

> Today you don't have so many of those procedures, those
> obligations that Party members used to take on . . . They
> used to go looking for duties, and then there was meeting
> after meeting, often. And that's hard for a mother, with
> a house, say, and children; it was pretty hard. In those
> days you didn't have those child-care centers, and if you
> had a meeting, well, maybe your husband could take
> care of the kids, but if he dozed off, then who was looking
> after them? And the meetings lasted a long time, maybe
> one hour, maybe two, that's the way it was.
>
> And then those obligations! Maybe somebody wanted
> to set himself up, maybe he would have liked to be a
> Party member, but maybe he couldn't, precisely because
> of these obligations! And then with kids, it's awkward. But
> today for sure it's a mass thing; today it's completely dif-
> ferent already.

8 Savez komunista Srbije, *Statut* [Statute] (Belgrade, 1970), p. 13.

So the majority of voters' meeting participants may be Party members who come out of a sense of obligation, as 'leading members' in the society, but the massive responsibility that this entails — in terms of both time and tasks — has been declining since the early fifties.

Aside from the Establishment activists whose offices or Party obligations compel their attendance, another group of participants comes to the meetings out of specific interest. These are the issue activists, who attend meetings when the agenda includes a topic in which they have a vested interest, say, as homeowners. The meetings of 1,000 persons to which Djordjević refers usually include on the agenda questions on sewer construction, schools, or parking lots. This probably indicates that in a city, new community, or community whose pattern of everyday communication and supply is threatened with serious disruption, voters' meetings have the highest attendance. Even Djordjević agrees with that view. Typical of the issue activist's attitude is Milutin Filipović's assertion that he goes to voters' meetings only when they are discussing 'communal questions — building without a permit, supplies, transportation, street-cleaning'. Filipović, an accountant, built his own house in Belgrade five years ago.[9] The issue activists are too amorphous a group to share a single political orientation. But in their argumentation at voters' meetings, issue activists most often represent the official line, except when they are trying to demand better services from the commune. Then they may criticize a general policy which they see as blocking the necessary funds. We may assume that their confidence in effecting political decision-making on the local level — why else would they come to specific voters' meetings? — is part of a general sense of well-being, linked in turn to an acceptance of the current policy line. So we can see that the 'official line' orientation is shared to some degree by two distinct groups of political actors: the 'Establishment' of office-holders and the issue activists.

9 Radivoje Marinković finds that high attendance at voters' meetings is related to three factors: (1) a low level of urbanization (since, according to Marinković, needs and interests in rural areas are usually fulfilled by personal participation and individual contributions, while in the city they are satisfied 'institutionally'); (2) in towns, when the discussion concerns communal improvements; and (3) when a high degree of education prevails among the voters. Marinković, *Ko odlučuje*, pp. 156–7, 198–9.

Stratification of activists

The third group of political actors is comprised of citizen-partisans. These citizens, many of whom are living on pensions, consistently attend voters' meetings and bring into the discussion their personal problems, which happen also to be societal problems, e.g. the housing shortage, veterans' pensions, incomes, and social services. We could call them citizen-partisans because of the Yugoslav Partisan movement, which was the first means of social mobilization to activate many of them. Also, in a more common sense of 'partisan', they are individuals who speak for the interests of the masses. Their argumentation's emphasis on the state's responsibility for broad social welfare, including greater economic equality, recalls the political orientation of Titoism II. Because their primary experience in socialist participation probably took place in Partisan and post-Partisan milieux, their argumentation shows influence by the social reality of that time.

In contrast to these three groups of political actors, the unmobilized masses constitute the great majority of the population. They consider politics boring or uninteresting or beyond their control, so they do not attend meetings. The unmobilized masses thus include poorly educated as well as well educated citizens, mystics as well as skeptics. Despite their heterogeneity, we can find represented among them, as this description implies, the political orientations that we have called social democracy and utopianism. Without their presence, the voters' meeting essentially presents interaction between the 'official line' orientation (Titoism III) of the Establishment and issue activists and the 'socialist backlash' (Titoism II) of the citizen-partisans. This indicates, on a very basic level, the parameters within which public, political discourse occurs.

The seating pattern at voters' meetings accentuates the separation of the three groups of participants. Thus Establishment activists sit in the front rows, citizen-partisans sit at the rear, and issue activists sit in the middle. They themselves choose these seats. Because they sit at the front, the Establishment activists must turn around if they want to face a speaker from among the issue activists or the citizen-partisans. This necessary act may put them at the physical disadvantage of a crick in the neck, but at the same time they hold a psychological advantage, for they are facing the same way as and in close proximity to the chairman and secretary. They are looking toward the masses, often over a few rows of empty seats which affirm the barrier. Along this line a Zagreb worker describes a typical Party meeting in his enterprise:

> The secretary sits at the table, in the first row is the director, the deputy director etc. The secretary opens the meeting of the basic organization and looks at the director like he sees a holy object in him. And how is this secretary elected? Everything's carried out real fast and they regularly elect the one who suits the higher-ups.[10]

Two other aspects of physical behavior differentiate the groups of participants. First, the front-row participants are usually better groomed and younger than those in the back row. Second, the forte of the front row is reading or citing the printed report, usually filled with numbers. However, the back rows often express themelves by shouting out; mumbling audibly, if not aggressively; and applauding each other in a show of social support.

This physical differentiation of groups of participants portends a difference also in their argumentation. As my definitions imply, the citizen-partisans are the most radical group of participants, for they appear ready to accept vast social changes in the systematic pursuit of socialist justice and equality. While the Establishment activists speak in terms of specific, preformulated proposals, and the issue activists speak for or against these proposals, the citizen-partisans for the most part bring their lives and their living problems into the discussion in a general, emotional way.[11] Despite the claims advanced by the self-management ideology and the communal approach to organization, most of the citizen-partisans' problems are too broad to be resolvable on a local level. They raise problems which are discussed almost daily in the press, problems of which everyone is aware but no one feels competent to handle. Since most citizen-partisans have

10 Mikecin, *Socijalizam*, pp. 101–2.
11 If we consider the voters' meeting as an act of communication, then the Establishment activists perform the role of the communicators. According to S. N. Eisenstadt's research, the communicator acts within several sets of institutional norms while the recipient acts in only one set of norms. S. N. Eisenstadt, 'Communications and Reference Group Behavior', in *Essays on Comparative Institutions* (New York: Wiley, 1965), p. 326. So this might explain the different argumentations of Establishment activists and other participants.

been socialized into this social awareness by communist ideology,
the partisan element of their consciousness is often apparent in
the way they treat their personal problems. Thus, they state that
their problems are those of either all Yugoslavs or the whole
working class and demand sweeping social reforms.

The terms of the citizen-partisans' argumentation are, first, a
global statement, usually about a promise unfulfilled: the promise
of socialism. Then, if they feel compelled to enter into an exchange with another participant who answers their criticism or
comment (usually an Establishment activist), they cite their own
experience. Sometimes they corroborate each other's statements
with personal experiences of their own. Often a citizen-partisan
speaks only once during a meeting, to bring up a problem, so we
must remember that we are looking at argumentation, not at a
two-sided argument.

Here are three examples of the problems that the citizen-partisans raise, projecting them onto an agenda where they do not
exist. These are concerned with the problems of unemployment,
income, the standard of living, and housing.

1. There are young people, people born after the war, in
the home of socialism, with a socialist upbringing. And
we send these people, mostly young people, to work
abroad. I read in the paper that we get more foreign
currency from our workers abroad than from tourism. It
might be unpleasant for me to say this, but I'll speak
freely. It would be better for us not to have this money
but to employ these people here . . . It's the city's responsibility to employ these people from the interior
without this or that, with nothing, and to stop the out-
pouring of the labor force abroad.

2. [The *mesna zajednica*'s representative to the Municipal
Assembly has urged the meeting to make proposals in
support of the federal government's new economic policy
of wage and price stabilization. The first speaker says:]
First there should be a limit on personal income — not
in the second stage of communism but now. We read in
the daily press about people with the same qualifications,
with the same success at work, getting vastly different
wages . . . I'm not for *uravnilovka* ['leveling', i.e. egali-

tarianism associated with Stalinism], never for that but differences within the same enterprise are too great . . .

3. I want to talk about pensions for fighters (*borci*) [referring to Partisan veterans]. We gave blood, we sacrificed for this country, and nobody asks how it is with us . . . It's hard to exist . . . and every day there are fewer and fewer of us.

(From voters' meeting in Braća Jerković, Commune of Voždovac, 11 December 1970)

In response to this kind of argumentation, the Establishment activists of the front rows use several types of put-downs. These are all based on support of a predetermined or established policy, proposal, or program — established by the government and the *mesna zajednica*'s higher organs, i.e. the Commune and Municipal assemblies. Since the *mesna zajednica* sends representatives to these organs, the Establishment kind of argumentation raises the question of who is being represented to whom. In other words, the elective function of Establishment activists is to represent the basic unit — it's proposals, its desires, its hopes — to the higher organs, but their argumentation indicates that they represent to a possibly greater extent the viewpoint of the higher organs toward the basic unit.[12] Their argumentation in the voters' meeting consists of, first, reading verbatim a printed re-

12 The problem of representation of the lowest commune organs, i.e. the voters' meetings, to higher organs has been noted by Yugoslav social researchers, also. Their data show that the voters exert no influence through their representatives. Moreover, these representatives are often out of touch with their constituents and uninformed about their opinions. See Marinković, *Ko odlučuje*, pp. 210–12.

Nor has the problem of representation been solved at any other level of political organization (except possibly in the Party, where the constituency may not be so heterogeneous). A plant psychologist, for example, documents this conflict between 'transmission representative' and 'independent representative' role components in a study of roles and role-conflict within the self-management organs in the large *Crvena zastava* (Fiat) factory in Serbia over a two-year period. He finds that over 60 percent of the fifty workers' council respondents think that they should vote in accord with their own opinions, while only 31 percent think that they should vote the way their constituents seem to be thinking. See Branislav Čukić, 'Patologija, tehnologija i kultura samoupravljača' [The pathology, technology, and culture of self-managers] (Report delivered at First Meeting of Self-managers of 'Crveni barjak', Kragujevac, 15–17 February 1969), p. 11.

port from the higher organ and, second, quelling the remarks of the other participants.

To answer the criticisms of the citizen-partisans, the Establishment activists use eight forms of put-downs. These replies constitute put-downs because they show that they do not seriously accept the argumentation of the citizen-partisans, i.e. the general statement of societal problems. Ostensibly replying to the citizen-partisans' argumentation, they are actually negating it. Moreover, the Establishment activists' put-downs implicitly claim the authority of superior knowledge — the kind for which experts are employed and statistics are piled up, and for which ordinary citizens find little use. This indicates the stratification of the groups of participants that I have been discussing, with Establishment activists not only at the front of the room but also in the ranks of an incipient technocratic elite. As we shall see later, the group of Establishment activists itself is stratified. However, the argumentation within that group which is revealed to the public is so shrouded by ideological jargon that it is usually difficult to recognize the put-downs.

To put down other participants, first, the Establishment activist may declare them out of order or ignore them. Since the citizen-partisans often speak out unrecognized by the chair and, as I have already said, irrelevant to a particular point on the agenda, this put-down is like a common parliamentary tactic. The second put-down is no more sophisticated but slightly less direct. With this tactic, the Establishment activist instructs the citizen-partisans that they do not really know what they are talking about. The form of the put-down is, 'This is socialism, Comrade Jovanović!' For example, when a citizen-partisan asserts that the Municipal Transportation Company should operate at a loss so that bus fares could be lowered, an Establishment activist answers with the counter-assertion that 'Capitalist society can afford that, but socialist society cannot'. (From voters' meeting on Zadarska Street, Commune of Stari Grad, 10 December 1970.) This is a neat reversal of the terms of the usual argument against government subsidies for public works in capitalist countries. Such a put-down refers to the superior knowledge — practically the omniscience — of the Establishment activists.

The next three forms of put-downs are also intended as instruction in essentials of the historical situation. The third put-down consists of the reminder that 'Present economic conditions in our self-managing society do not permit . . .' This blank can be filled in with relief of the social problem that the citizen-partisan has brought up, e.g. full employment or housing construction. In the fourth put-down, the Establishment activist reminds the citizen-partisans of their obligations vis-à-vis the historical epoch. He may say, 'We must live up to the demands of modernization' or of some other process associated with economic development. In one case, for example, 'the demands of modernization' include building a certain recreation center proposed for the commune. (From voters' meeting on Zadarska Street, Commune of Stari Grad, 10 December 1970.) Thus the Establishment activists implicitly allude to the tenets of the official ideology, which emphasize the 'practical' goal of economic growth over the 'pure' objective of socialist raising of consciousness. Meanwhile, the fifth put-down reminds the citizen-partisan that '. . . ing', e.g. proposing, discussing, or another activity limited to the meeting situation, 'is the citizens' obligation'. For example, an Establishment activist says to the participants, 'If we don't accept the suggested fare rise, then our representatives to the Municipal Assembly will be obliged to find a resolution. The Municipal Assembly must make a decision. It's easiest to be for or against something but hardest to make a concrete proposal.' (From voters' meeting on Zadarska Street, Commune of Stari Grad, 10 December 1970.) In this case, the proposal that he sought from the participants would ask for a fare rise on city buses and trolleys. That was an issue on which the voters wanted to take no action or even to 'regress', i.e. to press for lowered fares. They emphatically did not want to suggest that they should take more money out of their own pockets. This case illustrates a practical conflict between self-interest and self-management.

The next two put-downs constitute a typical defense of the status quo in any society: appeals to law and to past action. For example, the Establishment activist gets around all the criticism of the housing shortage and the need for free housing for poor people by citing 'a law that no one can use an apartment without paying for it'. He also negates criticism of social services and the quality of police protection by stating that 'this commune has done more for . . . [the given problem] than any other commune in Belgrade'. (From voters' meeting of Svetog Save, Commune of Vračar, 25 February 1971.)

Finally, the Establishment activist uses as a put-down the universal appeal to the authority of specialized knowledge. I have already said that the Establishment activist's forte is the printed report replete with numbers. His statements are couched in exact terms (whether right or wrong); he loves to cite the reports, to return to the reports, to offer to go into more precise detail. The other participants usually reject this offer. However, the combination of figures and categorical assertions give the Establishment activist an authority which ordinary citizens, i.e. the citizen-partisans and the unmobilized masses, cannot combat. As one citizen-partisan says, expressing his incompetence and relinquishing the field to the Establishment activists, 'Budget questions are too complicated for me — I leave them to Comrade Tomić and Comrade Petrović [Establishment activists].' (From voters' meeting on Zadarska Street, Commune of Stari Grad, 10 December 1970.) This attitude of leaving the 'complicated' matters to experts indicates that even problems which are presently resolvable on the local level are being increasingly confined to a narrow circle of experts and officials rather than to the broad body of citizens. However, at least one citizen-partisan is less docile about his relative incompetence. He says, 'As a citizen I'm interested, but I don't see the budget policy. The first part [of the proposal] is too declarative, and the second part gives figures in such a way that the budget policy isn't apparent.' (From voters' meeting of Svetog Save, Commune of Vračar, 25 February 1971.) But at least this citizen-partisan stands up in the meeting and expresses his doubts. Indeed, his mere attendance differentiates him from the unmobilized masses who probably feel even more incompetent to attend, let alone speak in, the meetings of 'their' self-management organs.[13]

Although Yugoslav survey research in the field of political participation generally centers on workers' self-management

13 According to a sociologist from Ljubljana who has studied local politics in Slovenia, the single most crucial factor in the citizens' lack of participation in voters' meetings is this feeling of incompetence, the feeling that they are unable to express their opinions. Zdravko Mlinar, *The Social Participation of Citizens in the Local Community* [in Slovenian] (Ljubljana: Institut za sociologije in filozofije, 1965), p. 148, cited in Marinković, *Ko odlučuje*, p. 199.

rather than social self-government, those studies document the same type of stratification that I have described in the context of the voters' meeting. Thus the Yugoslavs usually differentiate between at least two groups of political actors. On the one hand, these groups are defined as Party members versus nonmembers; on the other, they appear as members (and former members) of workers' councils versus nonmembers. In other words, survey responses usually differentiate between political activists of any sort and the inactive. Despite the limitations in Yugoslav data-collection and analysis, they do indicate significant differences between activists and other citizens.[14]

Besides Party and workers' council membership, another factor associated with political activism is occupational skill level. White-collar and highly-skilled workers tend to be politically more active than manual workers as a whole and less-skilled workers. In fact, some researchers find that white-collar workers dominate political meetings in the *mesna zajednica* and occupy a disproportionately high number of seats in workers' self-management organs. Their participation in and socialization into activist roles seems to have bred among the white-collar and highly-skilled workers a 'professional' interest in self-management. Thus, when asked why they want to participate in the workers' council, they tend to describe or to couch their reasons in terms of a desire to 'straighten out' the work of the whole enterprise. However, less-skilled and unskilled workers who say that they want to be on the workers' council claim as their motivation the fact that they are curious about or interested in the details of how the enterprise is run.[15]

14 In very simple behavioral terms, Party members attend many more meetings than nonmembers — as many as thirty meetings in a month — and tend more than nonmembers to speak out at meetings. Jugoslav Stanković, 'Gradjanin i politička aktivnost: Rezultati jedne ankete' [The citizen and political activity: Results of a survey], *Sociologija* 7, no. 3 (1965): 83–9.

15 Milos Ilić, ed., *Socijalna struktura i pokretljivost radničke klase Jugoslavije* [Social structure and mobility of the working class of Yugoslavia] (Belgrade: Institut društvenih nauka, 1963), I: 69–70, 58–9. See also S. Matić, M. Poček, and G. Bosanac, *Aktivnost radnih ljudi u samoupravljanju radnom organizacijom: Jedan pokušaj istraživanja na području komune Varaždin* [The activity of working people in self-management through the work organization: An attempt at research on the territory of the commune of Varaždin] (Zagreb: Institut za društveno upravljanje N. R. H., n.d. [1962]), pp. 65–9, 92–104; Stane Možina, 'Zainteresiranost samoupravljača za odlučivanje, kontrolu,

Stratification of activists

Whether we view political participation in Yugoslav self-management through the prism of Party membership, occupational skill level, or actual behavior, it is evident that, as in other political systems, there is some form of stratification separating activists and masses. This is the social reality that many Yugoslavs face with great candor as, for example, workers polled in two Slovenian enterprises say that those individuals who are most interested in self-management are not the workers themselves but their Party and union leaders.[16] We don't know which of the participants at voters' meetings are Party leaders or even members, but from the style and content of their participation we can see four strata of political actors: Establishment activists, issue activists, citizen-partisans, and unmobilized masses. In the first two strata the orientation toward the official line that we spoke about appears dominant, while the citizen-partisans seem to represent a 'backlash' of sorts toward the policy of an earlier era in Yugoslav socialism (Titoism II). Among the unmobilized masses are utopians, 'social democrats', and others.

PERSONAL RESPONSIBILITY

In their argumentation at voters' meetings, issue activists as well as citizen-partisans often try to affix personal blame for certain problems and conditions which irk them. The fruitless attempt to find where the buck — or the dinar — stops obviously exasperates them. So their statements have the air of gripes rather than reasoned arguments, particularly because the Establishment activists generally eschew fault-finding and shunt off the criticism.

The proposal to raise fares on Belgrade buses and trolleys, a problem that every voters' meetings had to consider and comment on at the beginning of 1971, brings out three major kinds of argumentation. One of these excoriates the irresponsibility of persons in the employ of the Municipal Transportation Company. The second argues against the proposed fare rise (by citing poor human conditions), and the third argues for the fare rise (by citing

davanje prijedloga i dobijanje informacija' [Self-managers' interest in decision-making, control, making proposals and getting information], *Sociologija* 10, no. 3 (1968): 27–36; Stanković, 'Gradjanin', pp. 87–8; and Županov, *Samoupravljanje*, pt. 1.

16 Vladimir Arzenšek, 'Analiza ankete o kadrovskoj politici' [Analysis of a survey on cadre policy], *Moderna organizacija* 1, no. 7 (1967), cited in idem, 'Samoupravljanje'.

operating expenses and enterprise deficits). The only participants who argue *for* the fare rise are the Establishment activists. Their argumentation is buttressed by an almost mournful presentation of facts and figures delivered by the Transportation Company representatives (dare we call them public relations men?) who travel around the city to speak at all the voters' meetings. Arguing against the fare rise, issue activists and citizen-partisans alike use the second kind of argumentation, i.e. the reasoning that poor pay and bad bus service make a fare rise an unnecessary hardship. The argumentation that some citizen-partisans use to try to counter the fare rise requires the least preparation or forethought. They simply allege irresponsibility or mismanagement on the part of the persons and company seeking the increased fares.

Because this argumentation typifies the approach of the citizen-partisans, that is, their fruitless attempt to affix personal responsibility for societal ills, we should look at some brief samples of their statements. Citizen-partisans at a voters' meeting say:

1. You ask the conductor why the bus is late and he says, 'Ask my boss.' I say, 'The bosses are responsible.'

2. I want Comrade Pešić [the representative to the Municipal Assembly] and the others from the Municipal Assembly to go to the enterprise and see who is guilty for the 4,000,000 [deficit].

3. When the bus is crowded, when people have to wait a long time and don't get to work on time, people say, 'If the directors of the Municipal Transportation Enterprise had to go to work on these buses instead of in their limousines, then some changes would be made.' [Murmurs of 'That's so, that's so.']

4. There isn't good organization in the enterprise. Are there experts there? [Murmurs: 'There are, there are.'] Then who are the leaders? The leaders are non-experts and there are engineers *under them!* [From the voters' meeting of Braća Jerković, Commune of Voždovac, 11 December 1970.]

Citizen-partisans often make very brief statements like these in the form of complaints which do not refer to any item on the agenda. Establishment activists usually ignore them unless the citizen-partisan or his comrades develop the gripe into a series of related statements on one topic, then a proposal (usually condensed and formulated by the chairman or another Establishment activist), and finally an acceptance of this proposal by voice vote. At that point the resolution is jotted down and noted for transmission to the higher organs.

Several other examples of these unplanned, i.e. non-agenda, statements, in which citizen-partisans spontaneously try to fix responsibility on known or unknown persons, refer to a wide range of everyday problems. The citizens who raise these problems do not know where else to turn but to the voters' meeting.

1. I've lived in this area for twenty-two years, and I want to ask, What's a house council for? What can it accomplish? [17] People are always worried about the house, but no one'll buy anything for it. I've been thinking about this, I've even been talking with the director and with the office workers *who are responsible for this,* and they say, 'You know, we don't have the means to buy a light-bulb that busts or to fix the stairs.' So who's going to come to us? And we pay rent . . .

I'm the president of my house council. *The others make the proposals, but I do the work.* Nobody wants to do any work. We have to start from the bottom up.

Another man adds: I don't know from personal experience. *Sometimes I'm afraid to make any suggestions, to have it written down, because I know that then I would have to do some work.*

The biggest problem is when the light-bulb in the elevator breaks, and people get disturbed about it. There has to be some arrangement for service. First you got no money and then you got the trouble to call up and get someone to fix it. [From voters' meeting of Svetog Save, Commune of Vračar, 9 March 1971.]

2. There's an institution here in this commune that deals with the problems of all of Belgrade. It would be natural for people to come there on foot, but they live far away so they come by public transportation. And so we see a

17 The house council consists of all the tenants in each socially-owned apartment house. It is responsible for upkeep and repairs, either directly or through the superintendent whom it may hire and pay.

crowd there, in front of the building, and sometimes there are even blows. And the people inside see this through their windows. *They take their salary; they should be obliged to come to these meetings.* [From same voters' meeting.]

3. Building inspection interests us citizens. Why aren't the inspection services more efficient? *The Commune Assembly should concern itself with this problem, then report back to the voters' meeting* . . . Let's investigate our rich construction enterprises. [From same voters' meeting, 25 February 1971.]

It is reasonable to ask why citizen-partisans use this kind of argumentation at voters' meetings. For one thing, they do not have access to specialized information as Establishment activists do. So they cannot cite figures and reports. But three other factors, all related to the nature of Yugoslav political organization, also influence the choice of argumentation. These factors are the earlier socialization of citizen-partisans into certain meeting norms, the unclear demarcation of responsibility between various self-management organs, and the catch-all functions of a basic-level meeting such as the voters' meeting in the *mesna zajednica*.

Because the citizen-partisans are generally the oldest participants in the voters' meeting, men between fifty and sixty years old, they are used to meetings where they can speak out on what ails them and appeal to the whole body for a solution. They expect this body to applaud points that they make, to voice their approval or disapproval by gestures and mutters outside the parliamentary speaking process. This kind of interaction characterizes the 'old-style, down-home' political meetings into which these men were socialized when they first began attending meetings where decisions are made. Whether they were peasants or workers, they probably attended meetings of this type. On the one hand, if they were peasants early in life, they no doubt participated in collective decision making of the 'old-style, down-home' type in their villages. On the other hand, if they were workers, or when they migrated to the city and became workers, they probably took part in or at least observed meetings organized by trade unions and the Communist Party. Since such organizations were hostile to the prewar regime, their meetings undoubtedly featured public criticism and airing of grievances. These kinds of statements are also typical of organizational interaction during a period of high mobilization such as the reconstruction period following World War II. Thus the oldest participants have experience in meeting situations which are structured by a personal kind of argumentation.

The second factor which influences the choice of this kind of argumentation is the unclear demarcation of responsibility between various self-management organs. This amorphous situation is in turn the product of the continual working out of the self-management system, both as an ideology and an institution, and also of the obscure language which declaims ideological goals. Because no one is sure which body is responsible for regulating certain social phenomena, the citizen-partisans bring up their problems and complaints in the political situation which is most accessible to them, that is, the voters' meeting.

Moreover, because the voters' meeting is supposed to be the most accessible organ of self-management to all citizens, including unemployed persons and pensioners who are thus excluded from workers' self-management, it encourages the expression of all kinds of political and social grievances. In other words, the basic-level meeting situation channels the cathartic outpour of social criticism which might otherwise result in alienation from the political system and 'antisocial acts'.

A final consideration vis-à-vis style and content is that there is no reward for using the kind of argumentation that the Establishment activists urge the citizen-partisans to adopt, i.e. the precise formulation of proposals. For when they do make precise formulations, the problems with which they deal are so deep that they are not soluble on the *mesna zajednica* level. Furthermore, the citizens never get any feedback to their proposed solutions from the higher organs.

ABSENCE OF FEEDBACK

From time to time during the voters' meeting, citizen-partisans express mild dissatisfaction or annoyance that the gathering has received no feedback from higher organs about proposals that they have made. They may only allude to the absence of feedback, as, for example, one citizen-partisan says during a discussion on the commune budget, 'I suggest that we go back to the previous decisions of this and other bodies.' (From voters' meeting on Zadarska Street, Commune of Stari Grad, 10 December 1970.) Or the plaintiff may tone down his remark, perhaps to mollify the Establishment activists, as when another citizen-partisan says, 'We should get answers to the suggestions we have made at past voters' and other-level meetings. Now, *I'm not criticizing the comrades at the front* [i.e. the Establishment activists], but we should get answers from the Municipal Assembly and so on.' (From voters' meeting of Braća Jerković, Commune of Voždovac, 11 December 1970. Emphasis added.)

Probably the citizen-partisans feel frustrated because the very problems that they have presumably 'resolved' at previous meetings turn up again and again on the agenda. On the one hand, their dissatisfaction with this situation indicates a certain political naïveté, for social problems are not so easily resolved, but on the other hand, it does seem that no one — neither man nor woman nor self-management organ — takes note of the voters' meeting proposals. A citizen-partisan illustrates both these problems when he says during discussion on the fare rise, 'I listened to the comrade, I read the material, but I remember that we discussed these matters two or three years ago at the voters' meeting . . . From the promises, the statements, we had the impression that we would have transportation without torture . . . but nothing ever came of it . . .' (From voters' meeting of Braća Jerković, Commune of Voždovac, 11 December 1970.)

Where is the break in the chain of self-government organs that cuts off feedback? After all, the *mesna zajednica*'s representatives are supposed to bring their constituents' proposals to the attention of the Commune and Municipal assemblies, and these organs are supposed to make policy accordingly. But observation of a Commune Assembly, only one link up in the chain of representation from the voters' meeting, indicates that at least the first break occurs here, at a level relatively close to the citizens.[18]

18 See also Marinković, *Ko odlučuje*, pp. 208–13. According to Marinković (pp. 212–13), 'The voters' meeting's conclusions . . . most frequently, as a result of the underdevelopment of the communications system, do not reach the right place, and they even get lost on the way to the meeting of the Commune Assembly from the voters' meeting, or they first get into the hands of the experts . . . What is more important, *the committeemen are not much interested in the conclusions of the meetings of their constituent units, mainly because they do not know them.* However, we have noted that the [Commune] assemblies look these resolutions over and that, *when they relate to a concrete pro-*

Absence of feedback

The meeting of the Commune Assembly consists mostly of successive, sometimes unrelated, statements by representatives from various *mesna zajednicas*. There is no *visible* discussion and negotiation between representatives of divers constituencies and interests. Furthermore, the Commune Assembly president, who chairs the meetings, seems to be a disciple of the same school of rhetoric as the *mesna zajednica* president, for she answers and puts down the representatives much as the voters' meeting chairman speaks to his constituents. But sometimes the commune president's remarks resemble a coach's pep talk to his team or, I suspect, a political commissar's charge to his Partisan brigade. 'Remember', a commune president remarks in this way, 'it's not important how many meetings we had last year but whether we carried out the national tasks in changing the existing situation and whether we fulfilled the essential needs of the citizens.' (All examples of the Commune Assembly are from the Commune of Stari Grad, 15 March 1971.)

In general, the president's argumentation combines the typical Establishment motifs of criticism, instruction, and reassurance about the Establishment's beneficial role in making social policy. For example, in her concluding remarks the commune president manages to defend the openness of the political system — at least its openness to publicity, to reassure delegates about the interlocking directorates of political organizations, and to criticize lobbyists from outside the Establishment. 'When we have the most subtle questions of the citizens' interests at stake', she says, 'we fight for full publicity.' But she does not discuss the fact that debate on these 'subtle questions', like all political discourse, is carried on in terms set by the Establishment, between actors either from within or recognized by the Establishment. It's all right, the president reassures the Assembly, that she attends the meetings of other political organs and voluntary associations which sometimes act as pressure groups. Ultimately it comes to a question of trust: 'Believe me,' she says, 'you must believe that I have good intentions.'

Most representatives deliver brief, not to say terse, statements of the resolutions passed by their voters' meetings. Delegates from

posal, they take them into account.' Emphasis added. Cf. economist Branko Horvat on the lack of feedback to the initiatives of the basic Party organization. Branko Horvat, *An Essay on Yugoslav Society*, trans. Henry F. Mins (White Plains, New York: International Arts and Sciences Press, 1969), pp. 227–8.

a few *mesna zajednicas* speak excitedly and argue their constituents' opinions further. Nevertheless, most representatives attempt neither dialogue nor cross-discussion. This kind of interaction probably frustrates some committeemen, who may be citizen-partisans or issue activists who have managed to get elected as representatives. One of these committeemen says toward the end of the Commune Assembly meeting,

> I as a committeeman also have a responsibility to bring here the opinion of the citizens. The proposals from my voters' meeting were never acted upon. Previously we proposed that a traffic light be installed . . . The voters say, 'If we elect someone then he has to bring our opinions to the Commune Assembly.'

This remark suggests that there may be a division among Establishment activists between those who represent from the bottom up, like this committeeman, and those who represent from the top down, like the president.

Although the scope of this study does not extend to elite behavior, observation suggests that officeholders start to represent from the bottom up when, unexpectedly frustrated by other members of the Establishment from pursuing their own opinions, they begin to identify partially with strata outside the Establishment. They become frustrated when their creative participation — which may consist of a legally correct and ideologically legitimate initiative or course of action — is rebuffed and negated by their colleagues. In this way, some activists come to see in an immediate way how restricted participation and democracy still are for the society at large. So, like Milovan Djilas or like the citizen-partisans at voters' meetings, they protest the illusion of participatory democracy and 'retreat' from the specifics of the agenda to sweeping social problems. They also tend to interpret and express these problems personally. Some of them admit publicly that opportunities for political participation are more a matter of form than of content.

FORM OVER CONTENT

As the discussion so far indicates, the Establishment activists' interaction with citizen-partisans at voters' meetings is significant for understanding the relationship between various strata of political participants. We have seen how the chairman exerts control over the meeting situation in several ways: by manipulating the participants, by criticizing and instructing them, and by defending the Establishment's role in the political process. The chairman also controls the situation by conscientiously guiding the discussion in a certain way. He or she tries to get the voters' meeting to pass resolutions which affirm — rather than criticize, negate, or replace — (1) a proposal made by an Establishment activist, (2) some other preformulated proposal, or (3) general policy. If the participants appear recalcitrant or merely reluctant to 'resolve' anything in this way, then the chairman himself, or herself, formulates a resolution which compromises between the Establishment proposal and the mood of the voters' meeting. However, his or her resolution is weighted in favor of the former rather than the latter. In any case, the chairman shapes the resolutions so that the voters' meeting appears to affirm the official line.

This, for example, is how a chairman sums up the discussion at a voters' meeting on the proposed fare rise. The meeting's mood is against the fare rise, so the chairman's argumentation and the kind of compromise that he formulates are noteworthy. He says,

> We have to look at the problem *more realistically.* We have to solve the problem of transportation, not just that of the Municipal Transportation Company. How much does Belgrade's economy lose because of municipal transportation, how much do workers lose at their workplace because of lateness? . . . *The problem can't be solved by prices alone.*

> [An Establishment activist proposes a limited fare rise, not quite so much as the Municipal Transportation Company requests.]

> Comrade Stefanović proposed a limited price rise; I'm for that proposal.

> [Collective murmurs, 'We're for that proposal.' Meeting votes in favor and spontaneously adjourns.]

So what becomes of the citizen-partisans' criticism? It disappears like blown-off steam and emerges in condensed, essentially changed form as a compromise proposal. Then the citizen-partisan may feel resigned and defeated, if not by the chairman, then by all the events and higher organs beyond the voters' meeting's control. We see this mental shrug of the shoulders, for example, when a woman who has frequently voiced criticism during a discussion says, 'I think that we should agree with the price rise. *If we don't, they'll be raised anyway.*' (From voters' meeting on Zadarska Street, Commune of Stari Grad, 10 December 1970. Emphasis added.)[19]

The citizen's sense of resignation is reflected also in essentially passive conceptions of the individual self and his or her options for political action. Below the surface behavior of attending voters' meetings, the participants know that this gathering does not contend with the most urgent societal problems. They themselves suggest that this is the reason that many of the masses are unmobilized. For instance, a citizen-partisan says, 'It would make an interesting voters' meeting if we would take a stand on social problems. That would interest many more citizens than many of our voters' meetings.' (From voters' meeting of Svetog Save, Commune of Vračar, 25 February 1971.) So they are aware that they, as participants, form a minority compared to the unmobilized masses outside the political process. 'It's a peculiar psychoanalytic [sic] fact', another citizen-partisan says, 'that out of a *mesna zajednica* with 4,000 citizens [he means voters], only sixty show up. Socialism makes progress — what's it going to be like in twenty-five more years?!' He goes on, 'Maybe it'd be better if you got paid to come, or if you had to pay a tax if you didn't come.' (From same voters' meeting, 9 March 1971.)

Ironically, the chairman who admits that these meetings are uninteresting offers an excuse which only illustrates the limited sphere of action of the voters' meeting, for he blames the higher organs. He says, 'Who determines our agenda? We get our daily work from the Commune Assembly already printed and typed out. We post the agenda, the citizens see it, and they don't come.'[20] (From voters' meeting of Svetog Save, Commune of

19 Similarly, Branislav Čukić, social psychologist at the *Crvena zastava* enterprise, notes 'a strongly developed passivity of members of the management organs as an elected body'. He relates this passivity to the Establishment activists' — or *aktiv*'s — monopoly over political participation, which he sees as part of the 'pathology' of workers' self-management. Čukić, 'Patologija', pp. 1–4.

20 The agendas, printed on colored paper, are posted on the outside walls of apartment houses and other buildings.

Vračar, 25 February 1971.) In other words, the masses remain unmobilized because the content of their political action has already been determined. The problems that they are summoned to 'resolve' are neither burning issues of life and death nor even of potatoes versus meat on the dining table. Moreover, the citizen can rest assured that these issues will be resolved by other organs, other individuals. They know that their 'input', i.e. their agitation, criticisms, and complaints, will be transformed into a 'concrete proposal' that the Establishment will tolerate. Sooner or later their negativism will be turned into affirmation of the status quo by 'their' representatives. In a sense, then, by staying away from the voters' meeting, some part of the unmobilized masses is refusing to be manipulated.[21]

At least some citizens who realize that their participation is specious to the content of policy-making tend to keep their distance from political activity and political activists. These Yugoslavs see through the imagery of the official ideology to an underlying certitude of political manipulation. Rade Popović, a highly-skilled worker who used to be a Party and workers' council member, makes this point. He says,

> You know how things are decided. Maybe they're smart, and
> maybe they're not smart, but they're in power . . . And
> they want to put their thoughts into action. So they bring
> out the propaganda. And the group around them that has
> to agree agrees that this should be brought into action for
> the good of the nation, for socialism. Then they bring it
> down to the people, to the assemblymen, to the common

21 Yugoslav survey data confirm this point. In a survey of five Belgrade *mesna zajednicas*, a Yugoslav sociologist asked what people thought the purpose of the voters' meeting was. Most respondents — both Party members and non-members — replied that the purpose was *least* decision-making by the citizens. Those respondents who tended more than others to say that voters' meetings exist for this purpose turn out to be Party officials. Stanković, 'Gradjanin', pp. 91–2. Furthermore, most workers in a recent survey of eleven Serbian enterprises blame their non-participation in workers' self-management on their lack of influence: 'Everything is decided in advance by others, the powerful ones', they say. So they see no point in attending meetings. 'Vladar bez vlasti' [Powerless ruler], *NIN*, 9 May 1971, p. 31.

Only one other non-Yugoslav observer has drawn this logical conclusion, i.e. that some of the unmobilized masses are simply refusing to be manipulated. See Meister, *Où va*, pp. 30ff. Meister's analysis on the whole agrees with mine.

citizens, and the Party members are known — they're the ones who have to say first that they agree. There are some there who don't agree, I'm not saying that there aren't, but they're such a small number that it doesn't mean anything . . .

Similarly, Branislav Belić, a young lawyer, refuses to accept the leadership's interpretation of the decision-making process. He looks, for example, at the way the constitutional amendments of 1971 were proposed and propounded and he sees — manipulation. Belić feels that the political leadership is railroading through the amendments. So, in his eyes, their ratification is a foregone conclusion. Belić says,

> The amendments are being discussed with so much trouble because it's too short a time for what they want and for what they're going to do.
> Yesterday I came across a very interesting column in the paper. It says— '*When* the constitutional amendments are accepted' — but just now these amendments are supposedly being taken apart by the masses, which means that there's no question at all whether or not they'll be passed. Then to what purpose are the citizens being asked their opinion whether [the amendments] are right or wrong, if tomorrow already they're going to go ahead in a fixed way?
> And that's why I knew from the moment they rolled out the carpet on these amendments that they would be carried through.

For Belić and Popović, as for many other citizens, the political discourse of voters' meetings and the news media is empty verbiage. Or in the words of Miša Cvijić, a young, politically uninvolved, white-collar worker,

> They talk a lot, politicians. They don't do anything directly. The whole thing lacks concrete proposals, concrete actions that have to be carried out through various decisions. And it's all managed from the top down. The political opinions that have to be worked on now are imposed from the top. Nothing concrete. This city, say, is really dirty. First something has to be done to make this city clean; we have to take some action in this field. We talk about it, but we have to *do* something.

Form over content

That politicians run on at the mouth is not a uniquely South Slavic phenomenon. Nevertheless, some Yugoslavs complain that their country is now experiencing an inflation of political discourse, in which the number of political statements 'in circulation', rises while the value of what is said declines. Thus the news magazine *NIN* claims that 'public speech . . . is in constant expansion', and the writer Matija Bećković finds that *speaking* about politics is confused with *thinking* about politics. Bećković observes ironically,

> Here verbal explanation is identified with thinking. He who explains correctly more and oftener, also thinks correctly. There is no other logic.
>
> For work you get a salary, but for verbal explanations [you get] all the other social recognition. Work is carried into the account books, but verbal explanations into biography . . .
>
> It isn't important what and how you think so long as you speak.[22]

In contrast to the verbiage of propaganda-making for the broader public, the voters' meeting and the meeting of the work collective should be forums of frank, concrete criticism and self-criticism. According to the official ideology of self-management, individuals as citizens and as workers can air their grievances, can criticize anyone and everything at these basic-level meetings in the *mesna zajednica* and in the enterprise. But the Establishment activists at the voters' meeting put down criticism. Furthermore, the put-downs of such initiative in the enterprise appear to be serious negative sanctions against the worker who dares to criticize either the managerial or the political-activist Establishment. Rade Popović laughs and says,

> Maybe you expected something 'new' at the voters' meeting? You know how it is? *Looking back, we could say a lot. But today, it bothers them when you say something.* That's one side of it, and the other side, the side that destroyed people, is in the work organization. *I don't dare, for instance, to criticize the director of my shop.* Because they're going to wait for me, at the pass as they say, and I'm going to start

22 Frane Barbieri, 'Elite' [Elites], NIN, 11 July 1971, p. 7; Bećković, *Dr Janez Paćuka*, p. 17.

slowly falling down. Or if I make a mistake they'll show me the door, maybe not this year or next year, but one day they'll get revenge on me.

On the other hand, it wasn't always like this. We criticized whoever it was, we talked freely . . . Looking back, maybe five years ago, we all put our tongues between our teeth, as they say. People shut up. If someone did get up to say something at a meeting — only this [he claps his hands]. [Emphasis added.]

Other people whose political credentials place them among the Establishment activists confirm this point. For instance, an intellectual from Zagreb who does much of his work within the Party framework talks about his brother, a worker at a large electrical appliance factory in that city. In this enterprise, the Party leader and the union president are pushing a certain proposal to which most of the workers are opposed. The brother gets up in the meeting of the work collective and says that the workers can get another Party secretary and union president. Thus the brother loses his job.

Danilo Arandjelović, the Belgrade journalist and Establishment activist, puts this point in the perspective of an uncertain economic situation. He says,

That part of the population which is more conscious, which knows what self-management means, isn't prepared to risk anything because tomorrow they might wind up — not by force of circumstances but by various dishonest methods — either on a lower rung or unemployed altogether. No one is going either to ignore himself or to be continually on his guard. And that's a big reason why self-management hasn't developed to the degree that it was conceptualized. *You know, if a man could be sure that if he didn't like it here, that he could find the same or almost the same job tomorrow, then he'd stand up to the director or to the head of the workers' council or whomever.* But if he isn't sure that he can find work, if he isn't economically independent, then he's more careful, more on his guard about what he's going to say and how he's going to act. [Emphasis added.]

These statements indicate that the Establishment in the enterprise as well as in the commune stifles self-managing initiative

Form over content

when it comes in the form of serious criticism. In citing Popović, Arandjelović, and the Zagreb worker's brother, I do not intend to imply that the population is cowering and fearful. Rather, I am trying to emphasize the stratification of political actors, with workers and citizens on the one hand and an Establishment of leaders and directors on the other. These two groups are ultimately separated by their leaders' authority to dispense negative sanctions. Nor is this an authority to which any worker can aspire, for despite the promises of the official ideology, the Establishment in the enterprise shows few real signs of 'rotation' or turnover. Similarly, it does not appear susceptible to being voted out of office by dissatisfied worker-constituents; rather, the political plaintiffs seem to bear the brunt of the penalties when they try to make a case against their leaders.

Within the ranks of Party members, also, participants appear to be stratified into dominant leaders and submissive members. Indeed, a survey commissioned by the League of Communists to find out why 50,000 members left the Party in 1970 reveals that the primary reason for quitting is a sense of political impotence.[23] Furthermore, various social structures such as republics and industries appear to relate positively to the LC only insofar as the Party furthers their interests. Conversely, the individual Party member who feels that the Party ignores, or even threatens or negates, his interests, senses that he is as impotent within the Party as in society. This individual may then become alienated from both the Party and society. Reports from various Party gatherings describe how norms of interaction within the LC alienate members in this way. According to the Third Conference of the LC of Bosnia and Hercegovina, for example, such alienating norms are 'above all the lack of democratic practice, the pressure of technocratic forces on the consciousness and acts of the direct producers, the underrating of the workers' abilities to make decisions on development policy, the imposition of the opinions of individual leaders on the whole collective and the arbitrariness of individuals'. Also, according to the Executive Committee of the LC of Croatia, 'The workers [in the survey] most often answered like this: The working class doesn't decide, others decide in its name, but everyone swears in its interest.'

23 Data in this section are from 'Savez komunista: Ko vraća crvene knjižice' [League of Communists: Who returns the little red books], *NIN*, 4 July 1971, p. 12.

The structure of political participation

Likewise, the same reasons hold true for why members quit the LC of Serbia. These reasons include 'dissatisfaction with opportunities in society, the work organization and the LC; disagreement with the role and the manner of action of the LC in their environment; the lack of development of internal democratic relations in the LC . . .'

Such general reasons are echoed by individuals, such as these Croatian workers who quit the League of Communists in 1973:

> I joined the League of Communists in '52, when I was 28, and, for all I knew, I liked it as an organization. But from year to year the whole thing changed, it went bad. There wasn't any more of that communist ideal. A person could get pretty disillusioned, seeing what went on from day to day — I'm not talking about my factory, but in general — the problem was that the whole set-up wasn't what it claimed to be. There were programs, sure, but they weren't carried out. [A semiskilled worker]

> I can tell you right away, that even though I'm not a member any more, I haven't changed a bit. The Party created a mighty good path — it couldn't have done any better — but in that Party you've got people who aren't real communists. I'm not saying you haven't got a lot who are real communists, but even today — even though the Party purged itself of bureaucrats and so on — you got a group of people who're pulling for themselves. Me, for example, I was disillusioned most by the familiarity in a certain factory, that 'You scratch my back, I'll scratch yours.' That rubbed me the wrong way: with hiring, with apartments — the worker always got the least.
> When I quit the Party, the secretary asked me straight out whether I was leaving because they took them — you know who — out of office. No. I've never discriminated between Croats, Slovenes, Serbs. What bothered me was that uncommunist relationship between people. One time I spoke out at the workers' council, I upheld the workers. Afterwards, the leader waited for me — he was one of us, before — and he says, 'Why didn't you go along with us? You know you could lose your job.' Is that the way communists talk? If I see someone committing a robbery, should I

184

keep quiet? I've got to say that it's better now, but we'll have to see how its goes. [A highly-skilled baker in industry][24]

Obviously, it is up to the Party committees to take action on these criticisms. In the past, perhaps, local LC leaderships have not wanted to face up to their 'failure', as evidenced by a large exodus of members. According to a skilled factory worker from Zagreb who left the Party in 1965, the LC committee leaders asked for the reasons why he and others were quitting but finally recorded that these were 'generally not serious reasons'. His reason for quitting was disillusionment with the Party's weaknesses — a case reminiscent of respondent Rade Popović's and the other Croatian workers cited above.[25]

A sense of political impotence may emerge not only among ordinary citizens and rank-and-file Party members, but also within the milieu of elected officeholders. Indeed, close examination of the norms of participation in this milieu reveals that as 'Establishment' a group as republican legislators may succumb to a low sense of political efficacy when their initiatives are put down and their criticism is stifled. For example, a dispute within the Yugoslav political Establishment recently began with the Slovenian Republican Assembly's enactment of an amendment permitting any group of twenty-five delegates to nominate a candidate for the newly-created federal cabinet (the *Predsedništvo*). It ended with the Slovenian Party's expulsion of an assemblyman who, with twenty-four others, insisted on his right to do so. Statements by the respective parties to this dispute show that the underlying theme is the Establishment's monopoly over political action. This is expressed, first, by the Establishment itself.

At that meeting of the LC *aktiv* [a reporter writes], the president of the commune conference of the Socialist Alliance of Working People of Ljubljana-Šiška [district] posed the question, How is it at all possible that delegates in the Re-

24 Aside from placing the blame on society, some workers advance personal reasons for quitting the Party, e.g. high membership dues of 600 dinars (about $40, or 60 percent of a poverty-line monthly salary) a year; lack of time to fulfill Party obligations; failure to get help with career advancement, including additional schooling, through the Party. 'Razočaranja, nebriga, obitelj, a i članarina . . .' [Disillusionment, lack of concern, household, and even dues . . .], *Vjesnik u srijedu*, 28 November 1973.
25 See Mikecin, *Socijalizam*, pp. 101–3.

publican Assembly voted through an amendment *which
permits a group to set itself into decision-making outside
the organized public discussion and democratic elections,*
through some 'safety valves of democracy', as that amendment would be . . .[26]

On the other side, one of the twenty-five republican legislators
defends their initiative in light of the Establishment's usual
inertia. This delegate says,

> Did the commune conference of the SAWP [Socialist Alliance of Working People] have any kind of special nominating conference for the election of members of the Presidium? Obviously, no one informed me about it. Not one commune organ informed me of the opinions about nomination and not once during the two years that I've been a deputy has any organ in Šiška asked me to bring any opinion whatever to the Assembly. Even though I am often at Assembly meetings. The Assembly regulations foresee that the deputy may present and formulate his own opinions about things that the Commune Assembly hasn't formulated opinions about, or if they don't have any at all.

Since the delegates' initiative in nominating candidates implies a
denial of the Establishment's monopoly over political action, the
Establishment feels threatened. Some of its members who are
obviously closer to the centers of power, i.e. the Party and government executive branches, make the appropriate response to
the threat by stifling the initiative, even though the initiators
come from within their own ranks.

The political impotence of legislators may extend to the
federal level. According to a recent *NIN* survey of 145 members
of the Federal Assembly, even these high-level representatives of
the people feel powerless and uninformed about political decisions. Over 80 percent of them feel that the Federal Assembly's
role and influence in policy-making is unsatisfactory; 75 percent
are dissatisfied with their position as representatives. Despite the

26 This section is based on Peter Božić, 'Fenomeni: Parlamentarna ili
politička kolizija' [Phenomena: Parliamentary or political collision],
NIN, 8 August 1971, p. 13. Emphasis added. For a follow-up, see Miloš
Mišović, 'Konfrontacije: Nesporazum oko demokratije' [Confrontations: Misunderstanding about democracy], *NIN*, 19 September 1971,
pp. 11–13.

Decision-making

Federal Assembly's constitutional ascendancy over all other official and unofficial organs, the actual powers in policy-making center on the executive branch of the government, i.e. the cabinet, the federal bureaucracy, republican Party and government leaderships, and also on various industrial interests. Thus a representative in the Federal Assembly's Socio-political Chamber (the chamber with the broadest mandate) says,

> The conditions in which the deputies work do not offer the full chance of affirmation of various initiatives which would grow out of social praxis. Some conceptions and opinions which are limited by dogma also affect this . . . The gap between the constitutional position of the Assembly and political practice decreases the Assembly's creativity, making its role in some cases mere formalism.[27]

From observation of political gatherings like voters' meetings to statements by citizens, Party members, and legislators, Yugoslav experience suggests that participatory democracy still meets with two obstacles: the hierarchical relationship between Establishment and masses, and a resulting, widespread sense of political impotence. But perhaps if we looked closely at the decision-making process we would find more creative participants than we expected. Or does our assertion still hold: that the forms of participation overshadow its content?

DECISION-MAKING

Having done five case studies of decision-making in Serbian communes, political scientist Radivoje Marinković concludes that the greatest influence is exerted by the 'bearers of strategic functions', or what we have called the Establishment.[28] Most significant among these officials are the president and vice-president of the commune, and sometimes also the heads of advisory councils and administrative departments. Marinković says that these key Establishment figures are powerful because they coordinate and organize all the stages of the decision-making process. When, for

---

27 Miloš Mišović, 'Moć i nemoć poslanika' [Power and impotence of deputies], *NIN*, 14 March 1971, pp. 32–4, at 33. See also Mišović, '(Ne)obavčšteni poslanik' [The (un)informed deputy], *NIN*, 23 May 1971, pp. 35–7.
28 Marinković, *Ko odlučuje*, pp. 225–54, esp. 250–4.

example, they want to make an issue out of some problem or situation, they covertly get professional associations and political bodies in their commune to bring the matter to the public's attention. In one of Marinković's cases a commune president who wants to put a local hospital out of business first gets the medical association to condemn conditions in the hospital. So much for the 'initiation' of decisions. As for the consideration of various options in decision-making, the key Establishment figures control the gathering of information and the formulation of alternatives through the experts, e.g. administrators and economists, who are in their, or rather the commune's, employ. Apparently these specialized cadres consider themselves the president's advisors. The major office-holders also control the information and communications channels, so they decide which groups and individuals have access to the data necessary to decision-making. When it is time for a vote, the presidents selectively mobilize these groups and individuals to maximize the chances that their proposal will be passed. Thus Marinković calls the presidents 'the directors of decision-making situations in their entirety or of individual sequences'.

The 'bearers of strategic functions' — the *aktiv* or the Establishment — are secure in their monopoly over decision-making. The only limitation on the president of a commune is that 'he doesn't make a mistake in some basic socio-political principle or [that] he doesn't conflict with the opinion of some significant political organization or group in the commune'. In other words, as long as they do not attack any principle of the official ideology, transgress any of the norms of political life, or step on the toes of any big Party or government leader, the president of the commune and his *aktiv* can do pretty much what they want.[29]

29 Ibid., p. 252.
   In the decision-making study 'Structure of Influence in Commune', Janez Jerovšek comes to the same conclusions. Jerovšek studied decisions on the municipal budget, the town plan, the housing construction plan, financing of schools, electing the commune president, and electing the director of an important enterprise in seventeen Slovenian communes. He finds that the professional councils of the Municipal Assembly exert the greatest influence on these decisions. According to Jerovšek, these councils have such great influence because their professional methods of work and high degree of informedness allow them to work out precise draft proposals which convince less-informed, busy office-holders. Also, their professional function gives the council members a sense of competence vis-à-vis the other socio-political bodies. After these councils, the next most influential group is comprised of

Decision-making

We find the same pattern of stratification and influence in the enterprise as in the commune. All Yugoslav research on collective decision-making in the enterprise shows that the distribution of influence is hierarchical, with executives at the top and workers at the bottom.[30] Despite this harsh reality, the majority of workers on all skill levels, from unskilled workers to executives, say that the distribution of power *ought* to be different. According to sociologist Josip Županov, workers want a democratic, or at least a polyarchic, structure of participation in decision-making. But the practice — as distinct from the theory — of self-management has made them diverge from the idea of equal participation through workers' councils. Thus Slovenian sociologist Veljko Rus finds that attitudes toward workers' self-management changed drastically during the 1960s. At the beginning of the decade, Rus says, workers felt that all members of the enterprise should participate equally in decision-making. By the end of the sixties, however, workers had accepted the hierarchical status quo and no longer *wanted* equal participation. According to Rus, the workers *want* only as much power as they already *have*.[31] Perhaps they are afraid of losing more control in enterprise decision-making, so they wish to keep what gains they have made relative to the pre-self-management era.

the president and the vice-president of the Municipal Assembly, for the same reasons that Marinković gives (see above). The third most influential group in decision-making is the municipal administrative apparatus. These administrators 'exert a much greater influence on the selected decisions, and thus on social life in the commune, than voters' meetings, local communities, or political organizations'. Janez Jerovšek, 'Structure of Influence in Commune', in *Sociologija: Selected Articles 1959–1969* (Belgrade: Yugoslav Sociological Association, 1970; translated and reprinted from *Sociologija* 11, no. 2 [1969]): 115–36.

30 See Županov, *Samoupravljanje*; Veljko Rus, 'A Comparative Analysis of Communications, Power and Responsibility in Two Industrial Organizations' [in Slovenian] (Ljubljana: Institut za sociologije in filozofije, 1968); Rus, 'Problems of Responsibility in Self-managerial Industrial Organizations', in *Sociologija: Selected Articles 1959–1969* (Belgrade: Yugoslav Sociological Association, 1970; translated and reprinted from *Sociologija* 11, no. 3 [1969]), pp. 93–114, and 'Moć i struktura moći u jugoslovenskim preduzećima' [Power and the structure of power in Yugoslav enterprises], *Sociologija* 12, no. 2 (1970): 191–207. See the bibliography for the work of other industrial sociologists such as Janez Jerovšek, Stane Možina, Josip Obradović, and Živan Tanić.

31 Županov, *Samoupravljanje*, p. 104; Veljko Rus, 'Samoupravni egalitarizam i društvena diferencijacija' [Self-managing egalitarianism and social differentiation], *Praxis* 6, no. 5–6 (September–December 1969): 813. Rus's survey was done in Slovenia, Županov's in Croatia.

The structure of political participation

Before we despair of the workers' potential for self-management, let us consider this problem from another perspective. Put simply, workers are disenchanted with the way self-management has worked out: with the power of the *aktiv* and their own inability to influence decisions. So, like the unmobilized or disaffected masses who do not go to voters' meetings, workers who do not participate in self-management may be refusing to be manipulated by 'their' representatives and 'their' workers' councils. In fact, a survey of Serbian workers shows that they reject the workers' council as a means of increasing their influence in decision-making. Instead of going through the workers' council, they would opt for greater autonomy *for* their individual work units and greater power *within* these work units. Thus they would concentrate on decision-making in the immediate work situation. Perhaps workers have redefined the sphere of self-management to this level because of their lack of effect on the workers' council and their representatives' cooptation into the enterprise Establishment. This state of affairs makes the workers want to place self-management in a small enough situation so that they can 'manage' it themselves.[32]

Like the Establishment in the commune, the enterprise *aktiv* controls the means of communication, information, and mobilization vital to the firm's functioning. So sociologist Josip Županov reasons that, as long as organization is based on the division of labor, the *aktiv* will continue to assume the dominant role in decision making. Their high degree of administrative-political know-how — as distinct from technical knowledge — is indispensable to the enterprise as it negotiates and otherwise deals with commune and republic governments. Also, the high social status that directors have gained in Yugoslavia makes the idea of challenging their power remote. Over the years, Županov says, the power of workers' councils has grown, but at the same time the power of enterprise directors has not diminished.[33]

From voters' meetings to Party membership, from the limitations on republican legislators to the power of enterprise directors, Yugoslav politics suggest that in at least one aspect — the hierarchical relationship of Establishment to masses — socialist

32 'Vladar bez vlasti', p. 33. Cf. Pateman, *Participation and Democratic Theory*, p. 100.
33 Županov, *Samoupravljanje*, pp. 105–17, esp. 112, 110.

self-management has not yet improved upon other systems. Also, there is some discrepancy between the official ideology and the practice of self-management. Although access to political institutions is theoretically equally free to all citizens, some groups of participants apparently make better use of these opportunities. In fact, they monopolize political offices and manipulate the non-office-holding citizens.

Obviously, this is a situation that we know first-hand in our own political system. But we expected something more democratic from self-management. Unfortunately, the imperatives of economic development seem to bolster these patterns of political participation. Not only the actual decision-making power, but also the potential for sharing in this power — that is, by having the information necessary for making a rational decision — is restricted to the ranks of a political-cum-technical elite. Even in Yugoslavia, technocracy rears its head. But will it be given its head: can the dream of participatory democracy so easily cede to a vision of high GNP and creature comforts? Yugoslavs indicate that some compromise is reached between ideological and material goals, a compromise in which socialism becomes liberalism and the revolution is technological. This redefinition of terms and values has also brought about a realignment of political forces within the Establishment. As a Belgrade law professor describes the three 'wings' of the Serbian Party, there are the 'old politicians of the *čvrsta ruka* [firm hand] school'; there are the middle-aged, college-educated intellectuals 'who continue to play the political game'; and there are 'the technocrats, who will do anything you want them to in politics as long as you leave economic growth alone. The managers are powerful and charismatic, and they attract the workers because they can promise higher wages and a better standard of living.' If the contradictions in Yugoslav socialism render basic social problems unresolvable, then the two elite groups with firm bases of power and corresponding *modi operandi* — the old politicians and the new technocrats — will mount intense competition. They must appeal to the popular orientations we have already examined, especially the reversions to earlier, more severe expressions of Titoism. Although the battle may already have been joined, the outcome is not clear.

Who among us can claim to know how self-management should work in practice? After two decades of workers' councils, many Yugoslavs scoff at the idealistic foreigner who talks about equal participation. Who would you prefer to make the decisions in a hospital, they ask me, the surgeon or the janitor? Indeed, this is the conundrum of participatory democracy in a complex society. Perhaps in everyday life, where no particular expertise is needed, self-management works out differently.

6

PATTERNS OF PUBLIC INTERACTION

> Socialist humanism should be guided by a moral ideal —
> which was that of the early socialists — namely, the conception
> of a community of creative, equal, and self-governing indi-
> viduals, on a world scale; and at the same time by a scientific
> and experimental attitude toward social problems and toward
> social policies for the reform or replacement of social institutions.
>
> T. B. Bottomore,
> 'Industry, Work, Socialism'

Just as the ideology of self-management postulates an ideal of
universal political participation, so its orientation toward socialist humanism presupposes a certain norm of social interaction. Originating in Marx's vision of future society, the norm
of how communists treat their comrades is based on interdependence, mutual respect, and equality. In other words, this socialist ethic teaches both the collectivity and the objectivity of
human relations. First, as a collectivity, all comrades share the
social experience and hence the responsibility for its outcome.
They are obligated to work for the good of all, and the group
as a whole is obligated to take care of their individual needs.
Furthermore, in all objectivity, the needs, desires, and opinions
of one comrade count as much as the respective attributes of any
other comrade. Following logically from this, comrades who
have been reared by the socialist ethic should respect the persons
and personalities of their comrades. Mutual respect and mutual
responsibility should color all areas of social relations so that
comrades indeed become, in Bottomore's words, 'a community
of creative, equal, and self-governing individuals'.[1]

But what can 'self-governing' mean outside politics, particularly in the way people treat each other? Because this question
calls for some speculation, a socialist philosopher's description
of the self-governing individual may suggest a starting point.
Svetozar Stojanović, a philosophy professor at Belgrade Univer-

---

1 T. B. Bottomore, 'Industry, Work, and Socialism', in Erich Fromm,
ed., *Socialist Humanism* (Garden City, New York: Doubleday, Anchor
Books, 1966), p. 401.

sity, discusses the self-governing individual in terms of a 'demo-cratic-socialist character'.[2] In Stojanović's interpretation, such a character not only actualizes the Marxian socialist ethic, but it also manages implicitly to negate the behavior patterns associated with Stalinist and etatist phases of socialism, e.g. unthinking discipline, ignorance of individual and social rights, excessive legalism which conceals basic injustice. Speaking positively, however, 'the democratic-socialist character desires the synthesis of duty and right'. Just as he or she participates in making collective decisions, so he or she assumes the 'voluntary engagement of the personality in carrying out obligations to society'. Thus the norm of social action becomes 'personal self-initiating social engagement'. But this kind of social action must be carried out with full consciousness of the collectivity. 'Without *moral* concern and the responsibility of their members', Stojanović warns, 'these organs [of socialist democracy] may be turned into organized indifference and irresponsibility.'

Stojanović's interpretation of 'self-governing' turns on such terms as 'duty' and 'right', 'obligations', 'moral concern', and 'responsibility'. In his view, individuals must internalize these components of the socialist ethic to the extent that their commitment is self-initiating, i.e. requiring no outside force, no negative sanctions, no reward. In other words, the 'critical others' who initiate, monitor, and judge behavior are individuals, themselves. Moreover, they become in themselves a cybernetic mini-system, constantly adjusting their actions so that they not only accord with but also reflect the mores of the whole society. This other side of the self-governing individuals is just as important as their independence from external influences. Thus, the 'critical other' is more or less the voice of society transistorized into an inner ear.

ANALYTIC CONCEPTS

Once we understand this model, what sort of things do we look for in the way self-governing individuals treat each other? Such a question requires that we make some connection between politics and public interaction. Since Tocqueville, however, later and inferior work in this area has either shrouded itself in the veil of description, added to give color to straight analysis, or leaped

2 Stojanović, *Izmedju ideala i stvarnosti*, pp. 170–2.

prematurely out of the closet to expose something called national character. One might have thought — indeed hoped — that the scholars who developed the field of political culture would have trained their analytic sights on this ground so that by now there would be accepted lists of social concepts or categories to investigate in norms of public interaction. In lieu of such a model, several analytic concepts that these norms reflect might be helpful.

Looking at public behavior as a whole, we can ask whether the subjects seem to refer to certain others for guidance. (The concept of the 'critical other' has already appeared in the discussion of Stojanović's self-governing individual.) These others may shape behavior explicitly, as parents, teachers, and clerics intend to do by expostulation, or they may structure behavior through the control of positive rewards and negative sanctions, as bosses and, again, parents and teachers do. If the subjects have not internalized certain norms of public behavior and thus threaten to disrupt a particular situation, then others whose work depends upon their 'proper' functioning act as teachers, agents of socialization, or referees, for there are no critical others to moderate and control the threatening behavior. In the absence of a critical other, the Israeli sociologist Eisenstadt offers the example of the bus driver, who teaches newly-arrived immigrants how to behave as passengers: forming a line, paying the fare, refraining from unruliness, not annoying the driver.[3] Generally, the critical others impose their standards on the subjects so that these, in turn, respect certain proprieties of person, place, and time. We would expect to find them in several kinds of relationships with the subjects, e.g. giving the subjects negative sanctions, teaching the subjects, or being deferred to by the subjects. In such ways the critical others determine what behavior fits a situation, or what the relevant proprieties are. Stojanović indicates that the critical others in a self-managing society should be the society-in-each-self.[4]

The concept of propriety suggests in turn several other norms

3 E. Katz and S. N. Eisenstadt, 'Some Sociological Observations on the Responsibility of Israeli Organizations to New Immigrants', in S. N. Eisenstadt, *Essays on Comparative Institutions*, pp. 259–60.
4 The Soviets have developed several ways of institutionalizing the role of 'critical other', most durably, it seems, in the 'children's collective' of day-care centers and schools. Urie Bronfenbrenner, *Two Worlds of Childhood: U.S. and U.S.S.R.* (New York: Russell Sage Foundation, 1970), ch. 2.

of public behavior. Thus the observer could look for the degree of order upheld by behavior in various public situations. These situations may include an order of time (Is behavior based, say, on a first-come, first-served norm?), of space (Do subjects form lines?), of persons (Do they push and shove each other?), of noise (Do they talk loudly or softly in public?). These parenthetical questions only suggest the beginning of empirical inquiry. Furthermore, they do not imply that behavior in all public situations maintains the same degree or kind of order. For example, Englishmen waiting for a bus maintain a different degree of order than Englishmen playing rugby. Even in the same public situation, such as riding a train in Italy, the degree of order or noise, say, may vary according to the family and social class relations of the passengers. Moreover, the norms of public behavior certainly change over time, as the medieval practice of throwing garbage out the window or a comparison of the balcony and pit audiences today and in Shakespeare's time shows. Nevertheless, behavior in public situations as a whole creates an overall impression of the kind and degree of order that a society will not only tolerate but even regard as proper. The collectivity and objectivity of the socialist ethic imply a high degree of order founded on mutual deference rather than social hierarchy.

Another social concept reflected in public behavior is cooperation and its opposite side, competition. The observer could ask whether subjects work together easily for social goals, in business, and in all the little mutual accommodations that make life bearable. Or from another point of view, do the subjects seem to put themselves first, aiming toward self-advancement rather than amiability? A subtler distinction may be made if the subjects are cooperative in some kinds of situations but competitive in others. This poses the question of where competition rather than cooperation is not only legitimate but is the dominant norm. Moreover, the observer could go on to ask what the basis of this cooperative or competitive norm is. For instance, an American who resided for some time in Japan contrasts the cooperation of the home with the competition of the business world and even of driving in Tokyo traffic.[5] According to this author, Japanese drivers 'are reckless, totally lacking in driver courtesy, and simply do not know what they are doing . . . The "me-first" thrust

5 See Richard Halloran, *Japan: Images and Realities* (New York: Knopf, 1969), pp. 258–61.

of Japanese life comes fully to the surface.' Furthermore, Japanese drivers' recklessness and 'rudeness' never evoke negative sanctions from either the police or the courts or other drivers. The author suggests that the unbridled competition of driving is a consequence of the relative novelty of passenger cars in Japan. Because the overwhelming authority of custom has not yet grown up around driving, this is one area outside the tradition-oriented norms of cooperative public behavior. Self-managing society should provide a contrast to such norms, with all areas of social activity reflecting cooperation rather than egoistic competition.

A third concept involving the norms of public behavior is agreement, or the way in which mutual accommodations are made. Perhaps the form of public agreement which comes to our minds first is the business contract. Although economic development and its concomitant business forms have made contracts almost universal, not all societies place as much emphasis on their enumeration and execution as Americans do.[6] This in itself indicates something about public action. Besides the contract, two other ways of reaching agreements involve direct requests or orders and, as in Japanese life, custom. The observers could ask first how the subjects reach agreements about how to conduct public interaction, e.g. through contracts, orders, or custom.[7] Then they could examine adherence to the agreements reached, asking whether the subjects carry out the agreements unconditionally, or whether they defer to norms or to others outside the agreement situation. We would expect a self-managing society to make most agreements by a combination of all three forms, except that it would replace orders with requests and purge mutual accommodations of all elements of domination, coercion, and egotism.

A final concept in this brief outline of public behavior is responsibility. In many public interactions the observers should be able to determine for whom the subjects are assuming responsibility. According to the ideal of self-management, on the

6 According to Halloran, for example, the Japanese do not make explicit contracts at all. Ibid., pp. 153–6.
7 This is similar to Rigby's categorization of societies by modes of co-ordinating social activity, which is in turn based on Max Weber's typology of societies according to forms of domination. See T. H. Rigby, 'Traditional, Market, and Organizational Societies and the USSR', *World Politics* 16 (1964): 539–57.

one hand, the individual's public behavior reflects responsibility toward the society. On the other hand, in some other societies, the individuals may act as if they are responsible only to themselves, or to their immediate families, or to certain other persons in a quasi-feudal relationship. Let us consider a few familiar examples of particularistic responsibility. First, the capitalist business ethic, especially its 'dog-eat-dog' or 'cut-throat' competition, indicates that the responsibility of commercial actors is limited to their own firm. A second kind of 'exclusive' responsibility is responsibility to the immediate family, which shapes social interaction in face-to-face milieux such as those among southern Italians and Sicilians. Finally, responsibility or loyalty to individuals occurs in contemporary descriptions of gangs of teenagers as well as racketeers. But in contrast to these examples, subjects of the ideal self-managing society would show collectivistic responsibility, or responsibility to the whole society. They would actively and honestly participate in all public interaction. In no situations would they shirk this wide responsibility.

To review the discussion thus far, several analytic concepts that appear to be related to public behavior are

order (time, space, persons, noise);
cooperation (or competition);
agreement (contract, order, custom);
responsibility (individual, family, personal, social).

These concepts are neither exhaustive nor mutually exclusive. Indeed, a more elaborate statement would have to clarify the connections and the distinctions between them. But we can imagine that in the ideal self-managing society, the individual's public behavior would reflect concern for his comrades, responsibility toward the wide social order, respect for other persons and personalities, and a preference for agreement through cooperation. What I have found in Yugoslavia, and shall try to describe rather impressionistically here, is that norms of public behavior interpret these values so narrowly that they leave much to be desired between theory and practice.

Like political life, public life in Yugoslavia shows the influences of traditional face-to-face society, industrialization, and partial urbanization much more than any influence derived from socialist humanism. Yugoslav intellectuals do not deny this reality. They tend to blame current socio-economic conditions for

making it impossible to eliminate such behavioral traits as egotism, duplicity, and irresponsibility. According to Predrag Vranicki, a philosopher at Zagreb University,

> The occult power of the market and of money, and the
> hierarchy of status, are bound to have an alienating effect
> on the unstable structure of contemporary man . . . Ego-
> centricity, the division of the personality into an official and
> a private component . . . the *homo duplex* . . . the ef-
> fect of the external, the superficial, and the ephemeral in
> the form of the living standard, prestige, or only shallow
> amusement . . . The structure and physiognomy of con-
> temporary man is still primitive in many respects . . .[8]

The same line of analysis leads the Belgrade philosopher Stojanović to plead 'for *skromnost* [modesty or moderation], which
stands between asceticism and luxury based on a renascence of
the instinct (*nagon*) for possession, which is regenerated like the
hydra . . .'[9] Evidently, the society-in-each-self does not yet moderate conduct; thus, the self-managers adhere to more traditional
norms than those posed by the socialist ethic. Empirical observation should indicate how the actual norms compare to the ideal.

'CRITICAL OTHERS'

Persistent, methodical observation of Yugoslavs in the public
places of Belgrade forces an American to conclude that these
subjects respond to their own needs and desires rather than to
those of their comrades. Furthermore, there seems to be little
public presentation of self as we know it, for Yugoslavs in public situations create — and tolerate — a general disorder in which
proprieties of persons and places simply do not exist.[10] Those
who would try to enforce such proprieties, either by requests or
by negative sanctions, are regarded as introducing new, unnecessary restrictions on behavior, even as importing these restrictions
from the West. Most Yugoslavs either ignore or repulse the re-

8 Predrag Vranicki, 'Socialism and the Problem of Alienation', in Fromm,
  ed., *Socialist Humanism*, p. 311.
9 Stojanović, *Izmedju ideala i stvarnosti*, p. 172. Cf. Milovan Djilas,
  'Anatomy of a Moral', in *Anatomy of a Moral*, ed. Abraham Rothberg
  (New York: Praeger, 1959), pp. 145–76.
10 See Erving Goffman, *The Presentation of Self in Everyday Life*.

quests or sanctions that others, trying to become 'critical others', attempt. Thus the potential critical others who try to moderate public behavior bear the brunt of negative sanctions for disobeying the norms.

The emphasis on self-expression rather than self-control in public may uphold a traditional south Slavic value of fulfilling one's own needs. Perhaps the initial experience with this value occurs when parents indulge their children. As in many other societies, historically, Serbian and Montenegrin fathers rejoiced in the birth of sons to continue in their warrior avocations, especially because of their preoccupation with ending the Ottoman domination (from the fourteenth to the nineteenth century). This must have influenced the parents' attitude toward their children, particularly toward males. In addition, the Ottoman institution of *devshirme,* or the levy of one-fifth of their male children imposed on Christian subjects of the Empire every five years until 1676, probably also influenced the emotional tone of Serbian child-raising, although attitudes toward the *devshirme* and its certain outcome of high social status for the child thus taken into the administrative elite appear to have been ambivalent.[11] Whatever the historical causes, Serbian parents today demonstrate in various ways the high value in which they hold all their children. These ways include forms of physical and emotional fondling, the latter seen in the parents', especially the mother's, servitude to the children long past the time when they should be independent of parental aid. Within the home, parents are always giving and children receiving.

The major guise in which an outside, i.e. non-kin, observer enters the home is as a guest, and hospitality creates a situation in which the hosts and guests perpetuate the giving-receiving relationship. Serbian hospitality is much vaunted, especially by Serbs. Respondents and friends told me both obviously true and obviously apocryphal stories in which poor peasant hosts give either invited or unexpected guests the last crumb of bread, the slaughtered pig that they were saving to sell, or the richest yoghurt instead of the plain water that the guest requests. (Interestingly, all these examples of legendary hospitality seem to be drawn from the rural past rather than the urban present.) How-

11 L. S. Stavrianos, *The Balkans Since 1453* (New York: Holt, Rinehart and Winston, 1958), pp. 83ff.

ever, anyone who has been in the Serbian hospitality situation either repeatedly or over a long period of time realizes that definite rules of behavior and certain hidden motivations are involved.[12] Despite the hosts' protestations that they act only out of the joy of giving, Serbian hospitality expresses both the anticipation of reciprocity and the demonstration of social control. Where reciprocity is not immediately apparent, as, for example, when a peasant offers food to a foreign tourist driving through his village — although I suspect that this is a case which occurs less and less frequently, and not in my own experience — the reciprocal may be hidden in the past, e.g. the peasant host may feed a French tourist because the French were kind to him when he was there during World War I, or the host may be demonstrating one-up-manship to his neighbors. He does this in two ways, first by gaining the vicarious social prestige derived from a foreigner's presence in the home and then by retailing to his friends various bits of information that the foreigner has dropped in conversation. Furthermore, the force-feeding of guests, which prompted the anthropologist Hammel to compare Serbian hostesses with Jewish mothers, derives less from generosity than from a desire to control the guest and the whole hospitality situation. Demonstrating his ultimate control over the situation and independence from his guest, the host ostentatiously refuses any offer of payment for the fruits of hospitality. However, the host undoubtedly notes the refreshment and entertainment that the guest has consumed, calculates its value, and regards that obligation which the guest or his surrogate will someday repay as the basis of their relationship. Similarly, when grown-up children help their elderly parents financially, they may be considered as paying off an unstated primal debt. Yugoslavs have not yet cast off the responsibility of supporting elderly parents and relatives, although personal interaction, such as visits and letters, between well-to-do, well-educated urban residents and their 'country cousins' may be minimal.

To sum up our impressions, the unstinted giving of the parent or host is repaid by both the child's or the guest's recognition

12 For a similar description and analysis of this situation, see Eugene A. Hammel, 'The Jewish Mother in Serbia or *Les Structures alimentaires de la parenté*', in Kroeber Anthropological Society, *Essays in Balkan Ethnology*, Special Publications no. 1 (Berkeley, 1967), pp. 55–62.

of permanent obligation and his courteous adherence to the host's (or parent's) rules. So the host or parent who apparently caters to the guest or child actually controls the relationships within the home. In this way we can account for the contrast between parental indulgence of children on the one hand and, on the other, the autocratic authority that heads of households and enterprises have traditionally enjoyed — and still do.[13]

The main point here concerns the relationship with critical others. The order of the home, where subjects observe certain proprieties of persons, place, and noise, indicates that 'presentation of self' occurs more among familiars and close relatives than among strangers in public. Thus the familiars and close relatives make up the only critical others whose opinions moderate behavior. Influenced by their relationship with these critical others in the home, Yugoslavs probably come to depend on certain unstated aspects of their immediate social environment: mutual dependence and monitoring of behavior, great tolerance for egotistic pursuits, few or no negative sanctions, and a primal mutual debt or obligation. Yet when they leave the immediate milieu of familiars and enter the public domain, they refuse to recognize any critical others to check their behavior. Thus they do not bother to observe the proprieties that a public presentation of self entails. Their pushing and shoving to get into buses, for example, is an indication that they do not even conceive of a public self to defend from the onslaught of other bodies. Their public self is displayed at home rather than in public places. This behavioral norm contrasts with the Anglo-Saxon and, by extension, Western conception. According to the norm in our countries, persons are careful to present their selves and to respect other persons' selves in public places, but they 'relax' their guards and proprieties at home. The Yugoslav norm seems closer to Japanese and Arabic behavior than to ours. However, the lack of critical others outside the home may impede the development

13 See Vera St Erlich, *Family in Transition* (Princeton University Press, 1966); Branislav Čukić, *Radne i samoupravne uloge u industrijskom preduzeću* [Work and self-management roles in an industrial enterprise] (Belgrade: Institut društvenih nauka, 1968); and Božo Jušić, 'Autokratski i demokratski način rukovodjenja u samoupravljanju' [The autocratic and democratic way of leading in self-management], in Jovo Brekić, ed., *Organizacija rada u samoupravnim odnosima* [The organization of work in self-managing relations] (Zagreb: Narodne novine, 1970), pp. 427–41.

of the kind of public self — responsible, considerate — that socialist self-management requires.[14]

Yugoslavs recognize few surrogates for critical others in public situations. In several cases of pushing in buses and on the
street, for example, I attempted to give negative sanctions by
reprimanding the offender or by asking him about his conduct.
The subject who had offended norms that I considered proper
evidently felt that he had not misbehaved, for he either ignored
me or cursed me. Furthermore, I never observed other pedes-
trians, passengers, or bystanders trying to moderate behavior in
a similar way. This situation indicates either a lack of development of critical others, as in some nonurban societies, or a de-
generation of the norm, as in some American cities.

As the sociologist Eisenstadt has pointed out, bureaucrats and
other (uniformed) officials often socialize their organizations'
new clients into behavioral norms. Although his example of the
bus driver holds true to a point in Yugoslavia, Belgrade bus
drivers' requests and admonitions to their passengers, usually to
move back in the bus (*'Samo malo, samo malo'*: 'Just a little'),
do not evoke much compliance. Only on long-distance, i.e. inter-
city, buses do the passengers heed the conductor by respecting
the moving and breathing space of their fellow passengers. However, the duration of the inter-city bus ride may create a pseudo-
familiar atmosphere in which the same riders have to travel in
close, even face-to-face, proximity for an extended time. During
the longer ride, the other passengers take on the force of critical
others and proprieties must be observed. Also, the transportation
organization itself establishes certain norms which create order
for the inter-city bus ride. One of these norms, for example, is
that bus tickets are sold for definite seats. Thus a reservation
guarantees that the passenger will have a seat, i.e. a set amount of
space which 'belongs' to him. Often more tickets are sold than
there are seats in the bus, but in that case the organizational
norm assures that pushing leads to no reward. Indeed, people
who buy these 'extra' tickets may be told in advance that they
will have to stand.

A more successful surrogate for the critical other in public
situations is the waiter in a *kafana* or cafe. The convivial at-

14 Similarly, see Horvat, *An Essay on Yugoslav Society*, pp. 217–20. Cf.
Hall, *The Hidden Dimension*, chs. 11–12.

mosphere which first strikes the casual foreign visitor yields upon more detailed observation to an impression of general disorder. Perhaps the Serbian *kafana,* traditionally a bastion of male society, is a place where men 'relax' their inhibitions and release behavior which would offend their familiars at home.[15] At home, for example, no one sings or talks loudly, everyone eats when the mother or hostess offers food and eats what she offers and, since space is at a premium, no one litters. In a *kafana,* however, the patrons shout across tables and sing as they drink. Most patrons order *rakija* (brandy), which at home is restricted to ceremonial occasions or entertaining. Furthermore, Serbs follow the 'picturesque' custom of dashing their liquor glasses against the wall only in public, that is, in *kafanas,* for such behavior would be unthinkable at home.[16] But this custom finds its parallel in the tradition of clinking liquor glasses together after making a toast — which is properly done at home, not in public.

A Yugoslav journalist writing about *kafanas* in *NIN,* the Belgrade weekly news magazine, calls attention to additional norms of public behavior which admit proprieties of neither place nor order. According to his account, the Serbian *kafana* is a place where people can escape outside their selves — can be free from presenting a self — without fear of sanctions or consequences. Thus, the *kafana* is decorated and arranged 'so that the guest is psychologically strengthened in the belief that, whatever his (aggressive) behavior, he will not be brought into greater material injury'. In this way, the Serbian *kafana* is diametrically opposed to the Viennese-type cafe, which 'subsumes a whole series of obligations' from its patrons. The Yugoslav reporter says, 'In [Viennese cafes] one categorically cannot, say, sing, for this disturbs those who are reading newspapers (and newspapers are, as you know, not only part of the atmosphere, but also part of the inventory of a Viennese cafe). It's obvious: here there are few of those who read newspapers in *kafanas,* and many of those who go out to a *kafana* to sing!' In other words, the Serbian *kafana* is not a place for calm newspaper reading, thinking, or otherwise intellectualizing. Rather, it is a place for letting loose. Moreover, the reporter also makes the comparison between *kafana* norms

15 I have heard of a women's *kafana,* apparently a rarity, in the Serbian town of Kruševac.
16 Who knows what the political significance of this glass-breaking could be? After all, the Greek government banned such behavior in public in 1966.

and the norms of behavior in other public places, for the *kafana* patron 'behaves the same as on the street or in the bus: he does not take off his coat, he sits down at a table with complete strangers, shakes his cigarette ash off on the floor and the like'. Thus *kafana* behavior, like the street and bus behavior, tends to disregard the proprieties of order and mutual consideration.[17]

In my experience, the only 'other' to try to moderate *kafana* behavior is the waiter. Like the bus conductor or driver, he assures a minimal degree of order. Although the waiter does ask disorderly drunks to leave and loud singers to lower their voices, he never initiates such a request. Instead, he usually waits until another patron in the *kafana* complains about the behavior. Only then does he request that the offender change his seat or lower his tone. Furthermore, the waiter's requests are usually mild in manner. If the unruly patron is obstreperous and persists in unruly behavior, then the waiter either leaves him alone or appeals to the patron's friends to calm him down. So even the waiter is reluctant to be a critical other. Yet in the *kafana* only he attempts the role. Just as it is sheer folly for one passenger to try to reprove another passenger's shoving on the bus, so it is worthless for one patron to try to control another patron's behavior in the *kafana*. For example, one afternoon I was drinking coffee with a Serbian man at an outdoor *kafana* associated with a good Belgrade restaurant. Another patron, sitting at an adjacent table with his wife, turned up the volume on his portable tape recorder so that a Serbian folk song blared out for several minutes. Because this annoyed my Yugoslav friend (who spends most of his time in England) and me, he took steps to stop the noise. Rather than approach the offender directly, he called the waiter over, brought the loud music to his attention — for the waiter, like everyone else, has a certain inattention vis-à-vis the public behavior of others — and requested that he ask the other patron to lower the volume. This brief conversation occurred within four feet of the offender, whose wife noticed that we were annoyed. When she tried to get him to lower the volume, he rejected her appeal. Then, when the waiter made his request, he roared indignantly, 'This is a public place: Let 'er rip! (*Pusti*

---

17 Bogdan Tirnanić, 'Fajront za jednu mehanu' [Farewell to a tavern], *NIN*, 17 January 1971, pp. 37–8. Cf. the (polite) norms which apparently govern behavior in West European sidewalk cafes, in Joseph Wechsberg, 'The Sidewalk Cafe, a Flower in Europe's Streets, is Fading', *New York Times*, 12 March 1972.

ga!)' This appears to sum up a significant norm of Yugoslav public behavior.

Whether the subjects show indulgence (of parents toward children), tolerance (of friends toward social deviants like drunkards), or laxness (in buses or *kafanas*), their reluctance to act in public as critical others indicates that the ideal norms of self-management have not yet affected everyday life. As Stojanović says, the most elaborate sets of written rules cannot compensate for people's unwillingness to get involved. If Yugoslavs are unwilling to adopt — and respect — a public self, then the institutions of self-management remain limited in scope.

Aside from buses and *kafanas,* there are many more areas of public behavior where Yugoslavs simply do not assume the responsibility of critical others. These areas, centering on social and business agreements which involve an exchange of goods or services, reflect a norm of *korupcija,* or corruption. Although the Yugoslav government and press recognize that corruption is a widespread social problem, involving individuals in all social strata and all organizations, neither official agencies nor private citizens are willing to interfere in the illicit transactions. Of course, social factors have influenced the development of the various forms of corruption. First, illicit purveyors of certain goods or services, e.g. apartments, jobs, telephone hook-ups, do fulfill a need for these items. Second, as the respondent Milovan Vuković pointed out, the rapid elevation of untrained, ex-Partisan peasants to positions of executive responsibility after the war altered these men's expectations so that they started to live above their salaries and were then willing to cheat a little here and there to get it.[18]

Still, the forms of corruption are so varied and the norm so pervasive that they threaten the development of a self-managing consciousness. A recent series of articles by *Politika*'s investigative reporter Žika Živulović-Serafim documents the assertion that corruption pervades the private, public, and political spheres of interaction. Providing a multitude of factual examples, such as bribing an official or an old tenant to get an apartment, paying

18 Cf. Steven J. Staats, 'Corruption in the Soviet System', *Problems of Communism* 21, no. 1 (January–February 1972): 40–7. Also, Dankwart A. Rustow points out that few new governments 'can fully cope with the supposedly minimal functions of the nineteenth century "night watchman" state in Europe'. *A World of Nations* (Washington, D.C.: The Brookings Institution, 1967), p. 75.

a handyman a bonus above the cost of his work so that he will complete the job promptly, price-fixing and pocket-lining in business, encroachment on state forest land for personal use, bribing official inspectors and judges, Serafim and other reporters illuminate a society where nothing seems to function, nothing is produced, and nothing is sold except through illicit agreements. Another *Politika* reporter corroborates Serafim's picture, describing an 'atmosphere that everything is tolerated and allowed' because the 'legitimate' person is the one who ' "gets along", no matter how'. As Serafim's butcher says in the folk idiom, 'Round and round, at the little door, with the little man. Where it's thin, that's where it crumbles.' [19]

The motivation behind corruption suggests self-interest rather than self-management. Serafim suggests that the extent of corruption in Yugoslavia is related to the economic situation. 'What is happening before our eyes?' he asks. 'Are we in a position to state that in the people there is growing ever greater assurance that money is all-powerful, that it can open all doors, resolve all problems, buy conscience? Obviously, a [certain] psychology is being realized en masse.' Aside from economic causes, Serafim and other journalists blame the people themselves. In institutions like workers' councils, according to Serafim, they condone and cover up corruption in 'the interest of the work organization'. As individuals, too, they become passive collaborators in corruption because, knowing about such behavior, they refuse to censure it. 'We all constantly keep our eyes closed', says a popular Belgrade columnist writing about corruption, 'and we all think — let someone else do it.' As in other countries, this appears to be the attitude toward crimes against property. An American journalist recently reported, for example, how a man stole a car in broad daylight on Terazija, Belgrade's busiest intersection, in the unquestioned but unquestioning sight of hundreds of passers-by. Even the Serbian town of Svetozarevo has evidently given up on deterrence and negative sanctions, for the authorities there abolished a real estate law that no one seemed to obey.[20]

19 Žika Živulović-Serafim, 'Serafim istražuje korupciju' [Serafim investigates corruption], *Politika*, 7–14 January 1971; Vojislav Lalić, 'Zakoni: Sporovozna rešenja' [Laws: Conflicting resolutions], *NIN*, 25 April 1971, p. 15; Slavoljub Čukić, 'Društvena hronika: Nedelja borbe protiv — korupcije' [Social chronicle: A week of battle against — corruption], *Politika*, 24 January 1971, p. 9.
20 Yug Grizelj, 'Ti, ja i korupcija' [You, me and corruption], *Večernje novosti*, 10 December 1970, p. 5; Alfred Friendly, Jr, 'Belgrade is Mak-

Patterns of public interaction

Paradoxically, the institutions — notably the court system — that Yugoslavia has established, which have prompted at least one foreign observer to see the country as 'a communist *Rechtstaat*', have not yet engendered a rule of law. First of all, most ordinary Yugoslavs do not believe that court action will resolve their disputes. Lower-class and working-class people in particular are loath to get a lawyer and go to court. Although state-subsidized legal aid is available, these social strata are much less likely than the educated middle classes to seek a legal resolution. Instead, they tend to send pleas directly to political figures or union leaders, such as Tito, who have no jurisdiction to intervene. Furthermore, Yugoslavs of all social strata do not generally believe that court judgments are enforceable. This cynicism appears to be based in fact, as, for example, enterprises which are ordered by the court to rehire an illegally-fired worker usually ignore the court order. Especially in the enterprise, the legal and quasi-legal systems for redress of grievances seem to set the burden of proof on the individual plaintiff, who is often a manual worker; to emphasize informal 'diplomacy' rather than public, collective bargaining; and to fail to enforce decisions — such as may be obtained in the courts — against the management. Thus in the legal and quasi-legal spheres of public interaction also, formal institutions and official ideology cannot fill the traditional lack of critical others. In their absence, certain 'leading cadres' appear willing to exercise functions of arbitrary judgment and to reserve the right to dissociate themselves from the consequences.[21]

So the refusal to act as a critical other in public situations has social consequences more serious than pushing in buses and singing in *kafanas*. Although financial transactions, such as bribes

ing an Extra Effort to Hold Down Its Two Summertime Pests — Mosquitoes and Burglars', *New York Times*, 22 August 1971, p. 13; and Slavoljub Čukić, 'Vreme sadašnje: Upoznaj (ako stigneš) zakon svoj' [The current time: Get to know your own law (if you can)], *Politika*, 22 November 1970, p. 7.

21 Although this section is based on Slovenian and Croatian data on labor disputes, it seems to indicate the general situation. I am grateful to Professor Rudi Kyovsky of the Institute on Labor Law at the Law Faculty of Ljubljana University for information drawn from *Udeljavljanje pravic delavčev v delovnem razmerju*, 19 vols. (Ljubljana: Institut za javno upravo in delovna razmerju, 1966). See also Josip Županov, 'Two Patterns', pp. 222–3. Cf. Winston M. Fisk, 'A Communist *Rechtstaat?* — The Case of Yugoslav Constitutionalism', *Government and Opposition* 5, no. 1: 41–53.

and graft, do not occur on the same scale as in a rich country like America, several factors make the problem of corruption even more worrisome in Yugoslavia. First, the country *is* poor. Thus the dinars spent to assure a desired flow of goods and services could be better used in investment or construction. Also, many people who need vital goods and jobs are not only too poor, but they lack the *veze* (connections) to get them illicitly. Another reason why the problem of corruption is so important is that neither individuals nor institutions, e.g. workers' councils, legislatures, or communal and municipal agencies, have shown the necessary willingness and the moral force to censure illicit behavior. Thus there are no critical others to turn public behavior in the direction of mutual responsibility. Moreover, since everyone expects irresponsible behavior, everyone acts irresponsibly: the expectation and the norm are mutually fulfilling. This indicates a third reason why the problem is significant. Because public behavior runs counter to the official ideology, it denigrates and threatens the promise of self-management. The official ideology depends on mutual help, moral concern, and responsibility for self and others. So everyday behavior must reinforce the official ideology to make socialist self-management a realistic goal. Otherwise, as in the United States in recent years, the distance between official ideology and public behavior, particularly of officials, creates a climate of disbelief which makes effective collective action problematic.

The expectation of selfish behavior, double-dealing, and unenforceable agreements may also have serious repercussions on the country's national unity when different ethnic groups are involved. For example, according to a Slovenian sociologist, altercation of this type recently soured relations between the republics of Serbia and Slovenia. Enterprises in the two republics had concluded an agreement that the Slovenes would build a large industrial development in Serbia. Because this was to be an expensive undertaking, the Slovenian enterprises carefully calculated and planned their needs for several years in advance. Furthermore, they gradually changed their organization and supply system to fit these needs. A year or two passed during which the Slovenes did not hear from the Serbian parties. When they managed to contact them, the Serbian enterprises admitted that, after signing the contract with the Slovenes, they had awarded the job over again — to Serbian enterprises. This case represented a great financial loss to the Slovenian enterprises. However, they did not try to take the Serbs to court because there is no belief that a court decision, especially across republican lines, will ever be enforced. Cases like this, involving the republics' inability to work together and to trust each other, pose a threat to Yugoslavia's tenuous unity. One would think that the norms of self-managing behavior, e.g. mutual responsibility and interdependence, could overcome traditional ethnic misunderstandings, rooted in different norms and differing expectations of behavior. But traditional behavior prevails. As a Belgrade sociologist comments privately, the Serbs act out their frustrations much more readily than do the Croats or the Slovenes. So these ethnic groups always feel thwarted in their dealings with Serbs, individually as well as collectively. Until this pattern, and the expectation of this pattern, changes, the ethnic nationalities will continue to dispute matters of territory and finance. Despite differences in values and history, the ethnic groups could establish common ground for working together by adhering to and enforcing the norms of self-managing behavior. Not least among these would be the willingness to assume the role of critical other.

BUREAUCRACY AND BUREAUCRATS

Although Yugoslavs appear reluctant to act as critical others in most public situations, they assume the roles of bureaucrats with alacrity. Unfortunately, however, the bureaucratic mentality which goes along with these roles is incompatible with self-management. Over the past twenty years, the official ideology has constantly attacked bureaucracy, bureaucratism, and etatism, and to be called a bureaucrat in one of Tito's speeches is still a damaging epithet. Slowly but surely, decentralization and direct democracy are supposed to purge Yugoslavia of bureaucratic bureaucrats, those reactionary opponents to liberalization and progress. Yet in all situations where Yugoslav officials of 'service' organizations have to deal with Yugoslav clients, they maintain a bureaucratic attitude which negates the official ideology.

Perhaps the readiness with which Yugoslavs still assume a bureaucratic mentality is related to the high social status that clerks (*činovniks*) and administrators have traditionally enjoyed. Another reason might be that bureaucrats, especially those who deal with the public, can legitimately establish control over their clients' behavior, at least within the bureaucratic situation. In this context, they are both distant from and superior to their clients.

Participant-observation in these situations documents the bureaucratic mentality. In one case we see a college student assuming a bureaucratic role vis-à-vis his fellow students. As a student-monitor in Belgrade's liberal arts college, a student often guards the door between the second-floor hallway and the administrative wing where the secretaries work. Unlike the free access of American colleges, the student-monitor controls who may go in to see the secretaries and who may not. Some days the student-guard keeps a line of students waiting to get in because, as he tells them, everyone from the offices is at a meeting. After a couple of hours, he announces that the meeting will continue indefinitely, so office hours for the day are cancelled. That meetings are held during working-time is symptomatic of the bureaucratic mentality, for they prevent clients from getting access to officials. Ironically, Yugoslavs report that the topic of many such meetings is 'How to prevent the loss of working-time'. Another aspect of the over-bureaucratization of this situation is that no one remains in the office to deal with clients who have urgent problems. Finally, we could note the continuation of a traditional role in Balkan bureaucracy, that of the doorkeeper (*vratar*), who accentuates the distance and enforces the separation between officials and clients.

Another example of the way in which employees establish their independence from clients occurs in the situation when a customer tries to buy something. Often the clerk whose function is to sell the stock — even at a newsstand — makes the customer wait while he or she lengthily rearranges it on the counter. Thus there is little idea of 'service' in a service bureaucracy. This does not seem traceable to the belief that socialism 'kills the profit motive', for at least two reasons. First, under workers' self-management, the clerks and all other employees have an economic interest in selling their product. Second, the lack of 'service' accords with the traditional south Slavic interpretation of the bureaucrat's role, which seems to act as a model of organizational behavior. Yet at other times the service bureaucracy can be much more personalistic than a Westerner would expect. Even in Belgrade, a capital city of over 1,000,000 inhabitants, the Yugoslav Air Line may delay an international flight for half an hour because a couple who hold tickets have not yet checked in, and another passenger thinks that he has spotted them at the airport. The couple are paged several times over the loudspeaker. The other passengers and the stewardesses wait in good humor and, when the missing couple finally arrives, they cheer them.

Behavior like this, falling into the arbitrary extremes of either impersonality or personalism, indicates that Yugoslav bureaucracy is still irrational. Thus it adds to the insecurity bred by the general disorder in public situations as well as the frequent political reorganizations. Often, the distance between officials and clients increases citizens' and workers' alienation from the political system; obviously, it negates the idea of self-management. It is interesting that all the Yugoslav republics apparently suffer from the same bureaucratic mentality. For example, according to a survey conducted by Zagreb sociologist Pavle Novosel, Croatian citizens expect the government bureaucracy to act both personally and irrationally. A majority of the Croats indicated that they would expect worse treatment than others get from the public servants. Only a handful believe that a citizen can count on fair treatment if he has no personal or family *veze* (connections) to help him, and very few think that a civil servant would go so far as to consider their point of view if they tried to explain it to him. The Croats express similar opinions about the fairness of police behavior.[22] All in all, the persistence of the bureaucratic mentality does not further the development of self-managing consciousness and behavior.

'A SCIENTIFIC AND EXPERIMENTAL ATTITUDE'

According to Bottomore's description of socialist humanism, self-managers should have 'a scientific and experimental attitude toward social problems'. Yet in everyday life and work, Yugoslavs resist and even discourage efforts to find new solutions to social problems. Quite simply, innovators and inventors often get no rewards for their discoveries and suggestions. This is true not only of people who discover new products or invent new devices,

22 Pavle Novosel, 'Politička kultura u S. R. Hrvatskoj' [Political culture in S. R. Croatia], mimeographed (Zagreb, 1969), pp. 28–31. These observations should not be understood as a 'civic culture' argument, for similar behavior occurs in all bureaucratic systems, where people have devices for defending themselves from arbitrary applications of rules. This behavior, in contrast to 'the law', soon becomes 'the norm'.

but also of innovators who introduce new methods of work. Such behavior is counter-productive vis-à-vis two major societal goals — self-management and economic development.

In an essay on the 'egalitarian syndrome' and the 'anti-initiative mentality', sociologist Josip Županov says that attitudes from the pre-industrial past prevent Yugoslavs from developing new, productive patterns of behavior.[23] Like traditional peasants, according to Županov, Yugoslavs stubbornly resist innovation. They tend to think that the pace of change in recent years has accelerated too quickly. Despite the fact that many reorganizational schemes are carried out only on paper, Yugoslavs apparently resent the sheer volume of changes they have been forced to absorb. To illustrate his point, Županov cites cases in which innovative directors have aroused the censure and acrimony of their employees as a whole and of the workers' council in particular. One case, for example, concerns the director of Niš-Express, a transport company in southern Serbia, who instituted express buses for long-distance hauls. The workers' council removed him from his position, but a referendum of all the workers reinstated him. Someone then threw him bodily through the fence of the enterprise property. So much ill-feeling resulted that the director had to leave.

As Županov sees it, Yugoslavs structure the situation so that there is little or no reward for innovation. Because economically profitable innovation is, in effect, censured, societal goals like technological development and market success remain mere slogans. Furthermore, this situation gives the lie to the 'scientific and experimental attitude' which is supposed to develop under socialist humanism. This in turn defeats the creativity that self-management demands. As long as the official ideology sanctions material incentives, but norms in everyday situations of life and work fail to reward initiative, theory recedes further from practice.

In contrast to public behavior, models of ideal, 'self-managing' citizens continue to appear in the press and in the speeches of political leaders. The Yugoslav leadership does not utilize the mass media to inculcate official ideology as heavily as some other governments, such as the Chinese, do. But every few days, a didactic 'success' or 'failure' story is published which serves to un-

23 Josip Županov, 'Industrijalizam i egalitarizam' [Industrialism and egalitarianism], *Sociologija* 12, no. 1 (1970): 31–5.

derline behavior that the leadership feels contributes to economic and political development. 'Success stories' of this type generally affirm the norms that we have related to self-management and socialist humanism: responsibility, moral concern, and innovation. Thus we find at random in the Belgrade *Politika* human-interest stories about a profitable salami factory, a sympathetic social worker, and the upwardly mobile sons of workers in a certain mine.

While Županov's essay cites behavior which defeats professional innovation, the article about the salami factory lauds the expertise of the factory director, who has written a dissertation about dehydration and other factors related to the quality and durability of winter salami. The reporter writes, 'Thanks to the contribution of the experts from [this factory], salami production has passed from narrow pragmaticist decision making to the sure control of professionals.' The story about the social worker contrasts with another aspect of public behavior that we have examined: the official-client relationship. Rather than assume the usual bureaucratic role in this situation, a young female social worker shows a high degree of commitment to people in general and to her clients in particular. She tells the interviewer, for example, how she got money for a poor mother to bury her dead baby, how she approved foster parents for adopting a child, and how she coaxed an armed youth out of the house where he had barricaded himself. The third 'success story' recounts the social rise of the sons of a group of miners. As engineers and technicians, the sons replaced the foreign experts who had directed their fathers' mine when it was first founded. An engineer son says, 'That was our father's life's dream: to send us both to school! He took from his mouth . . . Afterwards a scholarship came along and removed that enormous weight from his shoulders.' In this minimal Horatio Alger story, the norm of responsibility dominates the account of the sons' relationship to their father, his ambitions and sacrifice for them, and — as a matter of national pride — the development of native professional cadres.[24]

24 R. Ranković, 'Kad proizvodnja i nauka idu ukorak: "Jugoslovenski tip" zimske salame' [When production and science march in step: 'Yugoslav type' of winter salami], *Politika*, 26 October 1970, p. 9; Vuk Trnavski, 'Priča socijalnog radnika: Milica i tri njena slučaja' [Story of a social worker: Milica and three of her cases], *Politika*, 10 November

'A scientific and experimental attitude'

The use of the mass media to promote such norms indicates that self-management in everyday behavior remains an ideal rather than a reality. Through observation and newspaper-reading, we have noted how behavior in public places contradicts self-management in at least three ways. First, the reluctance to act as critical others or to accept the authority of those persons and institutions which assume the role of critical others seems to impede the development of a nontraditional type of social responsibility. Second, the persistence of a bureaucratic mentality perpetuates discrimination, callousness, and feelings of inferiority in the relationship between officials and clients. Third, resistance to innovation aborts the 'scientific and experimental attitude' which should be part of socialist humanism. It is understandable that economic exigencies and priorities on the one hand, and the norms of traditional, face-to-face Yugoslav society on the other, contribute to the difficulty of raising behavior to the ideal level. Nevertheless, we should not shrink from trying to make a 'progress report' at this time, two decades after the introduction of self-management as a sweeping ideology, a political system, and, not least, a behavioral model. With this in mind I have introduced the official ideology of self-management and, in contrast to this theory, the practice of ordinary Yugoslavs going about their business, or 'self-managing'. Before coming to any conclusions about the separation of theory from practice, it would be useful to look at some constrictions on contemporary behavior set by traditional norms.

1970, p. 7; Vuk Trnavski, 'Sto godina "Kostolca": Sinovi kostolačkih rudara' [100 years of Kostolac: Sons of the Kostolac miners], *Politika*, 4 November 1970, p. 7.

7
CULTURAL PARAMETERS OF
YUGOSLAV SOCIETY

> If we're asked for justifications, we've got them: We have little
> knowledge, an Oriental mentality; We're still a culturally
> underdeveloped society; It's difficult for us to drag ourselves
> out of the bureaucratic mentality of togetherness; We're not
> rich enough to give a chance to those who are looking for one;
> We change everything too fast to retain the necessity of methodi-
> cal work and great passion.
>
> Života Djordjević,
> 'Zrelo i zeleno groždje',
> *NIN*, 15, August 1971,

From a survey of current behavior patterns, it seems as though
the historically-determined situations into which the Yugoslav
peoples have been thrust — especially peasant society and colonial domination — continue to structure their perceptions and
their norms. Indeed, the self-concepts and explanations to which
all the Yugoslav national minorities subscribe indicate their origins in the presocialist past. By continually citing their 'cultural
underdevelopment', 'Oriental mentality', and 'bureaucratic mentality', Yugoslavs suggest that the social reality in which they live
owes more to a pervasive, traditional culture than to an intensive, official ideology. Nevertheless, it is not only the weight of
the past which makes the learning of new behavior problematic.
Several other factors complicate the current situation: the paradox of trying to institutionalize a revolutionary peasant tradition,
the task of inculcating norms which logically contradict those of
the traditional base, and the inherent conflict between certain
norms of two basic areas of the new culture — industrialism and
socialism. Moreover, the development of a new culture to match
the official ideology of self-management might have consequences
for the social system which would not be acceptable to the political leadership.

This sort of discussion assumes that culture plays an important
role in linking conduct, morality, and social structure. Indeed,

in a broad sense, culture sets parameters for the establishment, the justification, and the continuity of all forms of social life. For a given group of people, culture acts to define and to typify the various kinds of social situations which are historically encountered, to codify the responses which are judged appropriate to these social situations, to symbolize the patterns set up in these situations, to legitimize and to perpetuate these patterns.[1]

First of all, culture represents a means of sifting through the myriad details of shared historical experiences and extracting common factors relevant to their definition. The most basic use of this sort of sifting is probably found in the definition of various kinds of social situations, e.g. the culturally-defined 'situation' of a people, or a nation. In this sense, the legends, customs, and traditions of a culture define the people who will form a 'society'. Not only does culture act upon social situations in this way but it emerges itself from these situations, for society also produces the legends, customs, and traditions of 'culture'.

Culture also defines the actions and the interactions appropriate to various social situations. Patterns of behavior are set up, for example, in encounters between men and women, among men and among women, between enemies, and between persons and gods. In the process of integrating these patterns of behavior with current experience, culture also offers a framework for developing symbols which make the patterns familiar. So the culturally recognized healer or doctor may wear a special mask or a uniform which sets that person apart from other individuals. The mask symbolizes the healer's special abilities and the healer's obligation to act — and to be responded to — in a certain way in certain social situations. Over time, the symbols come to entail several consequences, such as the rendering of deference or tribute to their bearers and the establishment of an office or an institution associated with the symbol-bearers, the symbols themselves, and the patterns of behavior that they originally symbolized. Furthermore, the symbols eventually spawn their own symbols through the rituals of language and etiquette. In this way, the culture socializes everyone into a more or less coherent image of society and of self in society.

1 Cf. Clyde Kluckhohn, 'The Concept of Culture', in *Culture and Behavior*, ed. Richard Kluckhohn (New York: Free Press, 1962), pp. 19–73. See also Hans Gerth and C. Wright Mills, *Character and Social Structure* (New York: Harcourt, Brace and World, 1953).

The social behavior and the self-image enacted by cultural symbols and rituals may outlive the existence of the original symbols. After the stone tablets crumble and the patriarch's staff splinters, the behavior and the images that they had legitimated are transferred to new office-holders and new followers. In this sense, it is obvious that ceremonial obeisance to a leader is intimately related to political obedience to a ruler. Similarly, deferential patterns of behavior associated with social stratification may also be related to deference to political power or to political authority. Socially established and culturally enshrined, such patterns of behavior may last a long time. They may even outlast the ideology within which they originally developed. Thus, even under socialist self-management we may find patterns of behavior associated with earlier forms of authoritarianism. In some cases, such norms may be considered theoretically undesirable but practically necessary; in other cases, people may see no theoretical objections to these norms, but they may find them personally unpalatable. In any case, people will find relevant models for their positions in the cultural past.

As the examination of public behavior indicated, observers of socialist development should be concerned with the relative strength of such patterns as deference and authority, rationality and superstition, innovation and conformity, collectivism and individualism, honesty and chicanery. An analysis of cultural models, symbols, and self-images related to these patterns should suggest some parameters of socialist development.

MODELS AND NORMS

For a period of guerrilla war and sustained self-sacrifice, the Yugoslav, especially the Serbian, past offers relevant models of cultural response. *Borba,* or 'struggle', has a specific historical content in the continued Serbian rebellion (1389–1878) against foreign domination, which has given *borbenost* (the quality of being able to fight or struggle) a traditionally positive value. So the Partisan movement of the 1940s can trace its inspiration to the Serbian *borac* (fighter, in the heroic sense). In view of their strong identification with the past, Yugoslavs were probably drawn to the Partisan effort as would-be *borci*. Just as the cultural model of the *borac* glorified self-sacrifice for the collective good, so the *borac's* historical alter-ego, the *hajduk* (highway-man), justified plunder as an expression of anti-Ottoman, anti-state, and anti-authoritarian resistance. During the nineteenth century, many tribes of *hajduks* came down from their mountain lairs to join with local chieftains and warrior priests in rebellion against the Ottomans. Thus the people tended to interpret the *hajduks'* mode of behavior as another aspect of *borbenost* and immortalized them, with the *borci,* in epics and ballads.

After the Partisans had utilized the cultural model of the *borac-hajduk,* the postwar leadership had to face the problem of adapting it to peacetime conditions. The leaders attempted to institutionalize the revolutionary, peasant tradition by concep-tualizing the self-manager as a *borac,* or fighter, for societal goals. This adaptation fits rather well within the generally-accepted scenario of the fight for communism in an underdeveloped coun-try: collective deprivation, mass egalitarianism and mass con-formity, satisfaction of the basic needs for physical and psycho-logical security. But when the Yugoslav leaders changed the premises of the script to economic individualism, noncoercive mobilization, and social differentiation, the people found that the *borac-hajduk* model was no longer salient. In the new context of self-management and market socialism, the cultural model became a rhetorical figure. Ordinary Yugoslavs could easily find the irony implicit in the leadership's call to 'continue the strug-gle' when many objective conditions pointed the way to a con-sumer society dominated by political experts or technocrats. If the cultural model of the Serbian past was to be relevant to the Yugoslav future, then could there be a white-collar *borac?* The Yugoslav leaders hope that there can be. With that adaptation in mind, they find fault with much current behavior.

Not only the leadership, but also the mass media, social critics, and ordinary Yugoslavs find fault with the modal personality type which apparently thrives in the current social reality. This type personifies certain problems inherent in the attempt to build a modern Western culture upon a traditional, Balkan peasant base. In the absence of a reward system based on either sacred lineage or demonstrated merit, conformity and cronyism become the means of advancement. Consequently, individuals become extremely knowledgeable about the process of making a career without also acquiring the substantive training to function successfully in new positions of responsibility. They are political rather than politicized. Much in the manner of horseplayers analyzing the scratch sheet, they are calculating, but because they lack control over the outcome of the situation on which they lay stakes, they do not have to develop norms of efficiency, innovation, and methodical work. The fact that they regard their wins or losses as the result of forces beyond their control also permits them a relatively guiltless escape from responsibility for how the race is run.

With some exaggeration, this analogy fits the condemnations that many Yugoslavs hurl at their own society. Although the political leadership, economists and executives, and sociologists prefer to ascribe the negative qualities that they find all too prevalent in Yugoslavia to the persistence of a peasant mentality, we might alternatively posit some connection between current social conditions and the type of behavior that they decry. Despite the convenience of blaming the past for present behavior, there must be some relationship between the modal personality type and actual norms, between current practice and current theory.

Essentially, the problem can be traced to an incompatibility between the two basic areas of Yugoslav self-management: their norms, their ideological interpretations, their principles of organization. As I have indicated throughout this book, the Yugoslavs are suffering through a conflict between industrialism and socialism and between the principles of hierarchy and equality. In the early postwar period of mass deprivation and collective self-sacrifice, industrialism and socialism stood as mutually reinforcing goals. The perspective they offered was that of the distant future; the eventual outcome that they promised made hardship bearable and heroic leadership possible. At some point, the two goals diverged, and the leadership indicated confusion about goals and means. Consequently, the leadership lost its heroic glow and turned to rationalistic explanations. Just as the collectivist premises of socialism began to conflict with the individualist norms of industrialism, so a democratic exercise of authority was set aside for the institutionalization of hierarchy. Thus the norms inculcated by the official ideology and the compromise between industrialism and socialism that self-management, in its present stage of both theory and practice, represents,

Models and norms

do not leave much of a realistic basis for the continuity of *borbenost* in the traditional sense.

A final consideration about the continuity of cultural models concerns the political, economic, and social consequences of really aligning norms in all areas with what traditional values are held to be. As sociologist Josip Županov points out, the Yugoslav leadership continually calls for making the social reality reflect the central value system, especially the values of *borbenost*, egalitarianism, and democracy which are associated with Yugoslav culture.[2] However, the leaders of the League of Communists and the government and economic bureaucracies would hardly give up the privileges which conflict with these values. So, Županov says, the demand for integrating traditional values with current practice is sublimated, at the very highest levels of privilege, into attacks on lower, but prospering, social strata, such as those of intellectuals, businessmen, and self-employed craftsmen. If, as the chapter on public behavior indicated, norms of interaction within the political elite and even between republics influence the behavior of ordinary citizens, then Yugoslavs will continue to reproduce throughout the society the split between culturally sanctified values and actual norms until their leaders find a resolution. In Yugoslavia as in other societies, the leadership must take the first step toward changing norms — or what they often prefer to visualize as changing 'human nature' — by altering the form of social organization. But changing the behavior of Yugoslavs, particularly in an effort to integrate traditional culture with official ideology, poses some threat to the established degree of authoritarianism and elitism in the society.

The parameters placed on social change by traditional culture present an interesting problem. In this context it may be important to consider how Yugoslavs evaluate their own cultural legacy, as well as how the events and situations of the past have structured behavior which must meet the challenges of self-management. Historically, the political systems which have been caught and reflected in cultural values and behavioral norms include a mythologized pastoral democracy, a vilified colonial rule (Ottoman and Austrian), a 'Stalinist' etatism and, moving up to the present, socialist self-management. This chapter does not offer a history of Yugoslav culture. Rather, I have selected

2 Županov, 'Industrijalizam i egalitarizam', p. 42.

221

those aspects of successive historical periods and their characteristic social structures which seem to have left a lasting imprint on behavior that we can observe today in political and other public situations. The values and models from Yugoslav history comprise a weighty cultural legacy. Nevertheless, some Yugoslavs have complained of a recent 'hunger for values' among the younger generation which has grown up under socialism. Their behavior often contrasts with the valuable role that youth played — as both model and catalyst — during the Partisan War. Because an examination of Yugoslav society must consider young people's deviance from, as well as the general continuity of, traditional norms, we shall start with common roots and end with contradictions.

Obviously a caveat is in order about the multi-national character of culture in Yugoslavia. The histories of Serbs, Croats, Slovenes, Montenegrins, Bosnians, Macedonians, and other groups cannot be added together, averaged out, and homogenized into a single Yugoslav culture. But 'Yugoslav culture' can be used to denote two things. First, this term refers to the values, norms, and models which emerged from both the theory and the practice of the Partisan and nation-building period (1945–50) and which continue to pervade many aspects of social reality. Of course, as long as the Yugoslav republics remain differentiated by the extent and the rapidity of economic development and the ability to dispose of earned resources, some significant political aspects of social reality will continue to be influenced greatly by ethnic identification. One political variable of this kind — the citizen's relationship to the state — appears differently in Belgrade, Zagreb, Ljubljana, Titograd, Sarajevo, Skoplje. However, two or more of the Yugoslav national regions have shared certain historical experiences shaped by political institutions: by colonialism, for example, and by the *Gemeinschaft* of peasant societies. So the term 'Yugoslav culture', as I use it here, also refers to these shared experiences with certain political structures and some common patterns of behavior which have emerged. For reasons explained in the appendix on methodology, I chose to work among Serbs living in Belgrade, so here I am most interested in Serbian culture. I shall use 'Serbian' when discussing specifically Serbian history, values, and behavior and 'Yugoslav' when referring to common experiences of the nineteenth and twentieth centuries.

SELF-STEREOTYPES

Yugoslavs indicate that they are aware of their continued reliance on traditional self-stereotypes by a certain way that they excuse their conduct. This excuse, which would be humorous if it were not so common, is that Serbs lived for '500 years under the Turks'. Not only Serbs, Macedonians, and Bosnians, who actually lived under Ottoman rule from the fourteenth to the twentieth century, but also to some extent the other Yugoslav nationalities use this as an excuse when discussing the country's underdevelopment. With some self-humor they even tell the joke about the Yugoslav who went to Istanbul and, surprised by the relatively low standard of living there, was told by the Turks, 'But you know, we ruled for 500 years over the Serbs'. As a colony of the Ottoman Empire, Serbia was haunted and humiliated by the memory of the battle in which the country lost its independence to the Ottoman Emperor. This was the Battle of Kosovo in 1389. Memories of medieval greatness which preceded this battle have left a psychological residue in Serbia. From the outsider's point of view, this residue appears rather negative: the lack of artifacts from the glorious past (one need only compare the collection of the National Museum in Belgrade with those of museums in the capitals of former colonial powers), undeveloped natural resources, and an inferiority complex vis-à-vis the Western countries which now wield great power but 'still ate with their fingers while our kings were eating with forks and knives' (this refers to a fresco depicting a meal at the time of Tsar Dušan in the fourteenth century). These few images suggest that the picture that many Serbs hold of themselves as a nation focuses on a people brutalized and victimized until only a memory of abundance remains both to taunt and to inspire them.

The same idioms that contemporary Yugoslavs use to describe themselves occur in an early twentieth-century work by the ethnographer Jovan Cvijić.[3] Cvijić apparently roamed the grassy hills and valleys filled with admiration for the sturdy, freedom-loving peasants of Yugoslavia, whose life he observed. Because his book was used as a textbook in Yugoslav high schools until a decade

---

3 Jovan Cvijić, *Balkansko poluostrvo i južnoslovenske zemlje* [The Balkan peninsula and the south Slavic lands], vol. 2, *Psihičke osobine južnih slovena* [Psychological characteristics of south Slavs] (Belgrade: Izdavačka knjižarnica Gece Kona, 1931).

ago and because Yugoslavs who have never even been to high school speak of themselves in the same terms that Cvijić used, his typifications are still relevant for us. Cvijić admired the Dinaric type of Yugoslav, particularly the Šumadian, whose habitat is the countryside (Šumadija, 'Forest country') around Belgrade. According to Cvijić, the Dinaric Yugoslav — the category which includes Serbs — has a lively soul, a keen intelligence, a lively and varied sensibility, a vivid and rich imagination. He says of the Dinarics in a kind of paean,

> they are usually inspired by impulses of a moral and spiritual sort; material interests have only a role of the second order. To call forth the greatest amount of their strength, one has to touch their sensibility, sensitivity, their individual and national pride; one has to emphasize the question of honor or the ideal of justice or freedom. These are the major causes of passion which activates Dinaric people as they are the causes of conflicts which appear among them . . .

Furthermore, Cvijić sees in the Dinarics a tremendous 'instinct for life and development', an instinct which can pull them out of snares and pitfalls. Thus, according to Cvijić, the Dinaric people's 'faith is unclouded, [their] confidence is unlimited'. They appear to need this faith and confidence, for, as Cvijić tells us, the major goal of every Dinaric man is to avenge the Battle of Kosovo. Nursed on tales of Serbian heroes and weaned on laments of national humiliation, Dinaric man develops a 'practically unlimited spirit of sacrifice and self-denial' on the nation's behalf. Moreover, according to Cvijić, 'he considers himself as a God chosen for the execution of the national task', i.e. liberation from the Ottomans.[4]

The Šumadian variety of Dinaric man represents the quintessence of this character. According to Cvijić, the Šumadian is active but sensitive, courageous but tender, a good timer but 'consciously' so, democratic in society but slightly autocratic in the family, free in speech sometimes to the point of demagogy, egalitarian to the point of lawlessness. In times of national crisis, which almost invariably takes the form of war, the Šumadian peasant never wavers in his dedication to the nation. At such

4 Ibid., p. 18. See also Dinko Tomašić, *Personality and Culture in East European Politics* (New York: George W. Stewart, 1948).

times the Šumadians pull together and stand fast: starving, killing the enemy, and preparing for Liberation Day.[5]

Other witnesses beside Cvijić testify to the immediacy of medieval tradition to twentieth-century Serbs. Vera Erlich, an anthropologist from Zagreb, tells of the Yugoslav ethnographer who traveled around Yugoslavia in the 1930s and found in a mountain area in Dalmatia two small girls, watching sheep and crying bitterly. The little girls told him that they were mourning Lazar and Miloš, Serbian princes who, as all Serbs know, fell at the Battle of Kosovo.[6] Furthermore, the English writer and south Slavophile Rebecca West reports the bewilderment of her husband, a banker, when he saw the anachronistic style of art chosen to decorate a twentieth-century mausoleum for the Karadjordjević dynasty of Serbian and Yugoslav rulers: these were mosaic reproductions of frescoes from medieval Orthodox monasteries. 'But why did this man want to hold up an encyclopedia of medieval Serbian art over his family vault?' West's husband asks. She replies, 'Well, that is all the remote past they have, and they came straight out of that glory into the misery of Turkish conquest.'[7]

Despite all the positive qualities that Cvijić found and all the assertive characteristics (including negative ones such as national and male chauvinism) to which Serbian self-stereotypes subscribe, there may be an element of insecurity behind the bravura. As one of my friends, a Serbian woman, says of their national character,

> In our people there is a history of hunger. And this hunger
> results in a great fear (*strah*) inside, very close to the
> surface. We never know what tomorrow will bring; we
> are afraid to plan for the future. This fear is expressed in
> many ways. When you go to a wedding in the country-
> side you'll be amazed at the way people are singing and
> carrying on — as if they were drugged. But that's just a
> way of expressing this fear inside them. Maybe that's why
> we have the tradition of breaking glasses (*razbijati*) when
> we are drinking and we are very happy; we have at the

5 Cvijić, *Balkansko poluostrvo*, pp. 38–42.
6 Vera St Erlich, 'Ljudske vrednote i kontakti kultura' [Human values and culture contacts], *Sociologija* 7, no. 3 (1965): 31.
7 Rebecca West, *Black Lamb and Grey Falcon* (1941; New York: Viking, 1958), p. 493.

same time the need to destroy — to feel more secure by destroying something. We're very close to the gypsy temperament. Maybe that's why we're so lenient toward the gypsies. The Russians and the others feel superior to the gypsies, but the Serbs, no, the Yugoslavs, know that they and the gypsies are soul-brothers (*blizanci*).

Thus the self-stereotype of the national hero, the warrior for freedom, and the destroyer of inequality may conceal a basic fear and an insecurity about the conditions of life. The simpler side of Serbian national character emerges in the architecture and design of a Serbian Orthodox church, less imposing and less ornate than a Roman Catholic Church, and less frightening, too, for the Serbian Orthodox Church features no morbid images of the suffering, flesh-torn Christ. Still, the predominant image of the Serbian self-stereotype remains that of the warrior against Ottoman oppression.

Aside from the psycho-cultural residues of belonging to a national, though relatively poor, church (like the Serbian Orthodox) or an international religious movement (like the Croatian and Slovenian Catholics or the Bosnian Moslems), there is a compelling similarity between the self-stereotypes of all the Yugoslav nationalities. The norms and values perpetuated in folk tales and the common idiom hark back to precolonial peasant society. In those days, the lines of authority were clear and hierarchical rather than diffuse and democratic.[8] There were those who counted — primarily older men, the heads of extended families (although sometimes older women became or were chosen *starešina* of the household), and men in the prime of life — and those who didn't count. At the same time, everyone worked, and everyone was entitled to a share of food and shelter. Despite what we would call today an economy of scarcity, goods seem to have been distributed on an egalitarian basis. In this sort of folk society, people were highly conscious of their collective identity, particularly in tribes tracing a common descent and sharing a past, a present, and — as far as they could tell — a future. On this basis arose a sense of pride in belonging to a particular tribe, a concept of tribal honor, and a motivation of sacrificing individual attributes — to death, if necessary — in order to protect the group.

8 See Rihtman-Auguštin, 'Samoupravljanje', p. 39.

Such cultural values as authoritarianism, egalitarianism, and self-sacrifice may contribute to as well as detract from present societal goals. Especially when modes of behavior or social institutions associated with one set of societal goals, such as socialism, may conflict with those of another, such as industrialism, people may experience confusion in determining just which traditional values are relevant to current situations — and in what proportions. How, for example, could Yugoslavs mix authoritarianism, egalitarianism, and self-sacrifice in order to create and uphold social self-management in a multinational state? To complicate further the problem of accommodating traditional values to present situations, there are other cultural norms which appear unambiguously dysfunctional to all societal goals. Two such values from peasant society are the lack of adjustment to productive work, particularly the production of a surplus for either deferred consumption or sale, and the preference for forced acquisition, especially through plunder, over market transactions. Moreover, certain values which emerged in response to colonial domination, particularly by the Ottomans, seem to have accentuated the problem of moving into an industrialized and socialized society.

RESPONSES TO OTTOMAN RULE

According to Vera Erlich, the Zagreb anthropologist, certain values become either operative or more visible during periods of conflict when different cultures come into contact within the same population.[9] Although it is often difficult to know which cultural traits developed in earlier times and which developed during 'culture contacts', Erlich contends that those areas which assimilated Ottoman values (such as Bosnia) still exhibit different modes of behavior from those areas (such as Montenegro) which struggled against such assimilation. Thus Bosnian culture shows definite Oriental influences, in contrast to Montenegro's typification — and possibly even reification — of indigenous Dinaric traits. Putting it crudely, the assumption which underlies Erlich's analysis — as well as the Yugoslav stereotype in general — is that Bosnia 'knuckled under' to a rather effete Ottoman cul-

9 See Erlich, 'Ljudske vrednote'. For a different analysis, see Stavrianos, *The Balkans Since 1453*.

ture, while Montenegro stiffened its resistance to the Ottomans by emphasizing the strong, essentially male, Serbian virtues.

The Bosnian nobility, which belonged to the Serbian ethnic and religious group, more or less accepted the political rule of the Ottomans. Previously, they had been persecuted by the Orthodox Church authorities for pursuing the Bogumil 'heresy', so Islam seemed to offer a more tolerant, and more distant, patriarchal authority. Both the nobles and the peasants whom they dominated adopted the Ottomans' religion — along with their language, lifestyle, and values. In the view of many Yugoslavs, the adoption of Islamic values made political resistance against the Ottomans impossible. Erlich emphasizes four values which were 'debilitating' in this way: concentration of all one's attention on the private sphere of life, thus ceasing to esteem the warrior spirit, and belief in fatality, which brought with it tolerance. Although she does not use a psychological vocabulary, Erlich also indicates that the Bosnian Moslems sublimated their passion in love. This was not the Serbian love of country, she says, but the Islamic love of women, who were now veiled and separated from men.

In contrast to the Bosnians, the Montenegrins developed a lifestyle and values which increasingly differentiated themselves from the Oriental. The Montenegrins' family organization and their strong sense of collective responsibility prevented the emergence of an ideal of romantic love on the one hand and, on the other, kept alive and real the ideal of avenging the Battle of Kosovo. Furthermore, in contrast to the Ottoman standard of judging a man on his merits, the Montenegrins emphasized tribal identifications and genealogies.

Since Serbia freed itself from Ottoman rule and Yugoslavia liberated itself from Axis Occupation through guerrilla warfare, the Montenegrin response to Ottoman invasion constitutes a significant model for contemporary Yugoslav culture. Aside from the vaunted warrior spirit, there is also a particular open-yet-closed quality in this model. Thus the community is closed to the outside enemy, yet each individual is open to the influence of others within the community. As Erlich says of the Montenegrins, 'Each individual continually feels responsible to the collectivity and completely open to the judgment of his brothers.' [10] This

10 Erlich, 'Ljudske vrednote', p. 31.

kind of solidarity seems congruent with (future) socialist attitudes, as well as with the kind of social equality that Tocqueville describes: 'When all the ranks of a community are nearly equal, as all men think and feel in nearly the same manner, each of them may judge in a moment of the sensations of all the others; he casts a rapid glance upon himself, and that is enough.'[11]

Differences in ecology and in political history account for some difference between the Serbian and Montenegrin responses to the Ottomans. They share the sorrow of Kosovo and the national goal of avenging it — natives of both Serbia and Montenegro are ethnically Serbs — but Montenegro's mountainous terrain protected it while Belgrade's strategic and defenseless position kept Serbia under the control of the sultan and his pashas. In an enforced state of national dormancy, Serbs did not develop the desire to work hard, for they may have perceived their labor as contributing to the greatness of an alien power. Their contribution to the Serbian nation was made in terms of bloodshed, hunger, and religious conviction in ultimate victory. Moreover, these contributions were only sporadic, depending upon the accumulation of resources, including leadership and spirit, for a revolt. In their everyday work, the Serbs adopted and perfected the Ottoman quality of *javašluk* (in Serbian, from the Turkish *javaš*, 'slow', in the sense of the Mexican *mañana*). The behavioral norm associated with *javašluk* is that a person moves slowly if he or she must move at all. To this day, if a waiter or clerk in Serbia says in response to a plea for help, '*Odmah!*' (Immediately!), he means that he is coming in five or ten minutes; if he says, '*Sad ću doći!*' (I'm coming now!), he means that he will be even longer in arriving. In this case, the excuse of '500 years under the Turks' blames the Ottomans and their descendants for two things: for not having allowed the Serbs to develop their natural resources, including talent, and for inculcating the leisurely work habits of *javašluk*. Whether or not a Serb became a *javašluk* in passive resistance to the Ottomans, leisurely execution of work tasks and obligations has become a positive value in itself.

Although Serbian response to the Ottomans may appear destructive from one angle, from the view of the 'oppressed' population it seems positive, for the nation did survive and did

11 Alexis de Tocqueville, *Democracy in America* (New York: Vintage Books, 1960), 2: 175–6.

eventually regain its freedom. Two more behavioral norms which may have emerged as a response to foreign conquest could be described as positive in this way. These norms are what the Serbs call *moba* and *inat*. *Moba* means, simply, mutual help. Under a foreign oppressor it is easy to regard all fellow-oppressed subjects, particularly of the same ethnic origin, as brothers. When brothers of this kind are persecuted and murdered — often because of the common ethnic origin — people offer help and shelter, which they half-expect, half-fear will be needed some day in return. Thus a tradition of *moba* or mutual help develops. *Inat,* on the other hand, refers to action out of a kind of spite. According to this norm, a person attempts to do something that someone else claims is impossible, unfeasible, unwise, or disastrous. For example, if a friend says that it is impossible to walk across Niagara Falls on a tightrope, then I decide to do that precisely because he says that it is impossible. 'You can't do that!' he says. '*Bas hoću, iz inata!*' I reply: 'I'm going to do just that, out of spite.'

No other ethnic group in Yugoslavia adheres to this norm of *inat*. According to Serbs, though, *inat* is still a strong motivating force, even on the political level. For instance, the Serbs and Montenegrins are spearheading, contributing to, investing in, and by and large building by themselves the Belgrade–Bar railroad line, which is a tortuous track over high mountains. When I asked a Serb why, aside from the belief that the railroad would make both republics more wealthy, the Serbs and the Montenegrins are so insistent about this railroad, he said simply, 'It's *inat*.'

ETATISM

Yugoslavs probably have ambivalent feelings about state bureaucracy, for in the past it has represented both the oppression of the peasant population — especially by a foreign power and the native ruling class that it trains — and a means of upward social mobility for the scions of those peasants. Yugoslav peasants, like most European peasants, have usually perceived the state bureaucracy as strong, corrupt, and exploitative. This view is understandable when we consider that the only contacts the peasants had with the bureaucracy consisted of paying taxes and fines, serving in the military, and contributing *corvée* work. Yet the peasants attempted at every opportunity to enter the state bureaucracy themselves or to get their sons positions in it, evidently trying to reduce their economic insecurity.

Yugoslav political independence in 1918 did not reduce the power and corruption of the state bureaucracy. Because there was little industry, the largest employer was the state. As before, peasants could hope to reduce their poverty only by gaining a foothold in the civil service, thus allying themselves with the king, the rich, and the cartels. Once in that position, former peasants became harsh oppressors of their brothers. A Yugoslav writer in the interwar period describes the attitude of the peasant who has latched onto the security of the civil service:

> As forester, county chief, or a member of the parliament, as a simple clerk or as a sergeant in the *gendarmerie,* he will understand nothing and will not want to understand anything of the dismal conditions of his native community. On the contrary, in the unbridled way of a barbarian and a *nouveau riche,* he will jump on the back of his hungry people and soil even the bloody spot which he hit with his forehead when his mother gave him birth in a field furrow.[12]

To some extent this attitude seems to have prevailed even in the socialist republic. Yugoslavs today, highly critical of bureaucrats and bureaucratism, blame these excesses on both the Ottoman legacy and the postwar attempt to create a socialist Yugoslavia on the Stalinist model. Having abandoned that model with the introduction of workers' self-management in 1949–50, followed by various economic reforms from 1950 to 1965, the Yugoslavs feel free to castigate the features that they have rejected as 'etatism', a perversion of socialism. These features include a centralized state apparatus (with which the Yugoslavs are gradually dispensing in many areas), central economic planning and investment, and strong state controls over social life which rely on police enforcement and secret-police information. In this sense the 1966 ousting of Aleksandar Ranković — Minister of the Interior, head of the secret police, and a Party leader — from the highest official, as well as from Party, ranks, signified a rejection of 'etatist' practice. Nevertheless, even today, Yugo-

12 Dr Branimir Gusić, 'Today's Hercegovina', *Nova Evropa*, no. 7–8 (July–August 1936): 207, in Jozo Tomasevich, *Peasants, Politics, and Economic Change in Yugoslavia* (Stanford University Press, 1955).

slavs regard a *činovnik* (administrator) as 'a man who occupies a good position, in which there is little or no work, and who with all this has power and a good income'.[13]

THE CULTURE OF SOCIALIST SELF-MANAGEMENT

A population which successively lives under the rule of a colonial power, a dominant state bureaucracy, and a strong political party may find it difficult to develop behaviorial norms which adhere to the ideals of socialist self-management. That is, the norms of passivity and sporadic revolt which characterized the Yugoslavs' social behavior over the past five centuries must yield to norms of mutual responsibility, activism, conscious and conscientious work. To this end the official ideology of the political leadership promotes certain values which link traditional and contemporary ideals. Along with national independence, the fulfillment of mutual interests, and general progress, the official ideology of self-management advocates 'modern' goals in terms of socialist and economic development. Thus the Yugoslav psychologist-cum-ethnologist Dunja Rihtman-Auguštin has found that the 1963 Yugoslav Constitution describes *socialist culture* in terms of

> socialist social relations and defense of the socialist social system; national freedom and independence; *bratstvo i jedinstvo* ['brotherhood and unity', a Partisan slogan from the war] of the nations and nationalities and solidarity of the working people; possibilities and freedoms for the all-round development of the human personality and for bringing people and nations closer in harmony with their interests and desires on the road to creating an even richer culture and civilization of socialist society; unifying and harmonizing endeavors to develop the material foundations of the social community and human welfare; allying our own efforts with the progressive desires of mankind; a single basis for the economic and political system so that mutual interests and equality of nations and nationalities and people may be realized.[14]

13 Pavle Novosel, 'Reforma, samoupravljanje i socijalna psihologija preindustrijalskog mentaliteta' [Reform, self-management and the social psychology of preindustrial mentality], *Naše teme* 11 (1967): 2164.
14 Dunja Rihtman-Auguštin, 'Vrednote i današnji trenutak' [Values and the present], *Naše teme* 15 (1971): 246–7.

The culture of socialist self-management

Analyzing another document of the official ideology, i.e. the resolutions of the IX Congress (1969) of the League of Communists of Yugoslavia, Rihtman again finds the juxtaposition of traditional and contemporary values. These resolutions promote the model of the self-manager which Yugoslavs should emulate, an ideal type which combines elements of the traditional Serbian warrior and the Yugoslav desire for national unity, of socialist solidarity, and of the old-time American entrepreneur as well as the modern industrial manager. Thus the IX Party Congress envisions the self-manager as

> a fighter for self-managing relations, for the affirmation of knowledge, for new modern technology and contemporary business manners, for distribution on the basis of the results of work, for solidarity between people, for solidarity in business relationships . . . [He should be] communicative and cooperative but he should also follow through [on commitments].[15]

Turning from ideal to actual work norms, we find two key areas in which tradition appears to dominate over the official ideology of self-management. These areas are decision-making and distribution. As we have already seen, studies done in enterprises and communes show that small, informal groups (cliques or *aktivs*) and their hired experts control all aspects of decision-making.[16] According to Dunja Rihtman, this represents a continuation of traditional patterns of autocratic decision-making in the household, where the *starešina* (elder) made all the decisions, and in the village, where all the adult males who were interested in a particular issue decided its outcome. In both cases, the larger social group, i.e. the household and the village, accepted the decisions as legitimate and binding. Issues which could not be resolved through discussion were settled by more drastic means. Rihtman points out that, traditionally, peasant society offers various informal means of expressing disagreement with the content of decisions which are made autocratically. For example, an informal means of opposition is simply gossip. To combat the opposing opinions, which are expressed in this way, the decision-makers usually try to degrade them and so to dismiss them out of hand. Generally, the traditional decision-mak-

15 Rihtman, 'Samoupravljanje', p. 45.
16 See chapter 5.

ers could degrade gossip as being a 'female' pastime, hence personal and inconsequential. Similarly, Rihtman observes, Yugoslavs today have a tendency to blame enterprise failure on "interpersonal relations'. Gossip still continues to be an informal channel for the communication of information and opposition to managerial decisions.[17]

Distribution in traditional Yugoslav society also differed from today's official ideology. Traditionally, the distribution norm was based on the number of people to be fed rather than on the amount of work they did. But according to the official ideology of self-management, distribution depends on 'the results of work'. Although the traditional idea that the collective should take care of its members' needs seems consonant with socialist theory, the Yugoslavs have opted for the more 'modern' norm as a way of raising productivity. Thus the official ideology considers that material incentives will motivate Yugoslavs to work harder and longer. However, Rihtman and her senior colleague, sociologist Josip Županov, argue that here, again, traditional values dominate over the officially-inspired culture of self-management. In this case, the values of peasant society, especially the egalitarian ethic and the concept of limited good, negate the utility of material incentives. According to Rihtman and Županov, Yugoslavs tend to despise, rather than to emulate, people who get rich through their own hard work. In Croatian public opinion surveys, the idea of *bogaćenje* (getting rich) evokes extremely negative responses. In Serbia, too, public attention often focuses upon the local artisan or merchant, or the international trader or importer, whose ingenuity in fulfilling consumers' needs often results in financial success. Rihtman and Županov conclude that Yugoslavs accept *bogaćenje* only on the most elementary level, i.e. that of raising one's standard of living above the poverty level. Although this appears to contradict the *trka za dinarom* (running after dinars) that Yugoslavs talk about, Županov has related the anti-*bogaćenje* attitude to failure in industrialization and modernization.[18]

17 Rihtman, 'Samoupravljanje', pp. 48–9. Not all peasant households were equally autocratic. On workers' perceptions of enterprise leaders as autocratic authorities, see Čukić, *Radne i samoupravne uloge*.
18 See Rihtman, 'Samoupravljanje', pp. 42–50 and Županov, 'Industrijalizam i egalitarizam'. Županov's interpretation of Yugoslavs' supposedly peasant-like penchant for egalitarianism, which he sees as detrimental to industrialization, stirred a storm of protest at the 1970 con-

Youth as model and catalyst

Despite the many continuities between traditional and contemporary values, self-management would never have got off the ground if behavior patterns had remained completely mired in the past. Somehow passivity was transformed — at least for a time — into activism. During the social shock of World War II, Yugoslavs found that the organization of guerrilla warfare was a galvanizing force. Not only did the Partisan movement unite the population behind the goal of national liberation, but it was able to continue to mobilize this fervor during the postwar period.[19] During the war, one factor in particular paved the way for later innovation by both altering behavior and affirming traditional values. This factor is represented by 'the SKOJ ethic' (the norms of the Yugoslav League of Communist Youth); it refers to the major role of young people in both the war effort and postwar reconstruction.

YOUTH AS MODEL AND CATALYST

Although the Communist Youth League, or SKOJ, had existed since 1919 and had participated in the Party's demonstrations and organizing activities through the twenties and thirties, the necessities of war really made SKOJ a significant force for cultural change. First, the brutality of the German Occupation provided the motive for thousands of young people to join SKOJ. Then, the demands of battle made them much more accepting of discipline, rules, and criticism than an outsider would have thought possible. It was precisely these rules and criticisms which made behavior conform to such norms as, in the words of a SKOJ member's wartime diary, 'comradeship, initiative, bravery, sacrifice, persistence, discipline, and conspiracy'. During the war SKOJ provided a legitimate opportunity for young people to bring to life the warrior tradition of the Yugoslav nations, avenging both the Battle of Kosovo and Hitler's bombing of Belgrade. The SKOJ ethic, in short, promulgated many of the norms which would later comprise the cultural model of the

vention of the Yugoslav Sociological Association. See Fuad Muhić, 'Hronika: IV Stručni sastanak jugoslovenskog udruženja za sociologiju' [Chronicle: Fourth Professional Meeting of the Yugoslav Sociological Association], *Sociologija* 12, no. 1 (1970): 136–45.

19 See, for example, Stephen Clissold, *Whirlwind: An Account of Marshal Tito's Rise to Power* (London: The Cresset Press, 1949) and Vladimir Dedijer, *Tito* (New York: Simon and Schuster, 1953).

self-manager: 'comradeship, humanity, heroism, discipline, modesty, persistence, daring, readiness for the greatest obedience, industriousness, activity in self-education and upbringing'.[20]

SKOJ also served at least two other latent functions. First, SKOJ offered a legitimate channel for youthful and national aggression and, second, it provided a means out of the village for many peasant youths. The legitimate activity of war — killing — channeled youthful aggression and hostility. Because such rules as the death penalty that the Partisans instituted against rape and theft limited this aggression to action against the enemy, the Partisan and SKOJ organizations acquired a certain mystique. This was the kind of mystique which surrounds any group that practices some form of self-abnegation. In this case, the self-abnegation consisted of limiting oneself to killing only the enemy and denying oneself the usual spoils of battle, e.g. plunder and enslavement. It might be pointed out that, since the battleground was Yugoslavia, the victors would be plundering and raping their own people. However, it is significant that the Partisans, alone among the so-called defenders of Yugoslavia, abstained from plunder, rape, and religious massacres.

The second of SKOJ's latent functions was to provide a means of geographical and social mobility. Teen-aged peasant boys and girls who had done nothing but tend sheep and livestock, looking forward only to endless rounds of farm chores, were able to join SKOJ and escape from their villages. Before the war many peasant youths had neither the means to transport themselves out of their birthplace nor the cunning to support themselves outside of it. SKOJ took them out and in many cases kept them out. Another aspect of this mobility is the equality that women comrades enjoyed in SKOJ and the Partisans. By joining SKOJ, women were able to leave their families and their villages without the threat of moral and physical dishonor.

SKOJ maintained its organization and its ethic after the war. Frequent meetings took the place of day-to-day combat, and military brigades changed into the uniforms of work brigades. Because the reconstruction period was an extraordinary time of

20 Radomir Konstadinović, *Crna Trava i Crnotravci* [Crna Trava and the Crnotravians] (Leskovac, 1968), p. 235, cited in Milan M. Miladinović, *Lik članova SKOJa u revoluciji* [The image of SKOJ members in the revolution] (Belgrade: The author, 1971), p. 7; Miladinović, *Lik članova SKOJa*, p. 85.

common social effort, the SKOJ ethic still dominated popular consciousness. To be an activist was still to be a hero. However, as the unified revolutionary spirit disassembled itself into the combination of patriotism, passivity, and anomie which holds a society together in unextraordinary times, so SKOJ's function also changed from channeling aggression to channeling constructive support and conservatism. Gradually the society settled down to pecuniary rather than spiritual rewards, and work brigades became outmoded. Youth leaders enjoyed the privileges of public office; they became an entrenched leadership, defensive of the established order. Indeed, many Party and government leaders emerged from their ranks, including some of the recent heads of the Belgrade Party organization, who were trained in the League of Students.

Yet, today, a generation after the rise of its 'ethic', the youth organization seems to have lost its purpose. Perhaps its major function now is to train future political leaders rather than to mobilize and discipline the masses. Its new name — SOJ (*Savez omladine Jugoslavije,* or the Yugoslav Youth League) — symbolizes its de-ideologization. Indeed, according to a Zagreb college student being interviewed in a magazine symposium on 'youth's hunger for values', the youth organization of the 1960s merely purveys the established values of the official ideology. This student says,

> I am afraid that the youth organization can't do much of anything. I can even say that I don't at all feel like a member of that organization. I was thrown out of an open meeting of the local CP [Party] organization. There was a discussion on the censure of the newspaper *Spiral* [put out by] five high schools. They kicked me out of the auditorium before I could speak. I suppose that my appearance didn't seem promising enough to them . . . The youth organization has tried for too long to guarantee contentment by various or always the same formulas. I think that it'll never again have the popularity that SKOJ had.[21]

21 Slobodan Šnajder in Matko Bradarić, 'Matko Bradarić razgovara s Katjom Vodopirčevom, Ivom Segulovom [i dr.] o mladima danas: Postoji li glad mladih za vrijednostima?' [Matko Bradarić talks with Katja Vodopirčeva, Ivo Segulov (and others) about youth today: Is there a hunger for values among young people?], *Encyclopaedia moderna* 2, no. 5–6 (September–December 1967): 181.

The SKOJ ethic which prevailed in popular consciousness during and immediately after World War II presented and inculcated several behavioral norms which were later transferred into the ideal of self-management: comradeship, self-sacrifice, discipline, modesty, industriousness. Through its organization and its organizational purpose during the war, SKOJ was able to weld new norms like these to traditional values such as the warrior image, solidarity, and equality. These positive, traditional values later found expression in the model of self-management posited by the official ideology. But despite the wealth of old and new cultural norms, Yugoslavs have noticed that the younger generation is showing confusion, disruption, and even skepticism. Although this behavior may be the result of strain between some elements of traditional and contemporary cultural models, as well as between the societal goals of 'economic development' and 'socialism', Yugoslavs call it a 'hunger for values'.

'HUNGER FOR VALUES'

Symptoms of strain in Yugoslavia, as in other countries in the process of rapid social change, include rising crime rates, especially juvenile delinquency, rape, and murder; declining authority of heads of families and older people in general; and the restriction of obligations to the immediate circle of the nuclear family and some friends instead of to an extended group of kinsmen and former townsmen. These phenomena tend to surprise Yugoslavs because of the important role that young people played — through SKOJ and the volunteer youth brigades — in a period of value affirmation and social regeneration. Looking at many young people today, Yugoslavs say that youth has 'changed'. They suspect as factors of this change the very hallmarks of the Yugoslav official ideology: market socialism, consumer-goods production, contacts with the West. But when outsiders criticize these factors, Yugoslavs remind them defensively that they lack the perspective of having lived in poverty, fought the Partisan War, and suffered for 500 years under the Turks.[22]

22 These collective historical experiences have contributed, particularly in Serbia and Montenegro, to parental desire to 'give their children everything'. Aside from providing the material advantages that they themselves did not have, Serbian parents also promote high aspirations for their children's educations and careers, even when they know that such

'Hunger for values'

Perhaps young Yugoslavs, like their contemporaries in many other societies, are reacting not so much against the norms of the official ideology as against the continued protestations on the part of their elders in general, their parents and the political leadership in particular, that they have maintained the collectivist orientation of the Partisan period. In short, as the Belgrade respondents and other Yugoslavs have indicated, young people may be disaffected with their elders' claims to respect and obedience on the basis of their, i.e. the elders', public spirit.[23] And disaffection often results in dissociation. This has been the case, for example, with Yugoslav workers quitting the League of Communists and a former leader like Milovan Djilas choosing social democracy over communism. Similarly, we have seen how some Yugoslavs, dissatisfied with the social gains that they have achieved relative to those of other groups, dissent from the official ideology and develop their own interpretations of socialism. Just as disaffection from the official ideology leads to the expression of different political orientations so, too, disaffection from the dominant cultural model leads to the expression of divergent — sometimes called deviant — behavior. Among young Yugoslavs, we can find behavior which conforms to the official model of the ideal self-manager and behavior which deviates from this model in at least three ways. In contrast to the official cultural model, young Yugoslavs also present the norms of hoodlums, of hippies, and of utopians. As with the expression of political orientations, the adoption of these cultural norms is related to social origins and social rewards.

The dominant cultural model of the self-manager, like the official political ideology, shows strong signs of a motivation to 'make it' in Yugoslav society. According to philosopher Dimitar Dimitrov's provocative interpretation of this ideal type, the self-

aspirations are unrealistic. Andjelka Milić, a sociologist who studies the family at Institut društvenih nauka, Belgrade, reports this as a finding of her survey of Serbian families (personal communication).

23 Cf. Barrington Moore, Jr on American society: 'All upper classes profess to act in the public spirit. They are generally successful only so long as by and large their members believe in their job and feel that their privileges do have solid justification. When this confidence wanes, a ruling class is generally finished. This confidence is rapidly waning among the children of the elite. Its loss may be the most significant aspect of the student revolt.' *Reflections on the Causes of Human Misery* (Boston: Beacon Press, 1973), p. 131.

239

manager is primarily an economic personage.[24] Indeed, Dimitrov
blames the official ideology for distending the 'economic-posses-
sive dimension' of the people's intellectual, political, moral, and
esthetic character. What Yugoslavs praise as an 'expert', says
Dimitrov, is not an intellectual but an empty shell, a 'mediocrity
. . . who is a demagogue in politics, a *homo duplex,* a utilitarian
in morals, a practitioner of *kitsch* in his spare time'. But this
type of personality develops within the social reality of the time.
As Dimitrov views Yugoslav society, he sees the ideals of classical
Marxism receding further and further from the onslaught of
the norms of market socialism. In this process,

> the general concept of socialism in proletarian ideology
> dissolves; the general proletarian interest implicit in op-
> position to the bourgeois class is destroyed; the working
> class is to a great extent de-classed; differentiation begins;
> the individual is included in a group, a stratum, a profes-
> sion; the group, stratum and profession in society, and
> every one of these categories has its own interest, and
> those individual and group interests, crossed with the in-
> fluence of the ideological tradition, makes for a specific
> manner of political behavior, for which [these] are char-
> acteristic: *(1) unreliability, (2) conformity, (3) opportunism,
> and (4) ideological rationalization of social practice.*

Each of these characteristics is related to a norm of the official
ideology. As Dimitrov sees it, a Yugoslav is 'unreliable' because
he or she wants to fulfill the conditions of classical socialism,
but the economic emphasis on self-interest in the official ideology
will not permit him or her to act like a real socialist. Second, this
'pragmatic' orientation compels the Yugoslav to ignore general social needs while he concentrates on satisfying his own interests. He
begins to interpret principles in light of what the situation can
offer. Thus, he becomes a 'conformist'. Furthermore, when he
does participate, or intervene, in social practice, his motives are
strictly selfish: he will destroy a good thing or promote a bad
thing as long as it is in his interests to do so. As Dimitrov observes
ironically, Yugoslavs call this behavior 'the struggle for existence'.
The third characteristic that he sees in Yugoslav political be-

24 See Dimitar Dimitrov, 'Jedan tip ličnosti u jugoslovenskom društvu'
[One personality type in Yugoslav society], *Filosofija,* no. 1 (1970): 113–
16. Emphasis added in citations.

havior is 'opportunism'. As the discussion so far makes clear, Dimitrov perceives Yugoslavs as subordinating the basic goals of socialism to personal economic interests. Thus the Yugoslav 'connects every one of his or her actions with its possible utility; he or she continually thinks about the opportuneness of his or her behavior'. Finally, in Dimitrov's view, 'political consciousness' makes up for the meaninglessness of principles and social goals to the individual by rationalizing this behavior as 'socialist'. Thus the official ideology destroys its own *raison d'être* by setting up a cultural model — that is, the ideal type of self-manager — which is unreliable, conformist, opportunistic, and rationalizing. The Yugoslavs who emulate this model, according to Dimitrov, are no longer socialists. Nevertheless, many young Yugoslavs, particularly blue-collar workers with some skills, may acquiesce in the existence of this model without necessarily acceding to it in their own behavior, or expressing deviant norms. In short, as in other societies, there may be much quiet acceptance of dominant cultural or political models by those who are preoccupied with their daily existence. If Yugoslavs who feel this way do express an orientation which diverges from the official ideology, then they probably prefer the SKOJ model of the past along with the stricter controls of an earlier form of Titoism.

Young Yugoslavs who in recent years have deviated from the dominant cultural model by developing a hippie lifestyle, do not usually dissent from the official political ideology. They have no quarrel with either the general values for which their parents fought, e.g. peace, freedom, human potential, or the norms and institutions of self-management — as long as they are exempt from any ascetic requirements and can finish their college educations before getting good jobs in Sweden or West Germany. They love their country and they are socialists — this must not be misunderstood — but they do not see any necessity for continuing the struggle of their parents' youth. They are able to project a hippie lifestyle, by buying bell-bottomed trousers, turtlenecks, and drugs; by making contacts with young people from other societies, mostly in Western Europe; and by traveling in leisure from Yugoslavia to other countries, because they are the children of *nouveaux riches* and political leaders. Frequently, their parents have been revolutionary heroes. The hippies prefer to actualize their parents' values through passive political support and active consumption.

Another form of deviant behavior is expressed by the utopians, who prior to the outcome of the student rebellion of 1968 shared the high social origins of the hippies.[25] Perhaps the lack of success of that social movement, or the cooptation of its dissidents into executive positions in various fields, or the general depoliticization of youth in Western Europe and the United States have contributed to a decrease in the attraction of utopianism to the children of the rich, the influential, or the merely comfortable. Since 1968, the utopian youths have seemed to come from lower social strata. This change in recruitment may also reflect the growing realization among Yugoslav youth that most channels of the upward social mobility associated with economic growth since the war have been constricted. Thus the utopians, mainly university activists, criticize government policy in both politics and economics. These activists press, usually in the college newspaper, for greater egalitarianism and more political freedom. They judge the society and its leadership to have failed in realizing the original goals of equality and freedom. Not only do the utopians tend to affirm the social values for which their Partisan parents fought, but they also accept the activism and the self-sacrifice of political struggle, which the hippies have rejected. So the young utopians are the only group to work actively at reviving the SKOJ model in contrast to the dominant cultural model.

A final group of young people who deviate from the official cultural model is that of hoodlums or juvenile delinquents. They usually come from poor families, often from families which have recently migrated to the city. Presumably they observe other young Yugoslavs enjoying the benefits of industrial development and the spread of consumer goods, but they lack the skills, the jobs, and the *veze* (connections) to gain access to them. Unemployed, they roam the city streets or just sit around. The 18-year-old son of the Živković family, among the Belgrade respondents, has drifted from job to job since completing the eighth grade. He spends time driving around the city with a friend, the son of prosperous peasants, who has a car. Like his parents and

25 Although there are no data on the numbers, the social origins, the motivations, or the eventual fates of any of the groups of young people who are described here, information on the social origins of the utopians is from Dunja Rihtman-Auguštin (private communication). The utopians' political orientation is explained more fully in chapter 4.

other families in the 'wild settlement' where they live, young Živković has not been integrated into the life of the city. He would seem to be the type of young person who might commit a crime on persons or property. Because young people of this type have no *veze* in the political leadership, they go to jail.

Older Yugoslavs as well as young people are aware that 'youth has changed'. They are also aware that 'society has changed', but they are not sure how to connect the one and the other. Dimitrov's critique of current social reality is almost unique in its objectivity. Most Yugoslavs have reached the conclusion that young people show a 'hunger for values', which has been created by a double standard in their parents' morality, and that of the official ideology.[26] They see a difference between what Yugoslavs say (theory) and what they do (practice). Rather than realign current practice with classical socialist theory, some critics would revise theory to complement the social reality. In particular, they castigate the continued existence of an ascetic socialist ethic. Since Yugoslavs for the most part are no longer compelled to live and die in poverty, they think that the value system should change to accommodate the new lifestyle. As a Belgrade professor of philosophy and ethics says, 'Little by little we are becoming a rich society and not a society which can and should hold itself to a completely ascetic ethic.' In contrast to Dimitrov's censure of social reality, this philosopher evidently approves of the ideal type of self-manager and says, in effect, more power to him! In his words,

> We don't have to be unhappy that the young want, for example, a *Fića* ['little Fiat']. Let them have it, but *in a nutshell we want young people to work, to achieve the right to that* Fića *and to earn the* Fića. We would not have dared to be for some ascetic attitude. We have no fear of expanding technologically. We have to develop even further technologically. And rest assured, this will not threaten spiritual values.[27]

In my view, there is another contradiction within the dominant value system represented by middle-aged Yugoslav parents and

26 See the remarks of Katja Vodopirčeva, director of the Criminological Institute at the Ljubljana Law Faculty, in Bradarić, 'Matko Bradarić razgovara', esp. p. 167.
27 Vuko Pavićević, professor at the Philosophy Faculty, Belgrade University, in ibid., pp. 179, 180. Emphasis added.

teachers who try to socialize children and younger adults into the official ideology. This is the contradiction between what people say and what they say, in other words, the lack of internal consistency between the various messages or instructions that people give out. Here I am referring also to the kind of double-talk which occurs when agents of socialization, like parents or political leaders, inculcate their charges, e.g. children or citizens, with contradictory messages about norms and values. This is a serious case of hypocrisy on the very basis of existence.[28] Among Yugoslavs, the parents of today's young adults were socialized into political consciousness during an extraordinary time, an era of self-sacrifice and heroism, of ideals and struggle in the name of these ideals. They try to instill the values of that time in their children. Not only do the children grow up in vastly different material conditions than those in which their parents did, but the parents themselves are living better than they ever have. They see that their children's future well-being, relatively speaking, lies in a professional or technological career. Thus they advise their children to go to school or college, to learn languages, to become engineers. They also try to give their children the best consumer comforts that they can buy. So the parents talk of socialism and solidarity, but they run to Trieste on shopping sprees. These conditions have an effect on the political ideologies of both older and younger generations (as described in chapter 4). Meanwhile, some young people may perceive the contradiction in their parents' and teachers' messages about the ideal society that they are supposedly building. They hear about a society of equals, but they observe a society of equals who drive Mercedes and *Fićas* and those who must ride the bus. The young people who perceive these contradictions may show doubt, skepticism, and deviance from the official ideology. Some become utopians in the Yugoslav context. At any rate, the situation appears much more complex today than when the Partisan generation came of age. Then there were two sides: that of the enemy and that of the patriot. Gradually the model of patriot became identified with the traditional warrior-image, then with the struggle for socialism and reconstruction, now with the 'struggle for a dinar'. Unresolved contradictions both within the official ideology of socialist self-management and between theory and practice indicate that

28 See the work of R. D. Laing, esp. the case studies in R. D. Laing and A. Esterson, *Sanity, Madness and the Family* (London: Tavistock, 1964).

the desired process of political development has only begun. In this sense the realism — rather than the 'pragmatism' — of many Yugoslav youths will be a positive force for continued change. As a student from Zagreb says apropos of the 'hunger for values', 'Look at 1941. The year was a year of determination. Then it was completely clear for which side a man was making a choice. Today it is . . . much harder.' [29]

In this chapter I have made a brief historical survey of certain norms and values which have shaped Serbian culture and have also influenced a recent, shared Yugoslav culture. As such, these norms and values have helped set the parameters of contemporary social change. Just as the official ideology of the political leadership establishes what change is seen as desirable, so culturally approved behavior determines what change is possible. Between official norms and traditional norms, we have examined perceptions of society, orientations toward politics, behavior in political situations, and behavior in public places. Now is the time to tie together the threads of social reality that we have explored and to come to an agreement on what we have seen.

29 Slobodan Šnajder, in Bradarić, 'Matko Bradarić razgovara', p. 181.

8

POLITICAL AND SOCIALIST
DEVELOPMENT

You see, the worker is badly paid and doesn't have any desire
whatsoever or any stimulation to work harder and better.
Precisely because he doesn't have that desire and because he
doesn't work as much as and the way he should and could,
production falls, his salary falls, and he becomes still more
desireless and apathetic. So we come to that diabolical circle,
where the cause is the consequence and the consequence the
cause.

> Nazmija Mikulovci, President
> of the Central Workers' Council,
> *Trepča* Corporation.

Workers' Council president Nazmija Mikulovci sees a vicious
circle in the Yugoslav worker's apathy toward work and the in-
adequate financial reward for working.[1] This metaphor, according to which the cause is the consequence and the consequence
the cause, also fits the political history of socialist Yugoslavia.
But this implies neither the kind of social stagnation in which
nothing changes nor the state of affairs in which *plus ça change,
plus c'est la même chose*. Rather, the vicious circle of Yugoslav
politics is that the solutions which are derived to resolve social
problems recreate the original problematic situation in slightly
more complex form.[2] In other words, the solutions themselves
have come to perpetuate the old cleavages, the familiar divisions
between 'haves' and 'have nots', and the traditional political
stances that such groups assume.

This circular development is more visible today, a generation
after the revolution, than at other times during the continual
organization and reorganization of political life. Despite a great
change in the living standard of almost the entire population
and also a profound awakening of these people to the possibili-

1 Cited in Vuk Drašković, 'Štrajk koji ne prestaje' [Strike that doesn't
  end], *NIN*, 5 September 1971, p. 18.
2 Cf. Frane Barbieri, 'Uvodnik: Kokoš ili jaje' [Editorial: The chicken
  or the egg], *NIN*, 31 October 1971, p. 7.

Political and socialist development

ties of socialism and self-management, the major areas of Yugoslav society today bear crosses similar to the problems of twenty-five years ago. New ideas have emerged and new forms of organization are still evolving, but the problems of Yugoslav common people remain. This study has touched on three of these political, economic, and social problems: effective participation in political life; economic equality versus egalitarianism; and the incomplete 'horizontal' integration of the working class as opposed to the sustained 'vertical' cleavages between enterprises and between national-ethnic groups.

Instead of participating in the politics of self-management, many workers are concentrating their time and energy on work or other arrangements which bring them the dinars they need and want. The relatively few citizens who have not withdrawn into private pursuits have to deal with the political Establishment and the opportunists who manage to survive in the Establishment's interstices. Although the citizen-partisans and the Establishment share the same societal goals, they differ on immediate objectives and hence in their modes of political action. While the citizen-partisans rely on the promises of socialism, the Establishment activists look to the most recent Party resolutions. Most of the time, the independent self-managers batter their principles against the Establishment's monopoly over political action and, defeated and disillusioned, withdraw from combat. So the apathy of a large part of the population, and the monopoly that their leaders hold over effective political action, comprise a vicious circle in which Yugoslav self-managers are trapped.

The official ideology, as it has been amended through the adoption of various policies, perpetuates the mechanism of this vicious circle. A characteristic which may contribute to the inhibition of self-management is the dominance of 'practical' over 'pure' ideology. That is, the official ideology has come to emphasize the industrialization over the socialization of consciousness. Self-management has been transformed, according to the official ideology, from the ultimate societal goal to the most efficient means toward another goal: economic growth through industrialization. In this way the primacy of economic development, symbolized by the worker's increased buying-power, becomes legitimate. The resulting cultural model is oriented toward individual gain rather than the radical transformation of society.

Political and socialist development

Because this evolution of the official ideology has taken twenty-five years, it parallels a generational change.[3] Mainly, the Partisan generation were — and still are — more active politically and more idealistic than their children. Their societal bogeys, of course, were, first, economic underdevelopment and, after 1947, what they understood as 'Stalinism'. The dispute with the Cominform created widespread Yugoslav antipathy toward Stalin and the socialist-bloc nations under his domination. Over the next few years, not without some confusion and some heresy, all the social groups which determine and promulgate the official ideology and the spirit of the times, i.e. the politicians, philosophers, writers, came to accept Stalinism as the negative model against which Yugoslav self-management had to prove its superiority.

Gradually the Yugoslav leadership built the negative model of Stalinism into an adversary for conflicts of both theory and practice. Originally, this negative model had only a political aspect. Stalinism stood for foreign domination; it was the negation of independence. Soon however, Stalinism came to represent not only external control, but also the domination of the top of a Party-state hierarchy over the mass base. Thus, the Yugoslavs countered Stalin's monolithic personal power with the freedom of choice that workers' councils were to insure. They also intended workers' councils to counterbalance and eventually supplant the Stalinist model of bureaucratic centralism. Just as Stalin's way required submission of both nations and individuals, so the Yugoslav way called for independence.

Eventually, the negative model of Stalinism also assumed certain economic traits. These were features that the Yugoslav leadership had come to consider incompatible with their 'way' and hence undesirable. However, the undesirable economic traits that they associated with the negative model of Stalinism did not accurately depict the actual state of affairs in the Soviet Union. Although the Soviet economic system was indeed a centralized bureaucracy, as the Yugoslavs made it out to be, the distribution of monetary and other social rewards was not based on an egalitarian norm. In fact, from the early 1930s on, Stalin had fostered an imbalance in favor of cadres and skilled workers. Neverthe-

3 On the 'second-generation crisis' in socialist societies, from the viewpoint of elite analysis, cf. Zygmunt Bauman, 'Twenty Years After: The Crisis of Soviet-Type Systems', *Problems of Communism* 20, no. 6: 45–53.

less, perhaps put off by the low living standard of most of the Soviet population, the Yugoslav leaders added *uravnilovka* (leveling) to the catalog of Stalinism's evils. To differentiate themselves from this feature of the negative model, they called for individual initiative in economic life as well as in politics. Thus, the distribution norm which started as 'Reward according to need' became first 'Reward according to work' and finally 'Reward according to the results of work'. Through similar ideological adjustments, they also replaced the egalitarianism of equal, though severely limited, means with an equal-opportunity credo familiar to Americans.[4]

The guiding-force behind this evolution has been the leadership's opportunism or pragmatism in pursuing certain goals. Unfortunately, there is also an element of self-delusion which has caused the muddling and, indeed, the muddying of key concepts. As we have seen, the Yugoslav leadership tends to equate political freedom and the freedom of the market place, political repression and economic egalitarianism, etatism and planning. This sort of conceptual confusion between politics and economics has characterized attempts to define the citizen's role in society from Marx's time to our town. As T. H. Marshall points out, we have not resolved whether the citizen's role is based on social right or market value. Because Western democratic ideology regards the citizen at times as an economic being and at other times as a social being, political leaders appeal to both the citizen's sense of personal gain and his civic duty. 'But', Marshall adds, 'these paradoxes are not the invention of muddled brains; they are inherent in our contemporary social system.'[5]

As part of this system, Yugoslavia has been caught on the horns of an old dilemma: between old economic man and new socialist man. It is not unreasonable to have expected that the Yugoslav model which has inspired hope in such disparate breasts as Roger Garaudy's and Robert Dahl's would have solved this dilemma. But the Yugoslav leadership has chosen, in part opportunistically and in part as though driven by historical necessity, a kind

4 On the *uravnilovka* debate in the Soviet Union and a Soviet-American comparison, see Stanislaw Ossowski, *Class Structure in the Social Consciousness*, trans. Sheila Patterson (London: Routledge and Kegan Paul, 1963), pp. 110ff.
5 T. H. Marshall, 'Citizenship and Social Class', in *Class, Citizenship, and Social Development* (Garden City, New York: Doubleday, 1964), pp. 111ff, at 115.

of compromise. They have instituted equality to the extent that citizens enjoy the same formal political rights, and liberty to the degree that people are free to be economically unequal. This compromise between liberty and equality is called liberalism. Liberalism hardly represents a breakthrough in socialist democracy. Rather, Yugoslav liberalism — the concern with industrialization and the political conditions which aid its development, the homage to the free hand of the market, the reinterpretation of equality to allow for material incentives, and, not least, the freedom that the state grants and controls in the interest of attaining its goals — all this suggests that Yugoslavia has not broken away from the old, pre-socialist contradictions. Yugoslav leaders suggest that these are the contradictions of our times and, as such, are inescapable. Thus they perpetuate yet another vicious circle in which politics relentlessly pursues economics, and the absence of liberty complements the lack of equality.[6]

The official ideology represents only one of several political orientations that Yugoslavs share. There are also two kinds of 'socialist backlash' based on the recent Yugoslav past: 'Stalinism', referring to the period from 1945 to 1947 (Titoism I), and Titoism II, referring to the first efforts to distinguish the Yugoslav way to socialism from the Soviet model (1947–52). There is also a 'backlash' of another sort, a throwback to the ideals of the social democratic parties of the early twentieth century. Finally, there is a 'utopianism' which adheres to the classical Marxist model. Of these, backlash and utopianism represent glances toward a golden past and a golden future, respectively. Curiously, the backlash toward an earlier model of Yugoslav socialism (Titoism II) and utopianism are becoming increasingly influential orientations, particularly as inflation soars and wages come under state controls. According to a knowledgeable observer, the

6 For a much sterner view of Yugoslav liberalism, ending in the verdict that self-management is dead, see Meister, *Où va*, esp. chs. 1, 9, and 10. For a much milder view, see Solomon John Rawin, 'Social Values and Managerial Structure: The Case of Yugoslavia and Poland', *Journal of Comparative Administration* 2, no. 2 (August 1970): 131–60. For a theoretical discussion of liberty and equality which seems to take the Yugoslav point of view, see Ralf Dahrendorf, 'Liberty and Equality', in *Essays in the Theory of Society* (Garden City, New York: Anchor Books, 1969), pp. 179–214. When I used to broach this critique to Yugoslavs, I had to point out in advance that I had never lived under socialism and so lacked the experience from which to criticize. This usually dispelled any ill-feeling, for the dominant Yugoslav view regards such a critique as naive.

editor-in-chief of *NIN,* Yugoslavs 'now find [them]selves before
the tendencies that [their] self-managing democracy should be
either "corrected" by some kind of bureaucratic restoration or
on the other hand "hastened along" by some variant of a cultural revolution'.[7] The two alternatives to which the journalist
is referring are what I have called, respectively, Titoism II and
utopianism. Both backlash and utopianism seem to originate in
dissatisfaction, even disillusion, with the leadership's failure to
achieve revolutionary goals. They are also responses to the confusion of constant reorganization, which has characterized the
leadership's attempt to set up a viable polity. Finally, the ero-
sion of both revolutionary and more traditional identities has
created a great deal of doubt about where the individual and the
society are heading. Backlash on the one hand and utopianism
on the other are efforts to resolve this doubt.

Both backlash and utopianism strive, more or less inchoately,
for a socialist Yugoslavia where goods and money would be more
equitably distributed. The backlash, however, is politically reactionary, for it looks back to a golden age when people knew
their place in the revolutionary order, the norms of political life
were clear and uncomplicated, and corruption was thought to
be extinct. This was the postwar period that people recall, as
Gunther Grass has described it in another milieu of reconstruction, with 'the romanticism of lost opportunities'.[8] In contrast to
backlash, utopianism is politically radical. It looks forward to the
socialization of consciousness in full economic equality and political freedom. Potential dissenters from these orientations have
been coopted, especially during the 1960s, into the Establishment. But more recent events — Tito's signal in a speech in
Labin in May 1971 that Party members should show more vigilance, the purge of Croatian politicians seven months later for
being 'soft' on nationalism, Tito's strong criticism of 'socialist

7 Frane Barbieri, 'Uvodnik: Kokoš ili jaje', p. 7.
8 Cf. Grass on postwar Germany: 'Today there are plenty of well-heeled
   critics of the economic miracle who proclaim nostalgically — and the
   less they remember about the situation in those days the more nos-
   talgic they become — "Ah, those were the days, before the currency
   reform! Then people were still alive! Their empty stomachs didn't prevent them from waiting in line for theater tickets. And the wonderful
   parties we used to improvise with two pretzels and a bottle of potato
   schnaps, so much more fun than the fancy doings today, with all their
   caviar and champagne." ' Gunther Grass, *The Tin Drum* (Greenwich,
   Connecticut: Fawcett Publications, 1964), pp. 420–1.

millionaires and billionaires' in a speech at Rijeka in September
1972 — indicate that public opinion is strong enough to impel
or encourage the coopted dissenters into bucking the official line.
Backlash finds its adherents not only among the masses, but also
within the leadership, from Tito and the Partisan generation on
down. Events indicate that when these leaders perceive a serious
threat to the state, as from Party members' laxity, national chauvinism, and serious inequities, they tend to initiate strong action
and tighten controls. In other words, they feel that to hold the
official line they must straighten out its deviations.

It is in this light that foreigners should understand the underlying reasons for the recent 'crackdowns' on two groups of intellectuals, notably eight sociologists and philosophers at Belgrade
University's Philosophy (liberal-arts) Faculty and the editorial
board of the Zagreb-based journal *Praxis*. Both groups had profited, after the economic reforms of 1965, from the Yugoslav leadership's tendency to connect the loosening of economic controls
with political 'liberalization'. Generally, Yugoslav professors used
the relatively relaxed atmosphere to establish the academic credentials of the social sciences, to legitimize empirical investigation, to disseminate the latest methodological innovations of
Western social scientists, and to sketch the outlines — for Yugoslavia — of the intellectual's historical role in European society
as social critic.

Although the Yugoslav leadership now indicates that these
activities exceed the scope of the intellectual's functions under
socialism, an outside observer might not consider the professors'
work and their theoretical underpinnings as inimical to the leaders' policies. Indeed, this book has cited two of the criticized
Belgrade professors as expressing the apparent mood behind
much of the official line from 1965 to 1972.[9] Moreover, except
for a few cases of individual, non-academic, social critics, Yugoslav intellectuals have held to the goal of developing both a
Marxist critique of society and Marxist disciplines of sociology,
philosophy, and anthropology. Unlike some of their socialist
colleagues, such as the Polish social scientists who are working
out a positivist approach to social reality, most Yugoslav sociologists and philosophers retain their theoretical base in classical
Marxism. Furthermore, their approach seemed to be compatible

9 See citations of Svetozar Stojanović (chapters 1 and 2) and Mihailo
   Marković (chapter 4).

with the Yugoslav 'variation on Marx'. Decisions taken by the Yugoslav leadership, in pursuit of economic development, self-management, and technological progress, enabled the intellectuals, briefly, to work within the official framework.

Then why would they arouse official ire? As I have indicated in discussing the official line, and particularly the possibility of official backlash, the political leadership's action against certain intellectuals is only part of a reaction against a much more widespread, and thus more dangerous, threat to the state: from laxity, from national chauvinism, from serious economic inequities. Like the Chinese leadership, the Yugoslavs may also use a campaign against intellectuals to signal to the whole population an increased vigilance on all fronts. This 'new' orientation requires an organization from which controls emanate. Unlike the Chinese, whose Cultural Revolution (1966 and 1974) by-passed the Communist Party to rely instead on military and para-military organizations, the Yugoslavs are trying to reinvest their ruling party with the will, the authority, and the power to exert social controls.

Not only is the Yugoslav League of Communists an available means of mobilization, but, because of the significance of nationalism in Yugoslav society, it is also the most reliable social organization for carrying out control functions. The Party's early history (in the 1920s and 1930s) and its role in the Partisan War established its all-Yugoslav character. With the 1971–2 purge of various Croatian and Serbian Party leaders on grounds of 'national chauvinism', the Party demonstrated the bounds of acceptable federalism for the Yugoslav republics. Moreover, the decisions to purge the republican leaderships could not have been made unilaterally by any national-ethnic group; in this sense, too, it was an all-Yugoslav Party action. Finally, Tito and the other leaders have always been very conscious of maintaining Party and other social controls over the army because of the constant armed threat to the country's integrity posed by both the probable desire of foreign powers to occupy its strategic geopolitical position and the possible wish of disgruntled Yugoslav republics to secede from the federation.

If the League of Communists is to exercise widespread social control then it must eliminate rivals, detractors, and groups or persons who might potentially claim the public's political attention or affection. The terms in which the mass media analyze the eight Belgrade professors indicate that this is indeed the impetus for the recent criticism. In a most instructive article on the connections between the Belgrade professors and the student movement at the liberal-arts faculties in Belgrade, Zagreb, and Ljubljana, the Croatian newspaper *Vjesnik u srijedu* says,

> Sharpening their conflict with the SKJ [the Party], one of the goals of these instructors is to create the illusion of an open, general conflict between the Party and the intelligentsia, for the Party, according to their texts, is the mainstay of the bureaucratic movement, while the intelligentsia — again, in their view — should have a special status within the Party. With such opinions they attempted to establish the belief, in a certain number of their students, that they were a 'social conscience'. *In the name of 'scientific autonomy', the departments of philosophy and sociology transformed themselves into polygons for the formation of their own political action.*[10]

The sort of political action that the Party leadership considers unsuitable includes, on the one hand, efforts to make the League of Students autonomous from Party control and, on the other, student strikes, demonstrations, and mass meetings.

From 1968 to 1971, the main provocation of Yugoslav student demonstrations was the economic inequities and the lack of democracy that the students perceived in their society.[11] Since 1971, however, much of the 'agitation' in the major university centers has also focused on the problematic definition of Yugoslav federalism. So college students have put themselves on the volcanic terrain of the national-ethnic conflict. As a potential force for both disruption and mobilization in this conflict, the college students represent a threat to the political leadership and the state. Moreover, their position in the national-ethnic conflict probably generates more support for the college students in the

10 M. Lolić, M. Stojanović, M. Singer, and V. Bluml, 'Politička igra: "Filozofski" trokot Beograd-Zagreb-Ljubljana; Pod "naučnim" plaštem' [Political game: The 'philosophical' triangle Belgrade-Zagreb-Ljubljana; Under 'scientific' guise], *Vjesnik u srijedu*, 13 February 1974. Emphasis added. Cf. the threat to the political leadership's monopoly over political action posed by the Slovenian republican legislators who tried to act out their legal right to nominate federal candidates (above, chapter 5).

11 See the discussion on 'utopianism', above, chapter 4.

general population than they could expect in disputes over the role of intellectuals or the right of dissent. The potential for an alliance between dissident students and dissatisfied citizens is increased because the students in each university center tend to defend the interests of that republic and that ethnic group. Thus, beginning with the public discussion of the Constitutional amendments in 1971, the students at Belgrade University advanced a relatively centralist interpretation of federalism, while the students in Zagreb and Ljubljana defended decentralization in the form of states' (i.e. republics') rights. Since the members of each ethnic group tend to receive all their education and to hold all their jobs within the republic and the ethnic milieu of their birth, the students' stand has an obvious base in socialization practices.[12] The increasing pressure from all social groups, including college students, on the unresolved national-ethnic question places the intensification of the Party's criticism of the eight Belgrade professors and certain professors from Zagreb (from 1971 through 1974) in a different context from that usually adopted in either the West or the East.[13]

The argument so far in this chapter establishes that the Yugoslav leaders' political solutions have tended to perpetuate old cleavages (economic and national-ethnic) and to leave unresolved

12 Unemployed workers and certain professionals, such as doctors and engineers, who migrate to either the more developed republics (Serbia, Croatia, Slovenia) or to Western countries in search of jobs and higher wages are exceptions to this generalization, although surveys and personal conversations establish that migration outside the home-republic and outside Yugoslavia is perceived not as a matter of choice, but a necessity. On the geographical restrictions of jobs, see Richard Rosen and Sharon Zukin, 'Career Patterns of the Yugoslav Political Elite' (Unpublished paper, Columbia University, 1970).

13 Cf., for example, 'The Repression at Belgrade University', *The New York Review of Books* 21 (7 February 1974): 32–3; Yugoslav Embassy, 'On the Ideological and Moral Fitness of Professors and Teaching Staff at Belgrade University', *Telos* 18 (Winter 1973–4): 156–8; and my note, 'The Case of the "Belgrade Eight"', *Telos* 19 (Spring 1974): 138–41.
   Foreigners place themselves in a position of double-jeopardy when considering the case of the eight Belgrade professors. If my interpretation of the social context of this case is correct, then we must view the attack on intellectuals — of which we disapprove — as part of a larger program which includes controls over economic excesses and inequities — a step toward the egalitarianism of which we approve. Similarly, support for current expressions of the Yugoslav student movement must reconcile issues such as the mode of expression (including the right to dissent) and the content of such dissent (ethnic nationalism).

the most basic social problems that such cleavages engender. Whatever the positions of the individual Belgrade professors on specific policies, their objectivity and their critical role — to the extent of holding practice up to the stern looking-glass of theory — draw attention to contradictions in the official line and to the lack of resolution of social problems. Thus some of the Belgrade professors have endorsed the government's late-1960s policy of social differentiation, and some have advocated economic equality. Just as the former now seem to stand in the way of increasing governmental attacks on those who have profited by the policy, so the latter seem to call attention to the government's failure to move sooner and more consistently in this direction.

With various intentions, some Yugoslavs also make an association between student movements, dissent, academic sociologists, and philosophers, and national chauvinism. *Vjesnik u srijedu*, for example, describes a student meeting at Zagreb's liberal-arts faculty, held as part of a protest against the attempted dismissal of the Belgrade professors, as taking place 'with much of an uproar and in a euphoric atmosphere like those from the time of nationalism'. The reporters explain that

> the association with nationalistic euphoria is not coinciden-
> tal, because the contributors to the creation of such an at-
> mosphere [included] students who are still not cured of
> their nationalism, whom the members of KOSS [*Koordi-
> nacioni odbor Saveza studenta*] and the group around it
> certainly didn't choose as their allies (because they don't
> stand for such positions), but they only 'stuck together' ar-
> bitrarily according to that well-known motto, 'The enemy
> of my enemy is my friend.' [14]

Here the press follows the same adage, lumping together for condemnation 'extremist' students, the Yugoslav 'New Left', and ethnic nationalists.

Both the case of the Belgrade professors and the suppression of a student movement striving for its independence raise significant, universal problems. But in the context of Yugoslav so-

14. M. Lolić et al., 'Politička igra: "Filozofski" trokot Beograd-Zagreb-Ljubljana; Pod "naučnim" plaštem'.

KOSS is a student-government group of the Zagreb liberal-arts faculty which supported the Belgrade students' protest against the professors' dismissal.

ciety, they relate to specific pressures and unresolved conflicts. These include national-ethnic cleavages, economic inequality, and the role of the Communist Party in the transition to both industrialism and socialism. That the complex inter-relationships between the general and the specific problems should induce a new form of etatism, similar to the postwar Yugoslav system, seems to close yet another vicious circle in recent Yugoslav history.

Significantly, the threats that the leadership seems to consider most serious emerge from traditional cleavages rather than from new, i.e. self-managing, political forms. The historical national-ethnic cleavage, reinforced by problems of allocation of resources and related to the ideology of self-management, probably represents the most potent disruptive force. But other, very old issues are also involved. In 1953, for example, the case of Milovan Djilas challenged the legitimacy of the ruling class. This was hardly a new issue. Again, the cases of Aleksandar Ranković in 1966 and the Croatian leaders in 1971 expressed old national grievances, for Ranković was seen as a spokesman for centralism and the Croats were seen as sympathizers with separatism. It would be advantageous if Yugoslavs could work out political institutions in which new interests and cleavages, particularly those of the industrial labor force, could be expressed. At present, the interests of the working class are expressed only fragmentarily, as in strikes against individual enterprises. But the workers have grievances which should cut across national-ethnic and enterprise lines. In many cases workers are fired without cause and otherwise mistreated by enterprises, wages are low, prices are high, essential goods like milk and heating fuel are sometimes in short supply, and low social-security benefits indicate that 'the economy does not feel responsible for social policy in the widest sense of the word'.[15]

Despite workers' self-management, no organizational form — neither in the state nor the Party nor the enterprise — allows the aggregation of the workers' interests to transcend the narrow bounds of specific situations, to become a national issue. Work-

15 Zvonko Simić, 'Dileme: Jednakosti suviše ili premalo' [Dilemmas: Too much or too little equality], *NIN*, 4 April 1971, pp. 30-5, at 35. On enterprises' abuse of workers, see B. Otašević, 'Zbog čega se žale radnici: Zakon se često krši i — svesno' [Why workers complain: The law is often broken, even — consciously], *Politika*, 16 April 1971; on living problems, see the daily press.

ers' grievances become an issue only when a strike lasts so long and includes so many workers that a whole town is affected and it hits the national press. There is reason to believe that, just as an Establishment of political activists 'directs' citizens' interests on the local level, so a political and politico-technocratic Establishment 'manages' workers' interests in the enterprise. We can find an extreme example of such 'management' in the director of the Niš Electronics Industry, whose daring and politico-technical acumen has made his corporation's profits soar while his local political clout has come to overshadow that of the usual organizations. For these reasons director Jasić is considered the archetype of a politically successful technocrat. When the Party committee in his commune tried to have him fired from his job, he had the Party committee replaced. He keeps one of his two personal secretaries on the floor of the Federal Assembly, to which he is a delegate, so that he can be called to the floor to vote on issues which affect the electronics industry. He is very popular with his workers because salaries are high and housing conditions good. However, his treatment of workers falls in the tradition of benevolent autocracy. He holds two hours a week open to hear workers' grievances. The workers must come to his office, speak for no more than three minutes, and limit their appeal to one grievance. Furthermore, he allows no chairs in the workers' council meeting-room because he believes that a sitting person tends to speak too long. Although Jasić may represent an extreme, American-educated case, his methods have achieved national acclaim. They point to the possible future orientation of the Yugoslav technocracy, at least until the self-managing millennium arrives.

The organization of the economic system has made the enterprise an effective means of aggregating and expressing interests, but these are its own — not the workers' — interests. In the eyes of the state, which links business prosperity with overall economic growth, the most profitable enterprises enjoy a protected status. Thus a European sociologist compares the Yugoslav economic system to traditional state protection of fledgling industry. He views the Yugoslav enterprises as an increasingly effective counterweight to all other social forces.[16] Seen in this way, Yu-

16 Meister, *Où va*, ch. 10. Cf. Barrington Moore's view that self-management 'cannot solve the general problems of social order. Each individual plant or economic unit tends to pursue its local and selfish

goslavia is divided 'vertically' into republics and enterprises which are all competing with one another on the market. Sharing in the contemporary confusion between economics and politics as a determining factor of existence, republics as well as enterprises define their relative status in terms of their market value. They have come to believe that they deserve certain rights and benefits if they are run profitably. So the fact that Croatia brings in more foreign currency than any other republic gives added force to traditional Croatian national grievances. Moreover, the decentralized forms that Yugoslavs have worked out to make what they consider a more viable polity, e.g. the 'veto' that republics exercise and the 'republican key' for their representation in federal executive organs, perpetuate divisions and inhibit compromise between the six republics and two autonomous regions. The material preoccupations of Yugoslav citizens find an echo in inter-republican political discourse.

There is very little 'horizontal' integration which would unite the working class over the boundaries of republic and enterprise. As long as this horizontal integration is hindered or wishfully ignored, the genuinely self-managing expression and fulfillment of needs is doomed. However, preventing this sort of horizontal integration is a way of making the society more viable. According to the Polish sociologist Ossowski, a political leadership can hold society together by preventing the expression of cleavages which contradict its basic assumptions.[17] So far, socialist countries have prevented workers, intellectuals, and other groups from expressing such cleavages. Even though Yugoslavia, for one, has been moving toward legitimizing conflicts like strikes, workers and citizens lack the positive means, that is, the organization, to express their grievances and influence politics. Where such or-

interests, as has been repeatedly discovered in practice. Pushed to its logical conclusion, when these selfish interests balance each other without outside intervention the system would amount to no more than the classic model of competitive capitalism ruled by an impersonal market.' *Reflections on the Causes of Human Misery* (Boston: Beacon Press, 1973), p. 68.

17 Ossowski, *Class Structure*, p. 154. Cf. Dankwart A. Rustow, 'Transitions to Democracy: Toward a Dynamic Model', *Comparative Politics* 2 (1970): 354. Rustow suggests that democratic polities resolve cleavages substantively instead of repressing them ideologically. He says, 'A country is likely to attain democracy not by copying the constitutional laws or parliamentary practices of some previous democracy, but rather by honestly facing up to its particular conflicts and by devising or adapting effective procedures for their accommodation.'

ganization — and the will to use it — exists, as with the liberal-arts students' associations in Belgrade, Zagreb, and Ljubljana, the government penalizes attempts at unified political action. Then, the leadership and the mass media denounce student solidarity-in-dissent for being divisive and destructive vis-à-vis the general good. Just as the political leaders enforce the organizational isolation of student groups with common interests, so they also forcefully integrate rebellious student associations with those more amenable to the Party's influence. In either case, the criterion for integration seems to be whether the self-managing unit is sufficiently 'manageable'.

Systemically and systematically, self-management's decentralized organization sets up or affirms competing communities of interest in parallel units, such as communes, republics, and enterprises. Thus institutions perpetuate partial — rather than general — interests. The only two institutions which speak for wider interests are the Party and the army, but even branches of the Communist Party have advocated local and republican economic interests and at least one republic has proposed separate republican armies.[18] Logically, the institution which should speak for the workers' interests is the trade union, but more ideological revaluation is necessary before unions can assume this role in a socialist country. The cleavages and conflicts which still exist indicate that the cooperative basis of social action must be reexamined.

That these vertical cleavages have been maintained for, or have reemerged in force after, twenty-five years recalls the gradual change which sometimes occurs within a postrevolutionary generation. Such a change reverses, in effect, the revolutionary program. Following Thermidor, energies flag, vigilance relaxes, and minds turn from the pursuit of history to the pursuit of bread. Thus in France and in the Soviet Union, republic has yielded at least once to empire. But this is a gradual change, for it occurs over a generation, partially in response to new stimuli, particularly from abroad. In Yugoslavia, change both within a tired Partisan generation and between that and the next generation has resulted in an evolution in social attitudes. Many people now believe in investment rather than voluntarism and act ac-

18 See Savo Stajić, 'Hoće li slovenci u vojsku' [Will the Slovenes go in the army], *NIN*, 31 October 1971, pp. 17–18.

cordingly. Not only do parents and children learn such behavior from each other, but they also learn from their own experience. A major fact that Yugoslavs have learned is that the opportunity structure — in politics as well as in economic life — is hinged to the Establishment set up twenty-five years ago. This Establishment exercises directorship over the political action of less authoritative persons, i.e. issue-activists, citizen-partisans, and apathetics. Moreover, the children of the Establishment cadres continue to hold a monopoly of university admissions and on technical and professional occupations with the social power that such positions entail. Thus the social structure created by the revolution has been sustained over a generation. A circle of privilege and reward links the society of the 1970s with that of 1946.

In another area, public interaction in everyday situations suggests once again that Yugoslavs have not yet internalized the norms of self-management. Public behavior implies that a generation is too short a time for so much political development. Instead of developing a sense of public responsibility to fellow citizens, Yugoslavs continue to regard as 'critical others' only members of the traditional groups to which they belong by birth. These are, most prominently, the family and the ethnic nationality. On the one hand, this indicates the continued resistance of *Gemeinschaft* mentality to the wider social loyalties that self-management and industrialization demand. Yet on the other hand, it also provides evidence of fundamental social change, for the critical group has grown progressively smaller. Thus, over the past century the scale of cooperation has shrunk from the *zadruga* and village cooperatives to the nuclear family in its small apartment in town. But such change hardly accords with the aims of socialist humanism. Indeed, it implies once again that industrialism has had more of an effect upon Yugoslav consciousness than socialism.

Many Yugoslav books do not presume to end in a conclusion. Rather, they use a nice expression for the last chapter: *umesto zaključka*, 'in place of a conclusion'. That is really what this section should be called. The body of this study has described the way politics and society appear in Yugoslavia; the social reality that the Arandjelovićes, the Popovićes, the Vukovićes see; and the official ideology, social democracy, and socialist backlash that such families represent. I have also indicated my own political preferences. But I cannot predict where Yugoslavia and self-management are heading. My observations and interviews have made me more cautious than Pašić, Garaudy, and perhaps even Dahl. Reacting, perhaps overreacting, against traits imputed to the 'Stalinist' model, the Yugoslavs have nonetheless established an order of elite and masses. We have seen how they stifle the feedback from the masses that communists such as Roger Garaudy and Rosa Luxemburg have prescribed for a socialism of the future. As Albert Meister ironically notes about the Yugoslav leadership's conception of its role, they comprise 'an administration so enlightened that it seems impossible to imagine that it emanates from this people so asleep'.[19] But the price of greater political and economic equality may be the surrender of some liberty to a strong state, which alone seems able to set up and insure equality. Thus, paradoxically, self-management must be backed up by the state. Considering the uncertainty in which this leaves us (as well as the Yugoslavs), we can appreciate the stand of those Yugoslavs who, like the editor-in-chief of *NIN*, argue for maintaining the present official line of *moderate* social control over both economy and polity. As the *NIN* editor says,

> Our problem is in that self-management is not yet offered the full opportunity of regulating [anarchy and particularism], and it is already argued how incompetent it is for this task and how for that reason everything has to be returned to the state. The mystification is in that there isn't anything to return to the state, when it hasn't even abandoned a good part of these functions . . .[20]

So, after all, Trollope's appraisal of the author's difficulty in drawing a conclusion is most satisfying:

> When everything is done, the kindest-hearted critic of them all invariably twits us with the incompetency and lameness of our conclusion. We have either become idle and neglected it, or tedious and over-labored it. It is insipid or

19 Meister, *Où va*, p. 260.
20 Frane Barbieri, 'Uvodnik: Kokoš ili jaje' [Editorial: The chicken or the egg], *NIN*, 31 October 1971, p. 7. Yet over the last two years Yugoslav leaders have accepted strong, national controls against regional chauvinism and economic equality. Perhaps this indicates that Yugoslavia is moving toward the relatively democratic but more egalitarian society that I have suggested.

unnatural, overstrained or imbecile. It means nothing, or attempts too much.[21]

No conclusion on self-management could escape this fate.

Just as this study was conceived as an analysis of some problems of establishing a socialist democracy, in this case, in an economically underdeveloped society, so it was also a reaction against what I saw as some 'mainstream' concerns of American social science. Primarily what disturbed me was a disregard for, even an exploitation of, the subjects of research. This tendency has been expressed in both the methodology and the conclusions of many current comparative studies, particularly in the functionalist 'school'. These social scientists treat their subjects as anonymous statistics or impersonal constructs — as 'homunculi', in Alfred Schutz's term. What I objected to is not spectres like quantitative research or behavioralism, but the lack of a simple, humanistic concern for the subjects of study.

At times various social scientists have presented an alternative methodology. Authors such as Schutz, Oscar Lewis, and Robert Lane have made methodological innovations which recognize the essential humanity of their subjects: their problems and prospects, and how their interpretation of social reality fits in with the working of social and political institutions. A significant part of Lewis's and Lane's research consisted of effacing the interviewer's or observer's externality by listening — really listening — to what the subjects said and how they thought. Thus Lewis and Lane realized that understanding the connections between the subjects' perceptions and thoughts was imperative to explaining, first, the subjective social reality in which formal institutions operate and, second, the relationship of the subjects to these institutions. This is what I have tried to do in my work.

I have felt free to create, name, and combine various analytic concepts and research methods so that I could present a social reality as I saw others living it. Perhaps this constitutes the book's greatest strength: that it has rejected the fetishism of 'the scientific method' and its alleged objectivity in favor of explanation 'grounded' in admittedly subjective interpretation. Aside from this methodological stance, three concepts and two methods

21 Anthony Trollope, *Barchester Towers* (New York: Signet Classics, 1963), pp. 505–6.

that I have utilized seem particularly suggestive for critical social science. These are the concepts of the stratification of political participation, public behavior, and the political generation; and the research methods of participant-observation of political gatherings and analyzing the life-stories of respondents.

First, the stratification of political participation implies that certain modes of action are available to some groups of citizens and are closed to others. These options and opportunities color the behavior and the argumentation — or the style and substance — of the various strata of political participants from elites to masses. Once we admit that political action in all societies, including the 'self-managed' one, is stratified in this way, then we can deal forthrightly with issues such as the monopoly of power, the contradiction between theory and practice, hypocrisy in political discourse, and the alienation of citizens from political life.

The second important concept in this work is that of public behavior. Here I have followed in the steps of G. H. Mead, the interaction 'school' of social psychologists, and Erving Goffman, among others, to suggest the possibility that the dominant political ideology may have ramifications on the way people treat each other in everyday life. So I have introduced observations of public behavior into the study of politics as yet another 'slice of data', together with more orthodox sources such as the written official ideology, interviews with selected respondents, and other studies. It is understood, I hope, that this kind of analysis, as a reproduction of field work, is a legitimate part of the study of society.

The third concept that I have adopted is that of the political generation. Although there are difficulties in arbitrarily defining generational boundaries, there is evidence for the influence of early socialization, even at the stage of transition to adulthood, on later political attitudes and behavior. This study has described intergenerational relationships in Yugoslavia, emphasizing the moderate continuity and discontinuity between age-groups. Because these political generations suggest a convenient way of grouping people's experiences, it would be useful if more empirical work were done on this theme. The areas, both empirical and analytic, which should be examined are, first, the changes in attitudes and behavior which come with aging and, second, the complex mutual learning process between parents and children.

Political and socialist development

Two of the research methods that I have used are participant-observation of low-level political meetings and recording the life-stories of respondents. As a research method, participant-observation has long been a staple of the anthropologist's field kit. It represents the best effort to get a picture of the totality of social forces, institutions, and other individuals that the subjects confront. If observers are 'objective' to the extent that they do not impose their theoretical categories on the subjects, then they can learn a lot. The low-level political meetings are not usually so supersensitive and impenetrable to outside observers as higher-level or elite organs. Thus they provide an open field where interaction between various kinds of political actors, as well as the strategies and stratagems of their action, can be observed. Such observations suggest, on the one hand, divers categories around which additional data can be organized and, on the other, hypotheses about the structure of political action as a whole. Obviously, they are not the unique data source in this or any other study. They may be combined, for example, with data from interviews, survey responses, decision-making studies, and public statements by political officials. Also useful is material from the life-stories of respondents selected to represent variation within certain parameters. These life-stories comprise records of — depending on the researcher's metaphor — social forces working on the subjects or the subjects' confrontation with social forces. At any rate, as the respondents narrate their life-stories they not only present a record of what has happened to them, how they have behaved in concrete situations, but they also indicate their personal ideology. Usually, they cannot avoid indicating the ongoing process by which they rationalize, interpret, and, in short, 'make sense' of the working of social institutions and their place within the framework of these institutions. Furthermore, the life-stories offer a chronological view of past behavior and experiences. Thus they can be used to study long-range processes like social mobility or alienation.

Finally, this study has integrated the researcher's political ideology and methodology. From the very choice of topic — participation, equality, and socialism in a post-revolutionary society — to the concluding chapter, I have made no secret of a bias toward participatory democracy and economic equality. Because the official ideology of the society that I examined also shows these tendencies, I was able to criticize the society from the point of view of the gap between theory and practice. The direction of my criticism would stamp me as a utopian (in the terms that I have created for current Yugoslav political orientations), for I favor that paradoxical combination of strong-weak state controls in the economy and polity, respectively. In fact, living in Yugoslavia for a year as a participant-observer caused me to become as angered by unjustified privilege in that society as in my own. Furthermore, the more I juxtaposed catchphrases like 'Reward according to the results of work' and 'clear accounts' (*'čisti računi'* — referring to putting inter-republican relations on the level of business relations among equals, all keeping books on the debits and credits) with the lives that I have described in this study, the more I became concerned about the distance between the theory and practice of a political ideology. This, again, has not been a concern of 'mainstream' political science and political sociology in America.

To present an authentic, multi-dimensional view of politics and society in Yugoslavia, I have provided lengthy excerpts from interviews and voters' meetings. I have examined individual lives and collective experiences; perceptions and attitudes; political and public behavior. Rather than a scholarly case study, this book is intended to be understandable to non-experts, to the subjects themselves. It has offered them, as well as other readers, several categories for thinking about and some standards for positively criticizing their society. Thus its social criticism has been grounded in an in-depth approach to life in an industrializing socialist country. If the work has indeed carried out these intentions, then it should not be faulted, in the words of Trollope's imaginary critic, because 'it means nothing, or attempts too much'.

APPENDIX

METHODOLOGY AND FIELD WORK

The obstetrical slap that starts us howling is flesh against flesh, not concept against concept.

Maurice Natanson

As the preceding work has made clear, its goal has been to make sense of a socialist society which has distinguished itself by certain contributions to the theory and practice of participatory democracy. This topic, and the methodology that it calls for, suit various concerns of social — and sociological — criticism that I share. As the reader may already have concluded from the empirical part of the study, my approach has tried to counter the imperialistic, quantitative social science which prevails in much comparative sociological and political research with a qualitative analysis of politics and society.

Studies in the mainstream of imperialistic social science share a common and interconnected orientation, methods, and content.[1] Turning the classical priorities of sociological research on their heads, practitioners in this field appear to place most emphasis on what we have lapsed into calling quantitative methodology. To this end they export to other countries large-scale projects based on hierarchically-organized team work, an awesome array of data-processing techniques, and quantitative rather than qualitative analysis. This sort of work has been compatible with policy formulation within the governments of certain wealthy countries and international organizations, which have become major sources of funding for both underdeveloped countries and social scientists. Just as certain problems tend to develop in these international relationships, so too do strains of condescension and exploitation appear in relations based on social science imperialism. For at least two reasons, this kind

1 The description which follows fits the dominant model of comparative sociological research at the present time. At other times, the model might be different, e.g. it might focus on qualitative analysis, or it might be more or less inclusive of different fields of knowledge, e.g. economics, history, psychology.

of study tends to exploit its subjects: first, by treating them as aggregate constructs without adequate consideration of the nature of social aggregates and, second, by choosing problems for research which are unrelated to either the life-problems of real people or the struggle toward universal and societal goals. Individuals, deprived of their biographies and their motivations, become cells in a matrix to be rotated on the social scientists' spit. Nor has this sort of analysis contributed a deeper understanding of the nature of social groups such as masses and classes. Moreover, social science imperialists often discourage critical analysis of the social systems that they are studying when such analysis proceeds from assumptions or theses which run counter to their own way of thinking. Thus many comparative studies develop mechanistic concepts and abstract categories rather than critical ideas about specific societies or social problems. As they unfold, concepts such as 'development' or 'political culture' lose their concrete, historical content and become vehicles for the propagation of more work in the current tradition of imperialistic social science.

My work intended, by inflating neither concepts nor rafts of hypotheses, to utilize past studies, intensive interviewing, participant-observation, social and economic data, and public statements in the mass media to get into the effects on ordinary people of the social structure and the official ideology of Yugoslav socialism. Admittedly, this represents only one way of approaching a social reality; for me, however, this seems a very basic way. This approach was influenced by the qualitative methodology of Alfred Schutz and Peter Berger and Thomas Luckmann, all of whom have carried out the Weberian dictum of *Verstehen* by seeking to analyze the meaning of social reality to and within the life of the individual living in and conceiving of this reality. And Berger and two of his later coauthors say,

> Society is viewed in this perspective as a dialectic between objective givenness and subjective meanings — that is, as being constituted by the reciprocal interaction of what is experienced as outside reality (specifically, the world of institutions that confronts the individual) and what is experienced as being within the consciousness of the individual. Put differently, *all social reality has an essential component of consciousness.* The *consciousness of everyday life* is the web of meanings that allow the individual to navigate his way through the ordinary events and encounters of his life with others. The totality of these meanings, which he shares

Methodology and field work

with others, makes up a particular social life-world . . .
Any particular *social life-world* is constructed by the meanings
of those who 'inhabit' it.[2]

Schutz advocates that, instead of creating and manipulating
models of social actors, social scientists should concentrate on
understanding the way their subjects think about the world.
In this aim Schutz is guided more by common sense than by
the quest for grand social theory, for he suggests that the resulting social-science models be constructed so that they make
sense to the subjects themselves and to all other lay readers.

Of course, seeking to explain the subjective meaning of a
social reality for some collectivity, especially for a whole society,
subsumes many kinds of knowledge, points of view, substances
and shadows. Mindful of the pitfalls that this implies, I have
provided observations, life-stories, and indications of behavior
in everyday conditions in order to reproduce, within a representative range, the experiences which comprise ordinary urban
Yugoslavs' stock of knowledge about society, the categories or
typifications into which they organize these experiences and
the expectations that they generate, the salience or relevance
which these commonly-accepted categories hold for different
people, and the various models of social reality that these Yugoslavs develop and identify with 'Yugoslav socialism'. Indeed,
as an observer in that society, I have indicated experiences,
categories, relevances, and models of my own.

The major problem with this sort of approach is that it
tends to present a static picture of social reality. Because it
emphasizes a quest for order and integration on the part of
both the individual and the social system, this approach leaves
change to the eye of the beholder. What sense, then, are we to
make of the recurrent changes in Yugoslav society? We have
seen ordinary Yugoslavs in a dialectical relationship with many
of the stated values, goals, and norms of their society. We have
also noted the contradictory implications which may arise from

2 Peter Berger, Brigitte Berger, and Hansfried Kellner, *The Homeless
Mind: Modernization and Consciousness* (New York: Vintage Books,
1974), p. 12. See Schutz, *Collected Papers*, esp. 'Common-Sense and
Scientific Interpretation of Human Action', 1: 3–47, and 'Concept and
Theory Formation in the Social Sciences', 1: 48–66; and Peter L. Berger
and Thomas Luckmann, *The Social Construction of Reality* (Garden
City, New York: Anchor Books, 1967). Cf. H. H. Gerth and C. Wright
Mills, *From Max Weber* (New York: Oxford University Press, 1958),
pp. 55–61 and the intentions behind Robert Pranger, *Action, Sym-
bolism, and Order: The Existential Dimensions of Politics in Modern
Citizenship* (Nashville: Vanderbilt University Press, 1968).

such social constructs as theory and practice, economics and ideology, egalitarianism and liberty, industrialism and socialism. These contradictions, which are reflected in every area of social life, require a social science methodology to comprehend rather than to minimize them. In this study, two problems in particular required the modification of the qualitative methodology we have been discussing: the construction of a revolutionary social order and the socialization, in a Marxian sense, of consciousness and behavior. To deal with these problems I have tried to make a more dynamic, more critical analysis than Schutz's methodology implies.

The dynamism with which we have been mainly concerned arises from four types of constantly changing relationships: (1) the relationship between the choice of social goals or social policies and the response to these choices, including the unanticipated consequences of pursuing certain objectives and the responses occasioned in turn by these unexpected results; (2) the relationship, structured by institutions and ideology, between the individual and collectivities of various dimensions; (3) the relationship between traditional and dominant, contemporary conceptions of morality, particularly those which define the individual's place in both present and future social orders; and, overarching these, (4) the relationship between morality and its practice. Taken together, these relationships establish a context of continual destabilization rather than order. So the most useful social science concepts should reflect not only the content of these relationships, but also the social conditions which structure them, the contradictions which emerge within and between institutions, and the attempts which are made to resolve the contradictions. These concepts should also comprehend the fact that the 'resolutions' — partially emergent and partially imposed — serve to redefine the relationships. In this examination of the social reality of Yugoslav socialism, I have used the four types of relationships, as well as the concept of generations, an idea about political stratification, and various relationships between economics and politics. However, these concepts represent only a step toward developing an adequate social-science methodology. The reader may find a return to Marx, to the Critical Theory of the Frankfort School, and to Mannheim very helpful here.

This work has also been influenced by several empirical studies, primarily by sociologists and anthropologists, which focus on the social relations, perceptions, and ideologies of ordinary people.[3] Even without abandoning political and sociological analysis for the examination of individual psyches, there is still much to be learned from in-depth work in these areas. Unfortunately, many social scientists have assumed that a few general and historical texts, followed by investigation through massive survey research, will provide a fairly complete basis for generalizing about any social or political system, its citizens, and its prospects. Thus, for the most part, they have relegated labor-intensive, self-involving research work and subjective measures to such specialists as the ethnologists and the ethnomethodologists, to case studies rather than general analyses.[4] But it may be argued that social scientists do not in fact understand those concepts and constructs which seem to be most basic to, most accepted in our everyday lives. Even as 'understood' a concept as American ideology has many more — and more complex — meanings than commonly appear in sociological and political discussions.[5] Especially when attempting to analyze a society in which we ourselves have not grown up, we should demand and cultivate a literature of 'basic research' on ordinary lives and commonly-derived cognitions and perceptions. An ironically unheeded suggestion for this type of research was made, several years ago, within a mainstream of political science, in Lucian Pye's remark that we should study politics by comparing collective history and individual biography.[6]

FIELD WORK

Utilized mostly by anthropologists, the study of families offers a research strategy which focuses on both individuals and collectivities. The family, at least as we know it today in nuclear form, is both a 'natural' and a 'social' unit, in which people

3 See, for example, Oscar Lewis, *Five Families* (New York: Mentor Books, 1959) and *La Vida*; Lane, *Political Ideology*; Herbert Gans, *The Urban Villagers* (New York: Free Press, 1962); Elliot Liebow, *Tally's Corner* (Boston: Little, Brown, 1967); Danilo Dolci, *Report From Palermo*, trans. P. D. Cummins (New York: Viking Press, 1970 [1959]).

4 Sociologists Barney Glaser and Anselm Strauss argue that the findings of such research as participant-observation are not merely preliminary to real knowledge: they do constitute real knowledge. *The Discovery of Grounded Theory: Strategies for Qualitative Research* (Chicago: Aldine, 1967), pp. 226–8.

5 See Lane, *Political Ideology* and Joan Huber and William H. Form, *Income and Ideology: An Analysis of the American Political Formula* (New York: Free Press, 1973).

6 In Lucian W. Pye and Sidney Verba, eds., *Political Culture and Political Development* (Princeton University Press, 1965), p. 8.

learn from each other how they should act in the larger society. Within the family a researcher can participate, on the one hand, in the subjects' private lives, and can observe, on the other, the way they integrate these private lives with their public roles. The family also provides a context for studying the inter-action and mutual learning between generations. Ideally, I wanted to 'get into' a small number of Yugoslav families by camping out with them, i.e. by living in their households for several weeks at a time. But that degree of participant-observa-tion does not work out in a city. The demands of city living — in terms of both time and space — result in the subjects' need for privacy and a certain sense of hurriedness. So I had to settle for series of extended conversations and multiple in-terviewing with the adult members of a small sample of families. A limit of ten families appeared reasonable in light of my time limitations (one year) and of the delay which accompanies most field projects, especially, it seems, in Yugoslavia. I wanted to make this sample as homogeneous as possible with regard to national-ethnic identification, which is Yugoslavia's major divid-ing line, so that I could view more clearly the effect of social factors and experience on political attitudes and behavior. Thus I limited the sample to ethnic Serbs residing in Belgrade.

Why Serbs? Why Belgrade? First of all, Serbs represent a middle level in many senses. Whenever the six Yugoslav re-publics are rank-ordered according to an economic indicator, e.g. industrial production, growth rate, or income, Serbia usu-ally comes out in the middle. Furthermore, Greater Serbia con-tains large areas at all levels of economic and urban develop-ment. Belgrade, for example, is the most populous city in the country, capital of both Serbia and Yugoslavia. Historically, also, Serbia represents a middle ground, for it was under foreign rule rather less than Bosnia and Macedonia but longer than Montenegro and the Dalmatian Coast area around Dubrovnik. Moreover, the Serbs did not buckle under to foreign rule so much as the Bosnians and the Croats, who provided members of a native elite identified with and imposed by the colonial power, i.e. the Ottoman and Austro-Hungarian empires in Bosnia, and the Austro-Hungarian Empire in Croatia.

My choice of Belgrade was also related to the ethnic cleavage and its political implications. Most Croats are still convinced that Belgrade is presiding over the demise of republican sover-eignty or states' rights, particularly through the monopoly of central banks and federal agencies located in the Yugoslav capital. Thus Croats feel bitter about the centralized state and the obligations that federalism entails. They object, for example, to sending their foreign currency to a central pool, from which much of it is allocated not to Croatia but to the less developed republics, so that they can buy machinery and technical equipment abroad. Because Croatian businesses, especially in the tourist industry, and Croats working abroad provide 40 percent of Yugoslavia's foreign currency, they think that Croatia should get a larger share. Concrete issues of national sovereignty such as this one combine with a traditional distrust of Belgrade politics and a national-ethnic rivalry with the Serbs. Thus Croatian citizens have a certain disaffection from the state which is not directly connected with socialism. The riots which occurred in Zagreb in 1971, involving students and older citizens and resulting in the forced resignations of many Croatian Party leaders, showed a unanimity of opposition on this point which has no counterpart in other republics. In contrast to the policy of the Croatian students, recent student politics in Belgrade (from 1971 on) have supported the federal government and opposed efforts to increase republican autonomy, even those embodied in the constitutional amendments designed by the political leadership. All in all, these grievances and the disaffection from the state that they cause do not make for an environment in which to study the effect of socialism on people's lives. A final, nontrivial reason for my choosing Serbs was language. Because I had learned the Serbian variant of Serbo-Croatian, I felt that Serbs would accept me more readily than Croats, at least on the nonprofessional level on which my interview relationships would be based. My language makes me a double foreigner in Croatia: a Serbian-speaking American.

The reasons that I chose Belgrade rather than another city or a village were also both methodological and personal. Because it is the biggest city in the country and still growing rapidly, Belgrade is the glass in which the future can be seen for Yugoslavia as a whole. As Belgrade has developed industrially and economically, so all Yugoslav towns want to develop.[7] Furthermore, Belgrade draws many immigrants from other areas of the country, mostly looking for jobs for themselves and schools for their children. They believe that Belgrade offers them the best material and cultural conditions available in Yugoslavia. (Croats migrate to Zagreb and Slovenes to Ljubljana.) Thus a research site in Belgrade can include many different kinds of people with diverse experiences. Neither a town nor a village

7 I must point out that Zagreb and Ljubljana are not only historically more developed as urban centers, but they seem better planned.

could provide such a milieu. For personal reasons, also, I thought that adjustment to a year of village life would be too hard for me psychologically. Finally, I knew something about Belgrade and had a few contacts there.

Although Belgrade was my main working site, I have also utilized the resources of other Yugoslav regions. As a traveler through the republics, I compared my impressions there with my systematic observations in Belgrade and Greater Serbia. As a student, I have compared my research findings with those of social scientists in Croatia and Slovenia who are exploring areas related to my concerns. I have tried wherever possible in the text to cite the work of these Yugoslavs. Despite the relatedness of our research problems, our samples were quite different: I worked with Serbs in Belgrade, while they worked (primarily through survey research) with Croats and Slovenes. Nevertheless, my interpretation of their findings — through interpolating them with my own observations and impressions and consulting with Croatian and Slovenian sociologists — has convinced me that much of their analysis is generalizable to other regions in the country. Thus I have ventured to call 'Yugoslav' those norms in values and behavior which seem to be shared by two or more divergent ethnic groups. Sometimes I have dared to term the behavior or orientations exemplified by my respondents (i.e. Serbs in Belgrade) 'Yugoslav'. I have done this in cases where I believe the wider term applies and is verifiable.

Although I had no trouble choosing Belgrade as a field for research, I had many problems in finding ten families for my sample. None of the Yugoslav social scientists with whom I established contact would help me here. My mentor, a political advisor and theorist, thought it would be better for me if I managed to meet my subjects informally rather than under his official aegis. However, every social scientist who does empirical work either kept silent on the subject of my sample or, once offering me help, then engaged in behavior which incenses students doing field work in other cultures but rarely attracts attention back home: the dilatory tactic.

After two months of reading Yugoslav studies on self-management, particularly on participation and socialization, I decided to request or to browbeat acquaintances who knew of — but did not know intimately — families which were absolutely ordinary, i.e. in which no member held high political office, and which would be willing to talk with me about the political system. Because I wanted five middle-class and five working-class families which would vary in terms of income, education, and length of time that they had lived in Belgrade, I selected or rejected families that were suggested until the sample fit these requirements. Thus I met Danilo Arandjelović through a friend of mine who had been his boss, Branislav Belić through a mutual friend, and Miša Cvijić through a mutual business acquaintance who also introduced me to Vesna Djordjević and Milutin Filipović, co-workers in his enterprise. I met Rade Popović and Jovan Zivković when a sociologist-friend of mine took me to a 'wild settlement' where his institute had done field work, and through the Zivkovićes I met the Stojanović family. Then, by presenting myself to a family in a different neighborhood that had been interviewed several months before by a Yugoslav friend, I met the Ristićes. Finally, I found a laundrywoman and her family (the Vukovićes) so friendly and talkative that I decided to use them as respondents. That is how I made up my sample.

Interviews

I tried to duplicate Oscar Lewis' combination of conversations, interview questions, life stories, daily routine, and participant-observation of family life with a sample of ten families, whom I visited as often as once a week.[8] We usually sat around and drank *rakija* (brandy) or *vinjak* (cognac) and coffee or, in the poorer homes, just coffee, while my respondents smoked cigarettes and I refused cigarettes, and they talked for me and my tape recorder. Except for three families (one of which I rejected), the Yugoslavs related very well to this technique. They were pleased to meet an American and, if my nationality inhibited them at first from presenting anything but a 'front' of some sort, my continued visits, I think, broke much of that down. Nor were they offended or puzzled by my use of a tape recorder. At the first meeting I asked whether they would object to my using it, and only one family objected.[9] Then, I brought the tape recorder to the second meeting and explained how it worked. To ease its acceptance, I taped a little bit of the opening civilities and played it back so that we could all hear how we sounded. Because Yugoslavs are now very caught up in technological progress, they were impressed and perhaps even proud to be tape-recorded. I do not think that this method

8 See Lewis, *La Vida*, pp. xviii–xxiv.
9 I took notes while interviewing this family. Their suspicion of me apparently arose from the fact that I had been introduced to them by the husband's superior at work. So they suspected me of being a kind of spy sent by his enterprise.

inhibited them from saying what they wanted to say. Sometimes they even forgot that I was taping the conversation.

My interviews with these ten families were tape-recorded in Belgrade between January and June 1971 at the respondents' homes (except for Arandjelović, whom I interviewed at work). I spent approximately sixty-five hours interviewing, dividing my time among the ten families as follows:

Arandjelović	2 hours	Popović	4 hours
Belić	8	Ristić	3
Cvijić	7	Stojanović	3
Djordjević	18	Vuković	7
Filipović	7½	Živković	6

Interviews were semi-structured, and most questions were included in all interviews within a conversational context.

From these prolonged contacts with families, I derived three kinds of data. First, by asking straightforward questions and looking around the home, I got inventory or census-type data about the family's composition, education, income, and life-style. Second, by asking roundabout questions, I got qualitative data about relations within the family, relations with relatives and friends outside the home, attachment to the residential community, adaptation to urban life, and daily routine. Third, by drawing the respondents out in conversation, I got what could be called dense qualitative data about lives and perceptions. The advantage of these extended conversations is that I drew the respondents into an almost stream-of-consciousness kind of speech, so that their comments about society and politics were always framed within the context of their lives and personalities. I have tried to reproduce this context in the study by using long excerpts from the interviews rather than brief quotations.

One component of these dense data consists of all the details that individuals associate with their life-stories.[10] I found that the interview relationship can go very well if the researcher asks for the respondents' life-stories near the beginning of the interview process, e.g. at the second meeting, for this becomes in most cases an ego-expanding experience for the respondents. Moreover, the interviewer can learn from the life-stories more history and more about the respondents than mere factual

10 Anthropologist Joel M. Halpern utilizes life-stories in 'The Process of Modernization as Reflected in Yugoslav Peasant Biographies', Kroeber Anthropological Society, *Essays in Balkan Ethnology*, Special Publications no. 1 (Berkeley, 1967), pp. 109–26.

questions indicate. Furthermore, the life-story includes elements
of social memory. In this way the interviewer can delve into
crystallizing experiences from the respondents' youth and their
present integration of all their past experiences. A third topic of
dense qualitative data is social consciousness. This topic refers to
whatever group consciousness the respondents share, their perceptions of present and possibly future society, their idealism,
their interpretation of their own place in societal changes, and
their reaction to these changes and pressures. Finally, the extensive conversations let the interviewer find out how the
respondents understand the effect that they have on other people and on institutions in society, indicating their objective
competence, their subjective efficacy, and ultimately their alienation from or integration into the social system. Although these
topics apply to most societies, the questions must be formulated
and arranged so that they are relevant to each particular
respondent. The experience of testing questions in the field,
coupled with a sensitivity to both the political situation and the
differences between the interviewer and the respondent, indicates
where the emphasis should lie, where the elliptical suggestion
is more in order than the broadside.

Voters' meetings

To supplement these interviews with more objective material,
I needed to observe political participation.[11] Ideally, I would
have observed the same respondents as they participated in politics, say, at meetings. This proved to be impossible. First, most
of them do not attend political meetings of any kind. Second,
I was not able to get permission to attend Party meetings, and
only one of the respondents belongs to a workers' council. Third,
passing myself off as a Yugoslav of voting age, I was allowed into
basic-level voters' meetings. So I settled for observation of
voters' meetings, an open political forum for both the masses
and me.

I attended voters' meetings around Belgrade but mostly in
the area where I lived for a period of six months, from December 1970 to June 1971. Because no stenographic record is
taken of these meetings, I took my own notes. No one ever
questioned who I was, let alone this note-taking. I tried to

11 Goffman, *Behavior in Public Places* and *The Presentation of Self in
Everyday Life* are very suggestive — even irresistible — for this type of
analysis. Curiously, few political scientists or political sociologists (possibly disdaining the everyday, the familiar, or the mass) depict participation in this way. An exception is Herbert Gans, *The Levittowners*
(New York: Vintage Books, 1967), chs. 12–13.

look at the meeting as if it were, according to one metaphor, a play. Thus I looked not only at its staging, i.e. the actors' use of space, but also at the way the participants presented themselves by their physical presence and their manner of speaking. Finally, I recorded the argumentation that all participants used, often in verbatim notes. Reflecting on these notes back in New York, I was able to see certain categories and to tie them to events in the larger political situation, i.e. the society. So my observation had to be joined with articles in the mass media, especially in *NIN*, the weekly news magazine published in Belgrade, and Yugoslav empirical studies.

Public behavior

The inclusion of participant-observation of public behavior is perhaps the most problematic feature of this study, but it appears justified for at least three reasons. First, public behavior is merely an extension of behavior in the political arena and, as such, offers a larger context for observation, comparison, and generalization. Second, public behavior reflects, in the broadest sense, culture and traditional images of self and others in society. Third, public behavior indicates actual norms rather than idealizations.[12] As such, the norms of public behavior can be compared with the idealizations of cultural stereotypes in traditional beliefs, on the one hand, and contemporary ideology, on the other. In addition to participant-observation in many public situations, from waiting for and riding in the bus to drinking coffee in a *kafana*, I noted parts of the interviews which touched on social norms and relationships with others outside the home and used two Yugoslav studies of the 'cultural norms' of self-management. Yugoslav ethnographic studies were also indispensable for background on traditional culture. To balance my jaundice, I tried to confirm my impressions through conversations with Yugoslavs and reading the daily press, thinking that if behavior which struck me as anomalous or rude also hit Yugoslavs as, to some extent, problematic, then I must indeed have found a contradiction between theory and practice, or at least a norm in transition. So the data in this study should not be considered merely as the anecdotes of a foreign visitor.

In summary, all the techniques of data-gathering were designed to 'get into' the consciousness of ordinary citizens. I have

12 Cf. Goffman, *Behavior in Public Places* and Hall, *The Hidden Dimension.*

found justification of my analysis in the fact that Yugoslavs whom I talked to shared some of my views on the way their society works. Furthermore, reading of the Yugoslav press since my departure from Belgrade indicates that the problems that I have emphasized continue to absorb political leaders and citizens. My ultimate purpose, in both research and writing, has been to understand Yugoslav social reality the way Yugoslavs do, and to consider the potential of self-management from that vantage-point.

BIBLIOGRAPHY

Adizes, Ichak. *Industrial Democracy: Yugoslav Style.* New York: Free Press, 1971.

Adler-Karlsson, Gunnar. *Functional Socialism: A Swedish Theory for Democratic Socialization.* Stockholm: Prisma, 1969. Condensed and published as 'Funkcionalni socijalizam' [Functional socialism]. *Gledišta* 8, no. 4 (1969): 533–51.

Almond, Gabriel A., and Verba, Sidney. *The Civic Culture.* Boston: Little, Brown, 1965.

Andrić, Ivo. *The Bridge on the Drina.* Translated by Lovett F. Edwards. New York: New American Library, 1967.

Antonijević, Zorka. 'Položaj u procesu proizvodnje kao činilac samoupravljanja' [Position in the production process as a factor of self-management]. *Gledišta* 8, no. 2 (1967): 179–86.

Arzenšek, Vladimir. 'Samoupravljanje kao motiv i socijalna vrednost' [Self-management as a motivation and a social value]. *Moderna organizacija* 2, no. 1 (1969): 23–32.

Auty, Phyllis. *Yugoslavia.* New York: Walker and Co., 1965.

Banfield, Edward C. *The Moral Basis of Backward Society.* New York: Free Press, 1958.

Barber, James David. *Citizen Politics: An Introduction to Political Behavior.* Chicago: Markham, 1969.

Bass, Robert, and Marbury, Elizabeth, eds. *The Soviet-Yugoslav Controversy 1948–1958: A Documentary Record.* New York: Prospect Books, for the East Europe Institute, 1959.

Becker, Howard S., and Geer, Blanche. 'The Analysis of Qualitative Field Data'. In *Human Organization Research,* edited by Richard N. Adams and Jack J. Preiss. Homewood, Illinois: Dorsey Press, 1960.

Bećković, Matija. *Dr Janez Paćuka o medjuvremenu* [Dr Janez Paćuka on the meantime]. Novi Sad: Matica Srpska, Biblioteka Danas, 1969.

[Belgrade.] Skupština grada Beograda, Gradska popisna komisija. *Informacija o izvršenju popisa stanovništva i stanova* [Information on carrying out the census of population and apartments]. Belgrade, 1971.

Skupština grada Beograda, Gradski zavod za statistiku, Služba društvenog knjigovodstva. *Mesečni statistički bilten Beograda* [Monthly statistical bulletin of Belgrade] 14, no. 1.

Benc, Milan. 'Politička kultura gradjana i anketna istraživanja u Hrvatskoj' [Political culture of the citizens and survey research in Croatia]. *Politička misao* 7, no. 1 (1970): 23–31.

Bibliography

Berger, Bennett M. 'How Long is a Generation?' *British Journal of Sociology* 11, no. 1 (1960): 10–23.

Berger, Peter L., and Luckmann, Thomas. *The Social Construction of Reality*. Garden City, New York: Anchor Books, 1967.

Berković, Eva. 'Differentiation of Personal Incomes'. *Yugoslav Survey* 10, no. 1 (1969): 81–90.

Bićanić, Rudolf. *Economic Policy in Socialist Yugoslavia*. Cambridge University Press, 1973.

'Proces podruštvljenja i socijalizam' [The socialization process and socialism]. *Praxis* 5, no. 1–2 (1968): 180–5.

Bilandžić, Dušan. *Borba za samoupravni socijalizam u Jugoslaviji: 1945–1969* [The struggle for self-managing socialism in Yugoslavia: 1945–1969]. Zagreb: Institut za historiju radničkog pokreta Hrvatske, 1969.

et al. 'Problemi ostvarivanja samoupravljanja' [Problems of realizing self-management]. *Naše teme* 10, no. 3 (1966): 517–94.

Blumberg, Paul. *Industrial Democracy*. New York: Schocken, 1969.

Bolčić, Silvano. 'Samoupravljanje — cilj ili sredstvo' [Self-management — end or means]. *Gledišta* 9, no. 2 (1968): 221–30.

Bradarić, Matko. 'Matko Bradarić razgovara s Katjom Vodopirčevom, Ivom Segulovom [i. dr.] o mladima danas: Postoji li glad mladih za vrijednostima?' [Matko Bradarić talks with Katja Vodopirčeva, Ivo Segulov (and others) about youth today: Is there a hunger for values among young people?] *Encyclopaedia moderna* 2, no. 5–6 (1967): 166–85.

Bročić, Manojlo. 'Omladina i politika' [Youth and politics]. *Gledišta* 8, no. 2 (1967): 161–78.

Broekmeyer, M. J., ed. *Yugoslav Workers' Self-Management*. Dordrecht: D. Reidel Publishing Co., 1970.

Burić, Olivera. 'Family, Education and Socialization'. Paper prepared for the International Symposium on the Educational Functions of the Family in the Contemporary World, 23–7 November 1970, in Warsaw. Mimeographed.

and Zečević, Andjelka. *Porodični život i društveni položaj porodice* [Family life and the social position of the family]. Belgrade: Institut društvenih nauka, 1969.

Cammett, John M. *Antonio Gramsci and the Origins of Italian Communism*. Stanford University Press, 1967.

Campbell, John C. *Tito's Separate Road: America and Yugoslavia in World Politics*. New York: Harper and Row, for the Council on Foreign Relations, 1967.

Clissold, Stephen, ed. *A Short History of Yugoslavia: From Early Times to 1966*. Cambridge University Press, 1966.

'Correspondence on the treatment of pro-Cominform Yugoslavs in 1948'. *Problems of Communism* 21, no. 5 (1972): 96.

Cronin, Constance. *The Sting of Change: Sicilians in Sicily and Australia*. University of Chicago Press, 1970.

Čukić, Branislav. 'Patologija, tehnologija i kultura samoupravljača' [The pathology, technology and culture of self-managers]. Paper

Bibliography

read at First Meeting of Self-managers of 'Crveni barjak', 15–17 February 1969, in Kragujevac. Mimeographed.

Radne i samoupravne uloge u industrijskom preduzeću [Work and self-managing roles in an industrial enterprise]. Belgrade: Institut društvenih nauka, 1968.

Ćulibrk, Svetozar. *Želje i strahovanja naroda Jugoslavije* [Wishes and fears of the Yugoslav nations]. Belgrade: Institut društvenih nauka, 1965.

Cvijić, Jovan. *Balkansko poluostrvo i južnoslovenske zemlje* [The Balkan peninsula and the south Slavic lands]. Vol. 2, *Psihičke osobine južnih slovena* [Psychological characteristics of the south Slavs]. Belgrade: Izdavačka knjižarnica Gece Kona, 1931.

Dahl, Robert A. *After the Revolution?* New Haven: Yale University Press, 1970.

Damjanović, Mijat. 'Birač kao subjekt izborne participacije' [The voter as a subject of electoral participation]. *Politička misao* 7, no. 1 (1970): 83–91.

Dimitrov, Dimitar. 'Jedan tip ličnosti u jugoslovenskom društvu' [One personality type in Yugoslav society]. *Filosofija*, no. 1 (1970): 107–19.

'Diskusija: samoupravljanje i efikasnost rada i odlučivanja' [Discussion: self-management and the efficiency of work and of decision making]. *Gledišta* 11, no. 3 (1970): 405–65.

Djilas, Milovan. *Anatomy of a Moral.* Edited by Abraham Rothberg. New York: Praeger, 1959.

Conversations with Stalin. New York: Harcourt, Brace and World, 1962.

The New Class. New York: Praeger, 1957.

The Unperfect Society: Beyond the New Class. New York: Harcourt, Brace and World, 1969.

Djodan, Sime. 'Socijalizam i robno-novčani odnosi' [Socialism and goods-money relations]. *Praxis* 5, no. 1–2 (1968): 154–61.

Djordjević, Života. 'Grupašenja i demokratizacija komune' [Grouping and democratization of the commune]. *Gledišta* 9, no. 5 (1968): 771–5.

Djuretić, Jagoš. 'Dileme proleterskog konstituisanja vlasti' [Dilemmas of the proletarian constitution of power]. *Gledišta* 9, no. 4 (1968): 521–30.

Djurović, Djuro. 'Bespravna stambena izgradnja — jedna od karakteristika urbanog razvoja Beograda' [Illegal housing construction — one of the characteristics of Belgrade's urban development]. *Sociologija* 12, no. 3–4 (1970): 499–507.

Društvena nejednakost u socijalizmu [Social inequality in socialism]. Belgrade: Komunist, 1968.

Eisenstadt, S. N. *Essays on Comparative Institutions.* New York: John Wiley and Sons, 1965.

Erlich, Vera St. *Family in Transition.* Princeton University Press, 1966.

'Ljudske vrednote i kontakti kultura' [Human values and culture contacts]. *Sociologija* 7, no. 3 (1965): 27–42.

'L'expérience yougoslave'. *Revue de l'Est* 3, no. 2 (1972).

Bibliography

Filipović, Dragomir. 'Workers' Universities: 1959–1968'. *Yugoslav Survey* 10, no. 4 (1969): 1119–28.

Fisher, Jack. *Yugoslavia: A Multinational State*. San Francisco: Chandler Publishing Co., 1966.

Fisk, Winston M. 'A Communist *Rechtstaat?* — The Case of Yugoslav Constitutionalism'. *Government and Opposition* 5, no. 1 (1969–70): 41–53.

Fromm, Erich, ed. *Socialist Humanism*. Garden City, New York: Doubleday, Anchor Books, 1966.

Gans, Herbert J. *The Urban Villagers: Group and Class in the Life of Italian-Americans*. New York: Free Press, 1962.

Garaudy, Roger. *The Crisis in Communism: The Turning-Point of Socialism*. Translated by Peter and Betty Ross. New York: Grove Press; London: Fontana/Collins, 1970.

Glaser, Barney G., and Strauss, Anselm L. *The Discovery of Grounded Theory: Strategies for Qualitative Research*. Chicago: Aldine, 1967.

Goffman, Erving. *Behavior in Public Places*. New York: Free Press, 1963.

The Presentation of Self in Everyday Life. New York: Doubleday, Anchor Books, 1959.

Greenstein, Fred I. 'A Note on the Ambiguity of "Political Socialization": Definitions, Criticisms, and Strategies of Inquiry'. *Journal of Politics* 32, no. 4 (1970): 969–78.

Hall, Edward T. *The Hidden Dimension*. Garden City, New York: Anchor Books, 1969.

Halpern, Joel M. 'Peasant Culture and Urbanization in Yugoslavia'. *Human Organization* 24, no. 2 (1965): 162–74.

'The Process of Modernization as Reflected in Yugoslav Peasant Biographies'. In Kroeber Anthropological Society, *Essays in Balkan Ethnology*, William G. Lockwood, special editor. Special Publications no. 1 (1967). Berkeley.

A Serbian Village. Rev. ed. New York: Harper and Row, Harper Colophon Books, 1967.

Hammel, Eugene A. *Alternative Social Structures and Ritual Relations in the Balkans*. Englewood Cliffs, New Jersey: Prentice-Hall, 1968.

'The Jewish Mother in Serbia or *Les structures alimentaires de la parenté*. In Kroeber Anthropological Society, *Essays in Balkan Ethnology*, William G. Lockwood, special editor. Special Publications no. 1 (1967). Berkeley.

The Pink Yo-Yo. Institute of International Studies (Berkeley) Research Series, no. 13 (1969).

Hoffman, George W., and Neal, Fred Warner. *Yugoslavia and the New Communism*. New York: Twentieth Century Fund, 1962.

Horowitz, Irving Louis. 'Anthropology for Sociologists: Cross-Disciplinary Research as Scientific Humanism'. In *Professing Sociology*. Chicago: Aldine, 1968.

Horvat, Branko. *Ogled o jugoslavenskom društvu* [An examination of Yugoslav society]. Zagreb: Mladost, 1969.

Bibliography

Also published as *An Essay on Yugoslav Society*. Translated by Henry F. Mins. White Plains, N.Y.: International Arts and Sciences Press, 1969.

Hunnius, Gerry. 'Workers' Self-Management in Yugoslavia'. In *Workers' Control: A Reader on Labor and Social Change*, edited by Gerry Hunnius, G. David Garson, and John Case. New York: Vintage Books, 1973.

Hyman, Herbert H. *Political Socialization*. New York: Free Press, 1959.

Ilić, Milos, ed. *Socijalna struktura i pokretljivost radničke klase Jugoslavije* [Social structure and mobility of the working class of Yugoslavia]. Vol. 1. Belgrade: Institut društvenih nauka, 1963.

Inkeles, Alex. 'Participant Citizenship in Six Developing Countries'. *American Political Science Review* 63, no. 4 (1969): 1120–41.

and Bauer, Raymond A. *The Soviet Citizen*. 1959. Reprint. New York: Atheneum, 1968.

Jambrek, Petar. 'Društveno-ekonomski razvoj i političke promjene: Empirijska analiza odlučivanja u šestnaest slovenskih općina' [Socio-economic development and political changes: An empirical analysis of decision-making in sixteen Slovenian communes]. *Sociologija sela*, no. 31–2 (1971): 42–7.

Janićijević, Milosav, et al. *Jugoslovenski studenti i socijalizam* [Yugoslav students and socialism]. Belgrade: Institut društvenih nauka, 1966.

Jerovšek, Janez. 'Konflikti u našem društvu' [Conflicts in our society]. *Sociologija* 10, no. 4 (1968): 160–7.

'Structure of Influence in Commune'. In *Sociologija: Selected Articles 1959–1969*. Belgrade: Yugoslav Sociological Association, 1970. Translated and reprinted from *Sociologija* 11, no. 2 (1969).

Johnson, A. Ross. 'The Dynamics of Communist Ideological Change in Yugoslavia: 1945–1953'. Ph.D. dissertation, Columbia University, 1967.

Jučić, Božo. 'Autokratski i demokratski način rukovodjenja u samoupravljanju' [The autocratic and democratic way of leading in self-management]. In *Organizacija rada u samoupravnim odnosima* [The organization of work in self-managing relations], edited by Jovo Brekić. Zagreb: Narodne novine, 1970.

'Motivacioni aspekti organizacionih uloga' [Motivational aspects of organizational roles]. In *Organizacija rada u samoupravnim odnosima* [The organization of work in self-managing relations], edited by Jovo Brekić. Zagreb: Narodne novine, 1970.

Kavran, Dragoljub. *Sastanci i odlučivanje* [Meetings and decision-making]. Belgrade: Radnička stampa, 1968.

Kermanuer, Taras. 'Kultura, umjetnost i prosječni gradjanin' [Culture, art and the average citizen]. Paper read at Fifth Meeting, Yugoslav Sociological Association, 11–13 February 1971, in Dubrovnik. Mimeographed.

Kirchheimer, Otto. 'Private Man and Society'. *Political Science Quarterly* 81, no. 1 (1966): 1–24.

285

Bibliography

Kolaja, Jiri. *Workers' Councils: The Yugoslav Experience*. London: Tavistock, 1965.

Kovačević, Milivoje. *Komunali sistem i komunalna politika* [The commune system and commune politics], 2nd ed. Belgrade: Zavod za izdavanje udžbenika S.R. Srbije, 1968.

Kožul, Franjo. 'Politička kultura i političko ponašanje u suvremenim političkim procesima' [Political culture and political behavior in modern political processes]. *Politička misao* 7, no. 1 (1970): 3–11.

Laing, R. D.; Phillipson, H.; and Lee, A. R. *Interpersonal Perception: A Theory and a Method of Research*. New York: Harper and Row, Perennial Library, 1972.

Landy, Paul. 'What Price Corruption?' *Problems of Communism* 10, no. 2 (1961): 18–25.

Lane, Robert E. *Political Ideology*. New York: Free Press, 1962.
Political Thinking and Consciousness: The Private Life of the Political Mind. Chicago: Markham, 1969.

Lewis, Oscar. 'An Anthropological Approach to Family Studies'. *American Journal of Sociology* 55, no. 5 (1950): 468–75.
'Controls and Experiments in Field Work'. In *Anthropology Today*, prepared under the chairmanship of A. L. Kroeber. University of Chicago Press, 1953.
Five Families. New York: Mentor Books, 1959.
La Vida: A Puerto Rican Family in the Culture of Poverty — San Juan and New York. New York: Random House, 1966.

Liebow, Elliot. *Tally's Corner: A Study of Negro Streetcorner Men*. Boston: Little, Brown, 1967.

McClellan, W. D. *Svetozar Marković and the Origins of Balkan Socialism*. Princeton University Press, 1964.

Madžar, Ljubomir; Ostračanin, Miodrag; and Kovačevic, Mladjen. 'Economic Development: 1947–1968'. *Yugoslav Survey* 11, no. 1 (1970): 23–42.

Mandić, Ivan. 'Psihološka analiza ekonomskog ponašanja proizvodjača' [A psychological analysis of the economic behavior of producers]. In *Organizacija rada u samcupravnim odnosima* [The organization of work in self-managing relations], edited by Jovo Brekić. Zagreb: Narodne novine, 1970.

Mannheim, Karl. *Ideology and Utopia*. New York: Harcourt, Brace and World, 1966 [1936].
'The Problem of Generations'. In Karl Mannheim, *Essays on the Sociology of Knowledge*, edited by Paul Kecskemeti. New York: Oxford University Press, 1952.

Marinković, Radivoje. *Ko odlučuje u komuni* [Who decides in the commune]. Belgrade: Institut društvenih nauka, 1971.

Marshall, T. H. "Citizenship and Social Class'. In *Class, Citizenship, and Social Development*. Garden City, New York: Doubleday, 1964.

Martić, Mirko. *Studenti Zagrebačkog sveučilišta: Sociološka ispitivanja 1959–1965* [Students of Zagreb University: Sociological research 1959–1965]. Zagreb: Institut za društvena istraživanja, 1967.

Bibliography

Matić, S.; Poček, M.; and Bosanac, G. *Aktivnost radnih ljudi u samoupravljanju radnom organizacijom: Jedan pokušaj istraživanja na području komune Varaždin* [The activity of working people in self-management through the work organization: A research attempt on the territory of the commune of Varaždin]. Zagreb: Institut za društveno upravljanje N. R. Hrvatske, n.d. [1962].

Meister, Albert. *Où va l'autogestion yougoslave?* Paris: Editions Anthropos, 1970.

Socialisme et autogestion: L'expérience yougoslave. Paris: Editions du Seuil, 1964.

Mikecin, Vjekoslav. *Socijalizam i revolucionarni subjekt* [Socialism and the revolutionary subject]. Zagreb: Kulturni radnik, 1970.

Miladinović, Milan M. *Lik članova SKOJa u revoluciji* [The image of SKOJ members in the revolution]. Belgrade: The author, 1971.

Milenkovitch, Deborah D. *Plan and Market in Yugoslav Economic Thought.* Yale Russian and East European Studies, no. 9. New Haven: Yale University Press, 1971.

Milić, Vojin. 'Osvrt na društvenu pokretljivost u Jugoslaviji' [A review of social mobility in Yugoslavia]. *Statistička revija* 10, no. 3–4 (1960): 184–235.

Milivojević, Dragoljub. *The Yugoslav Commune.* Belgrade: Medjunarodna Politika, 1965.

Milošević, Aleksandar, and Sizentić, Milan. 'Imports of Consumer Goods'. *Yugoslav Survey* 12, no. 3 (1971): 63–70.

Mlinar, Zdravko, and Toš, Niko. 'Individualno i kolektivno zadovoljavanje potreba' [Individual and collective satisfaction of needs]. *Sociologija* 12, no. 2 (1970): 179–89.

'Progresivne i konzervativne snage u našem društvenom razvoju' [Progressive and conservative forces in our social development]. *Naše teme* 14, no. 4 (1970): 658–95.

Možina, Stane. 'Pozitivne i negativne strane egalitarizma u našem društvu' [Positive and negative sides of egalitarianism in our society]. *Naše teme* 14, no. 6 (1970): 1277–81.

'Utjecaj samoupravne organizacije rada na poslovanje i odnose' [The influence of self-managing organization of work on business and relations]. In *Organizacija rada u samoupravnim odnosima* [The organization of work in self-managing relations], edited by Jovo Brekić. Zagreb: Narodne novine, 1970.

'Zainteresiranost samoupravljača za odlučivanje, kontrolu, davanje prijedloga i dobijanje informacija' [Self-managers' interest in decision-making, control, making proposals and getting information]. *Sociologija* 10, no. 3 (1968): 27–36.

Muhić, Fuad. 'Hronika: IV Stručni sastanak jugoslovenskog udruženja za sociologiju' [Chronicle: IV professional meeting of the Yugoslav Sociological Association]. *Sociologija* 12, no. 1 (1970): 136–45.

Neal, Fred Warner. 'Yugoslav Communist Theory'. *Slavic Review* 19, no. 1 (February 1960): 42–62.

and Winston M. Fisk. 'Yugoslavia: Towards a "Market Socialism"'. *Problems of Communism* 15, no. 6 (1966): 28–37.

287

Bibliography

Nikolić, Miloš, ed. *Savez komunista u uslovima samoupravljanja* [The League of Communists in conditions of self management]. Belgrade: Kultura, 1967.

Novosel, Pavle. 'Društvena stratifikacija i norma o prihodu' [Social stratification and the income norm]. *Naše teme* 10, no. 3 (1966): 617–30.

'Politička kultura u S. R. Hrvatskoj' [Political culture in S. R. Croatia]. Mimeographed. Zagreb, 1969.

'Reforma, samoupravljanje i socijalna psihologija preindustrijalskog mentaliteta' [Reform, self-management, and the social psychology of the preindustrial mentality]. *Naše teme* 11, no. 12 (1967): 2159–76.

Obradović, Josip. 'Participacije i motivacije u radničkom samoupravljanju obzirom na tehnološki nivo proizvodnja' [Participation and motivations in workers' self-management with regard to the technological level of production]. Mimeographed. Zagreb: Institut za društvena istraživanja, 1967.

Ossowski, Stanislaw. *Class Structure in the Social Consciousness.* Translated by Sheila Patterson. London: Routledge and Kegan Paul, 1963.

Pašić, Najdan. *Klase i politika* [Classes and politics]. Belgrade: Rad, 1968.

Političko organizovanje samoupravnog društva [Political organization of a self-managing society]. Belgrade: Komunist, 1970.

Pateman, Carole. *Participation and Democratic Theory.* Cambridge University Press, 1970.

Pečujlić, Miroslav. *Horizonti revolucije: Studije iz političke sociologije* [Revolutionary horizons: Studies from political sociology]. Belgrade: Institut za političke studije, 1970.

Klase i savremeno društvo [Classes and modern society]. Belgrade: Savremena administracija, 1967.

and Ničić, Dušan. 'Early Stage of Socialist Reconstruction and Awareness of It'. *Socialist Thought and Practice,* no. 29 (1968): 68–89.

Položaj i problemi porodice u procesu konstituisanja samoupravnog socijalističkog društva. [The position and problems of the family in the process of constituting the self-managing, socialist society]. 2 vols. Belgrade: Institut za političke studije, 1968.

Popov, Nebojša. 'Granice vlasti i mogućnosti socijalizma' [The limits of power and the possibilities of socialism]. *Gledišta* 9, no. 10 (1968): 1331–48.

Popović, Mihailo. 'Neusladjenosti i suprotnosti u procesu transformacije jugoslovenskog društva i njegove strukture' [Disagreements and contradictions in the process of transforming Yugoslav society and its structure]. *Sociologija* 12, no. 2 (1970): 161–78.

Popović, Nenad D. *Yugoslavia: The New Class in Crisis.* Syracuse University Press, 1968.

Pranger, Robert J. *Action, Symbolism, and Order: The Existential Di-*

Bibliography

mensions of Politics in Modern Citizenship. Nashville: Vanderbilt University Press, 1968.

Putnam, Robert D. 'Studying Elite Political Culture: The Case of "Ideology" '. *American Political Science Review* 65, no. 3 (1971): 651–81.

Pye, Lucian W., and Verba, Sidney, eds., *Political Culture and Political Development*. Princeton University Press, 1965.

Rawin, Solomon John. 'Social Values and Managerial Structure: The Case of Yugoslavia and Poland'. *Journal of Comparative Administration* 2, no. 2 (1970): 131–60.

'Razgovor u studiju: "Koncepcije robne privrede u socijalizmu" ' [Conversation in the studio: "The conception of a goods economy in socialism"]. *Treći program* 2, no. 3 (1970): 187–324.

Rihtman-Auguštin, Dunja. 'Samoupravljanje kao kulturno-antropološki fenomen' [Self-management as a cultural-anthropological phenomenon]. *Naše teme* 14, no. 1 (1970): 37–53.

'Štednja: Jedan uvid u motivacije i globalne orientacije' [Saving: A view into motivations and global orientations]. Mimeographed. Zagreb: Ekonomski institut, 1970.

'Vrednote i današnji trenutak' [Values and the present]. *Naše teme* 15, no. 2 (1971): 241–58.

'Vrijednosni aspekti organizacionih uloga' [The value aspects of organizational roles]. In *Organizacija rada u samoupravnim odnosima* [The organization of work in self-managing relations], edited by Jovo Brekić. Zagreb: Narodne novine, 1970.

Rose, Arnold M., ed. *Human Behavior and Social Processes: An Interactionist Approach*. Boston: Houghton Mifflin, 1962.

Rubinstein, Alvin Z. 'Reforms, Nonalignment and Pluralism'. *Problems of Communism* 17, no. 2 (1968): 31–41.

Rus, Veljko. 'Institutionalization of the Revolutionary Movement'. *Praxis*, intl. ed. 4, no. 2 (1967): 201–13.

'Moć i struktura moći u jugoslovenskim preduzećima' [Power and the structure of power in Yugoslav enterprises]. *Sociologija* 12, no. 2 (1970): 191–207.

'Problems of Responsibility in Self-managerial Industrial Organizations'. In *Sociologija: Selected Articles 1959–1969*. Belgrade: Yugoslav Sociological Association, 1970. Translated and reprinted from *Sociologija* 11, no. 3 (1969): 441–62.

'Samoupravni egalitarizam i društvena diferencijacija' [Self-managing egalitarianism and social differentiation]. *Praxis* 6, no. 5–6 (1969): 811–27.

Rustow, Dankwart A. 'Transitions to Democracy: Toward a Dynamic Model'. *Comparative Politics* 2, no. 3 (1970): 337–63.

A World of Nations. Washington, D.C.: The Brookings Institution, 1967.

Rytina, Joan Huber; Form, William H.; and Pease, John. 'Income and Stratification Ideology: Beliefs About the American Opportunity Structure'. *American Journal of Sociology* 75, no. 4, pt. 2 (1970): 703–16.

Bibliography

Savez komunista Srbije. *Statut* [Statute]. Belgrade: Komunist, 1970.

Schurmann, Franz. *Ideology and Organization in Communist China.* Berkeley and Los Angeles: University of California Press, 1968.

Schutz, Alfred. *Collected Papers.* 2 vols. The Hague: Martinus Nijhoff, 1964–7.

Shoup, Paul. 'The National Question in Yugoslavia'. *Problems of Communism* 21, no. 1 (1972): 18–29.

'Yugoslavia Today: The Evolution of a System'. *Problems of Communism* 18, no. 4–5 (1969): 67–77.

Smailagić, Nerkez. 'Samoupravljačka demokracija i politička kultura' [Self-managing democracy and political culture]. *Politička misao* 7, no. 1 (1970): 47–56.

Smiljković, Radoš, and Petrović, Milan, eds. *Samoupravljanje i socijalizam: Čitanka samoupravljača* [Self-management and socialism: A self-managers' reader]. Sarajevo: Zavod za izdavanje udžbenika, 1970.

Stalna konferencija gradova Jugoslavije. *Mesna zajednica u našem društveno-političkom sistemu* [The local community in our socio-political system]. Belgrade: Stalna konferencija gradova Jugoslavije, 1966.

Opština i samoupravna integracija društva [The commune and the self-managing integration of society]. Belgrade: Stalna konferencija gradova Jugoslavije, 1968.

Stanković, Jugoslav. 'Gradjanin i politička aktivnost: Rezultati jedne ankete' [The citizen and political activity: Results of a survey]. *Sociologija* 7, no. 3 (1965): 79–96.

Stavrianos, L. S. *The Balkans Since 1453.* New York: Holt, Rinehart and Winston, 1958.

Stojanović, Svetozar. *Izmedju ideala i stvarnosti* [Between ideals and reality]. Belgrade: Prosveta, 1969. Also published as *Between Ideals and Reality.* Translated by Gerson S. Sher. New York: Oxford University Press, 1973.

Stojić, Ljubomir M. 'Opažanje motivacije za prisustvovanje političkim sastancima i za odsustvovanje sa njih' [Observation of motivations for attendance at political meetings and absence from them]. *Politička misao* 7, no. 1 (1970): 75–81.

Supek, Rudi. 'Motivation and Evolution of Attitudes in Youth Movement Work-Groups'. In *Sociologija: Selected Articles 1959–1969.* Belgrade: Yugoslav Sociological Association, 1970. Translated and reprinted from *Sociologija* 2, no. 1 (1959): 211–37.

'Robno-novčani odnosi i socijalistička ideologija' [Goods-money relations and socialist ideology]. *Praxis* 5, no. 1–2 (1968): 170–9.

Šuvar, Stipe, *Sociološki presjek jugoslavenskog društva* [A sociological crossview of Yugoslav society]. Zagreb: Školska knjiga, 1970.

'Urbanizacija, socijalna diferencijacija i socijalna segregacija u našem društvu'. [Urbanization, social differentiation and social segregation in our society]. Paper read at Fifth Meeting of Yugoslav Sociological Association, 11–13 February 1971, in Dubrovnik. Mimeographed.

Bibliography

Tadić, Ljubomir. *Poredak i sloboda* [Order and freedom]. Belgrade: Kultura, 1967.

Tanić, Živan. *Tehnika, rad, organizacija* [Technology, work, organization]. Belgrade: Institut društvenih nauka, 1968.

and Vuković, Olga. *Znanja i obaveštanost proizvodjača o radničkom samoupravljanju* [Knowledge and informedness of producers about self-management]. Belgrade: Institut društvenih nauka, 1968.

Todorović, Aleksandar. *Razvoj radničke svesti u socijalističkom društvu* [The development of working-class consciousness in socialist society]. Belgrade: Sociološki institut, 1967.

Tomac, Zdravko. 'Politička kultura i društveno-političke organizacije' [Political culture and socio-political organizations]. *Politička misao* 7, no. 1 (1970): 13–22.

Tomasevich, Jozo. *Peasants, Politics, and Economic Change in Yugoslavia*. Stanford University Press, 1955.

Tomašić, Dinko, *Personality and Culture in East European Politics*. New York: George Stewart, 1948.

Tomić, Stojan T. 'Potrebe i interesi društvenih grupa u lokalnim zajednicama' [Needs and interests of social groups in local communities]. Ph.D. dissertation, Visoka škola političkih nauka, Belgrade, 1967.

Trouton, Ruth. *Peasant Renaissance in Yugoslavia: 1900–1950*. London: Routledge and Kegan Paul, 1952.

Ulam, Adam. *Titoism and the Cominform*. Cambridge, Mass.: Harvard University Press, 1952.

Vidaković, Zoran. *Korak nazad, dva koraka napred* [One step back, two steps forward]. Belgrade: Komunist, 1971.

Vucinich, Wayne S., ed. *Contemporary Yugoslavia*. Berkeley and Los Angeles: University of California Press, 1969.

West, Rebecca. *Black Lamb and Grey Falcon*. New York: The Viking Press, 1958.

Worhers [sic] Management in Yugoslavia: 1950–1970, edited by Stanko Grozdanić and Momčilo Radosavljević. Belgrade: Medjunarodna politika, 1970.

Yugoslavia. Savezni zavod za statistiku. *Popis stanovništva 1961* [1961 Population census]. Vol. 6. *Vitalna, etnička i migraciona obeležja: Rezultati za opštine* [Vital, ethnic and migrational characteristics: Results for communes]. Belgrade, 1967.

Savezni zavod za statistiku. *Statistički godišnjak Jugoslavije.* [Yugoslav statistical yearbook]. Belgrade, annually.

Yugoslavia's Way: The Program of the League of Communists of Yugoslavia. Translated by Stoyan Pribechevich. New York: All Nations Press, 1958.

Zaninovich, M. George. *The Development of Socialist Yugoslavia*. Baltimore: Johns Hopkins Press, 1968.

Zeitlin, Maurice. *Revolutionary Politics and the Cuban Working Class*. Princeton University Press, 1967.

Živković, Miroslav. 'Jedan primer segregacije u razvoju naših gradova'

Bibliography

[An example of segregation in the development of our cities].
Sociologija 10, no. 3 (1968): 37–58.

'Kriza ili transformacija roditeljskog autoriteta' [Crisis or transformation of parental authority]. *Gledišta* 7, no. 12 (1966): 1496–1506.

Županov, Josip. 'Antinomije i planiranje razvoja industrijskog društva u Jugoslaviji' [Antinomy and planning of the development of industrial society in Yugoslavia]. *Sociologija* 12, no. 3–4 (1970): 449–56.

'Društvena pokretljivost i razvojne perspektive jugoslovenskog društva' [Social mobility and the developmental prospects of Yugoslav society]. *Gledišta* 12, no. 11–12 (1971): 1493–1503.

'Industrijalizam i egalitarizam' [Industrialism and egalitarianism]. *Sociologija* 12, no. 1 (1970): 5–45.

'Neke dileme u vezi s robno-novčanim odnosima' [Some dilemmas in connection with goods-money relations]. *Praxis* 5, no. 1–2 (1968): 165–9.

Samoupravljanje i društvena moć [Self-management and social power]. Zagreb: Naše teme, 1969.

'Two Patterns of Conflict Management in Industry.' *Industrial Relations* 12, no. 2 (1973): 213–23.

'Upravljanje industrijskim konfliktom u samoupravnom sistemu' [Management of industrial conflict in self-managing society]. *Sociologija* 13, no. 3 (1971): 427–47.

INDEX

activism, *see* political participation
activists, *see* Establishment *and* issue
   activists
aging, 28–9
aktiv, 21, 185, 190, 233
   see also Establishment
apathy, 31, 246
   following postwar reconstruction,
      21
   related to leadership, 12
   over time, 121–2, 261
   in sample, 96, 123ff
argumentation, 162–7, 169–73, 175–6,
      177–9
army, 95, 253, 260
Austro-Hungarian Empire, 33,
      221, 272
authoritarianism, 119, 218, 219, 226–
      7, 233–4

Baboeuf, F. N., 50
Bećković, Matija, 112–14, 146
Belgrade, 37, 52, 272–4
   bombing of, 235
   geographical position, 229
   lifestyle, 106, 107, 108
   migration to, 103
   Party organization, 237, 242
   public behavior in, 203, 207, 211–12
   surrounding area, 223–4
   'wild settlement' in, 102
Belgrade–Bar railroad, 129–30, 230
Belgrade University, 148–9, 211, 252–
      6, 260
Berger, Peter, 269
bogaćenje (enrichment), 234
Bogumil heresy, 227
borac (warrior)
   cultural model, 218–19
   Partisan veteran, 89, 111, 164,
      218

borbenost (the quality of being able
      to struggle), 218, 220, 221
Bosnia-Hercegovina, 85, 223,
      226, 227–8
   Party organization, 183
Bottomore, T. B., 193, 212
bourgeoisie, *see also* middle strata
   prewar, 39, 42, 52, 110
Bulgaria
   egalitarianism in, 24
   as occupying power, 84, 106
bureaucracy, 33, 230–1
   and bureaucratic behavior, 210–12,
      214
   and bureaucratic mentality, 216
   in Stalinist model, 12, 68, 248
buses, behavior in, 195, 202, 203, 206,
      208, 278

capitalism, 25, 74–5, 165, 198
Catholics, 226
centralization, 60, 231, 248, 257
Četniks, 52, 55, 85
children, relationship with parents,
      200–2
Chinese model, 18, 21, 62n, 213, 255
Church, *see* Islam; Roman Catholic
      Church; *and* Serbian Orthodox
      Church
citizen–partisans, 161, 162–5, 167,
      169ff, 247, 261
cleavages, 246ff
Code of Self-Managers (1971), 58, 66
collective entrepreneurs, 22, 61
collectivism, 9, 69, 134–5
Cominform, break with, 51, 116, 248
   leadership's response to, 61, 67, 68
   personal experience of, 78, 92–4,
      134
   and Yugoslav Stalinism, 53
commune, 60
   autonomy of, 21, 50, 61

Index

Index

Djilas, Milovan, 11, 17, 26, 176, 257
  choice of social democracy, 239
  idea of 'the new class', 5–7
  role in establishment of worker's councils, 51n
Dušan, Tsar, 223

economic development, 75, 81, 99, 150
  and desirable behavior, 214, 232–3
  as goal, 63–5, 67, 72, 243, 247, 248
  rationale, 20, 191
  relation to elitism, 72–3
  relation to market socialism, 22
  relation to self-management, 71, 98
  Western model, 18
economic reforms, 231
  1950–4, 60
  1965, 63, 118, 252
education
  college, 96, 133
  postwar period, 89–91
egalitarianism, 138, 247, 248–9
  campaign for, 150
  contrasted with industrialism, 213, 220, 234
  as ideal, 119, 135, 242
  leadership's perception of, 24, 68–9
  masses' perception of, 119, 147, 163–4, 234
  Party leadership's behavior, 9
  policy, 118
  in postwar period, 219
  preindustrial, 228
  as value, 221, 226, 227
Eisenstadt, S. N., 162n, 195, 203
elections, 124, 148
elitism, see decision-making; experts; idealism; instrumentalism; and technocracy
Engels, Friedrich, 50
enterprise
  autonomy of, 21, 59, 60
  in competition, 70, 247
  power structure in, 22–3, 189–90, 233–4
  and workers' self-management, 57, 60–1, 257–9
  see also decentralization; decision-

making; and workers' self-management
equality, see egalitarianism
Erlich, Vera St, 224, 227–8
Establishment, 158–9, 258, 261
  argumentation, 162–3, 170, 171, 173, 175, 176–7
  cooptation into, 251
  definition of, 158–9, 161, 167–9, 247
  and official line, 160
  power of, 188–91
  reaction to criticism, 181–3
  relationships with others, 164–7, 176–7, 181–3
  stratification within, 185–7
  within Party, 183–5
etatism, 119, 140, 221, 249, 257, 262
  contrasted with enterprise autonomy, 61
  contrasted with market socialism, 15
  contrasted with self-management, 12–13, 68–9
  and economic reforms, 60
  masses' perceptions of, 147, 150
  and Party, 12–13
  related to behavior, 194
  and Stalinism, 140
  and Titoism, 140
  in Yugoslav history, 230–1
ethnic nationalities, see national-ethnic minorities
experts, 22, 219, 233, 239–40
  in communes, 154, 155, 157, 187–8
  in enterprises, 21, 93, 214
  see also technocracy

factory councils, 53, 54
families
  in methodology, 271–2
  in sample, 37–45, 274–7
  see also zadruga
Federal Assembly, 123–4, 186–7
feedback, 173–6, 262
Filipović, Filip, 55

Garaudy, Roger, 1n, 249, 262
generations, political, 27–30, 264
  and other changes, 248

295

Index

Index

material incentives, 10, 61–3, 65, 213
  effect on behavior, 17, 25, 35–6
  and postwar reconstruction, 87
Mead, G. H., 264
meetings, *see* League of Communists of Yugoslavia; trade unions; *and* voters' meetings
Meister, Albert, 179n, 262
mesna zajednica (local community), 158, 178
  limitations of, 155–6, 164–5, 174–5
  as territorial unit, 32–3, 153–4
methodology, qualitative, 2–3, 30, 32–3, 36, 263–79
  see also life stories
middle strata (middle class), 20, 22
  criticism of, 149
  and political activism, 168
  in sample, 37–42, 99
  social origins of, 100
  in Soviet Union (1918–22), 58
  see also bourgeoisie, prewar
migration, 78
  in life stories, 90, 101–3, 106, 121, 127
  interrepublican, 255
  outside Yugoslavia, 137
Mijanović, Vladimir, 149
Miloš, Prince, 225
moba (mutual help), 229–30
mobilization, 151
  postwar, 86–92, 117
  through self-management, 21
Montenegro, 86, 145n, 200, 227–9
morality, 216
  leadership's, 5–7
  socialist, 193–4, 198–9, 206–10, 239–41
  teaching of, 243
  see also illicit activities
Moslems, *see* Islam
Municipal Assembly, 33, 153, 156, 164–6, 174
Municipal Transportation Company (Belgrade), 165, 166, 169–71, 174, 177–8

national chauvinism, 225, 253

national–ethnic minorities, 19, 120n, 216, 247, 252
  contractual agreements between, 209–10
  disputes of 1971–4, 141, 253–7
  and economic distribution, 118–9, 259
  and political institutions, 259
  shared experiences of, 222
  and traditional behavior patterns, 210, 230
national liberation
  from Ottomans, 218–19, 224, 226–30
  War of, *see* World War II
'new class', 5–7
Nikezić, Marko, 141
NIN (Nedeljne informativne novine), 278
  on extremism, 251
  on *kafanas*, 204–5
  on political controls, 262
  on public speech, 181
  survey of Federal Assembly members, 186–7
  survey of social ideals, 133–7
Novosel, Pavle, 212

Occupation, *see* World War II
opština (commune), *see* commune
Ossowski, Stanislaw, 259
Ottomans
  acculturation to, 227–8
  colonialism of, 33, 221, 223, 231, 238, 272
  influence on parent–child relations, 200
  influence on work habits, 229
  resistance to, 219, 224, 227, 228–9
ownership, 49
  individual, 109–10
  private, 74–5
  social, 15
  state, 6, 96

parents, relationship with children, 200–2
Paris Commune (1871), 49, 50, 53, 67
Partisan generation, 27–9, 132, 248, 252, 260

Index

Index